The Mindfulness and Acceptance Workbook for Anxiety combines the accumulated wisdom of the ages with up-to-date, cutting-edge developments in scientific psychology. In an easy-to-read and fun format, those suffering from anxiety in all of its guises will find the keys to breaking loose from its shackles. By emphasizing acceptance of toxic emotions (and illustrating ways to accomplish this), rather than struggling to overcome them, the person inside you may finally emerge to set your life on a new, productive, and valued course. Highly recommended for all those struggling with worry, anxiety, and fear.

—David H. Barlow, Ph.D., professor of psychology and psychiatry at Boston University and author of *Anxiety and Its Disorders*

Ably surfing the dual currents of traditional exposure and acceptance-based treatments for anxiety, the authors of this resourceful workbook illustrate the synergies to be found in their combination. Carefully structured charts and patient assignments support the core message that taking action to face one's fears is most effective if acceptance informs our starting point and values determine our destination. This book is a "must-read" for anyone encountering anxiety as a barrier to leading a fuller life.

—Zindel Segal, Ph.D., Morgan Firestone Chair in Psychotherapy, head of the Cognitive Behaviour Therapy Unit at the Centre for Addiction and Mental Health, and professor in the Departments of Psychiatry and Psychology, all at the University of Toronto, and author of *The Mindful Way Through Depression*

If you suffer with anxiety, Forsyth and Eifert have given you a gift. It is not a structured manual for how to get over your anxiety as much as it is a book of wisdom. They raise the inevitable truth that anxiety is a part of all of us, and they show us the way, through willingness, compassion, mindfulness, and acceptance of ourselves and others, to live a life worth the living, to understand our important values and to live in concert with them. This is a book well worth the reading, and its message is worth keeping close to your heart.

—Richard G. Heimberg, Ph.D., professor of psychology and director of the Adult Anxiety Clinic of Temple University

Steeped in the rich tradition of psychological theory, The Mindfulness and Acceptance Workbook for Anxiety *by Forsyth and Eifert represents a major advance for the practical treatment of anxiety and related conditions. This book will assist clinicians and patients in constructing a treatment plan that insures progress in overcoming the many obstacles associated with conquering fears. A major contribution to clinical care, this workbook will contribute to the growing knowledge base on acceptance and commitment therapy, joining other evidence-based approaches as a major tool for treating the disabling symptoms that accompany anxiety.*

—Terence M. Keane, Ph.D., chief of psychology service at the VA Boston Healthcare System, director of the Behavioral Science Division of the National Center for PTSD, and professor and vice-chair for research of the Division of Psychiatry at Boston University School of Medicine

In this impressive workbook, Forsyth and Eifert show how giving up your attempts to control anxiety and fear will help you to leave your anxiety problems behind and get on with your life. This clearly written book is packed with helpful suggestions. I will definitely use it with my own clients and students, and I recommend it highly for anyone who struggles with anxiety.

—Martin M. Antony, Ph.D., ABPP, professor and director of graduate training in the Department of Psychology at Ryerson University in Toronto, ON, Canada

This book presents a framework to orient you toward the rest of your life. You will be taken on a journey. Go. To uncouple from your anxious reactions to life, you will need to alter your consciousness. No small task! It takes a student's mind and a willingness to be coached. Fortunately, you will find these authors to be trustworthy and competent guides.

—Reid Wilson, Ph.D., author of *Don't Panic*

The
Mindfulness & Acceptance
Workbook for Anxiety

A Guide to Breaking Free from Anxiety, Phobias & Worry Using Acceptance & Commitment Therapy

JOHN P. FORSYTH, PH.D.
GEORG H. EIFERT, PH.D.

New Harbinger Publications, Inc.

Publisher's Note

Distributed in Canada by Raincoast Books

Copyright © 2007 by John Forsyth and Georg Eifert
        New Harbinger Publications, Inc.
        5674 Shattuck Avenue
        Oakland, CA 94609
        www.newharbinger.com

Cover design by Amy Shoup
Text design by Michele Waters-Kermes
Acquired by Catharine Sutker
Edited by Elisabeth Beller

Audio portion of the CD produced by Troy DuFrene

Library of Congress Cataloging-in-Publication Data

Forsyth, John P.
 The mindfulness and acceptance workbook for anxiety : a guide to breaking free from anxiety, phobias, and worry using acceptance and commitment therapy / John P. Forsyth and Georg H. Eifert.
    p. cm.
 Includes bibliographical references and index.
 ISBN-13: 978-1-57224-499-3 (pbk. : alk. paper)
 ISBN-10: 1-57224-499-2 (pbk. : alk. paper)
 1. Anxiety disorders--Treatment--Popular works. 2. Acceptance and commitment therapy--Popular works. I. Eifert, Georg H., 1952- II. Title.
RC531.F67 2008
616.85'2206--dc22

           2007041238

17   16   15

20   19   18   17   16   15

To our good friendship and support. With gratitude for fifteen years of collaboration, fun, sharing, and learning from each other. Writing this book together was a pure joy!
—JPF and GHE

To my parents, Russ and Ann,
for taking the risk to bring me into this world;
showing me the value of faith, hard work, kindness, and generosity;
and supporting each step of my journey.
Any difference this book makes in the lives of those who read it
is a testament to the difference they've made in my life.

And to my loving wife, Celine, and my three children
for giving me opportunities to nurture
patience, compassion, and love as vital antidotes to suffering.
This book is a reflection of the lessons I've learned through them.
—JPF

To my mother, Margarete, who taught me kindness and compassion through the way she treated me and other members of our family—and by acting with loving-kindness toward us regardless of what her mind may have told her about us at times.

And to my wife, Diana, and our two boys, Daniel and Leonardo, with gratitude for their love.
May we continue to learn to struggle less
and be more kind to ourselves and compassionate with our experience.
—GHE

Contents

Series Editor Letter   vii

Acknowledgments   ix

Introduction   1

PART 1: PREPARING THE WAY FOR SOMETHING NEW

CHAPTER 1   Choose a New Approach to Get a Different Outcome   11

CHAPTER 2   You Are Not Alone: Understanding Anxiety and Its Disorders   27

CHAPTER 3   Confronting the Core Problem: Living to Avoid Fear and Anxiety   51

CHAPTER 4   Myths About Anxiety and Its Disorders   57

CHAPTER 5   Letting Go of Old Myths Opens Up New Opportunities   67

PART 2: STARTING A NEW JOURNEY

CHAPTER 6   Facing the Costs to Take Charge of Your Life   81

CHAPTER 7   What Matters More to You: Managing Your Anxiety or Living a Good Life?   93

CHAPTER 8   Ending Your Struggle with Anxiety Is the Solution   105

CHAPTER 9   You Control Your Choices, Actions, and Destiny   121

CHAPTER 10   Getting into Your Life with Mindful Acceptance   135

CHAPTER 11   Learning Mindful Acceptance   147

PART 3: RECLAIMING YOUR LIFE AND LIVING IT

CHAPTER 12   Taking Control of Your Life   165

CHAPTER 13   Finding Your Values   177

CHAPTER 14   Getting Ready to Face Anxiety with Mindful Acceptance   187

CHAPTER 15   Bringing Compassion to Your Anxiety   201

CHAPTER 16   Developing Comfort in Your Own Skin   213

CHAPTER 17   Developing Comfort with Your Judgmental Mind   227

CHAPTER 18   Moving Toward a Valued Life   245

CHAPTER 19   Staying the Course   255

References, Further Readings, and Internet Resources   263

Dear Reader:

Welcome to New Harbinger Publications. New Harbinger is dedicated to publishing books based on acceptance and commitment therapy (ACT) and its application to specific areas. New Harbinger has a long-standing reputation as a publisher of quality, well-researched books for general and professional audiences.

Anxiety is often experienced much as one might experience a hand to the throat. When your air passage is restricted, only one thing seems important: getting free from the restriction. Life may allow thousands of wonderful things, in that moment—were the anxiety not there. You may know how to do scores of things that you would enjoy in that moment—were the anxiety not there. But since it *is* there, only one thing is important: getting that emotional and cognitive "hand on the throat" to release itself.

This metaphor is the ancient one on which the word "anxiety" was built. At one time, language was not developed enough even to speak of emotions, so they were spoken of metaphorically. The word "anxiety" came from a root word meaning "I cannot breathe" or "I'm choking."

Unfortunately, the human mind is not well built to deal with anxiety in a healthy way. The human mind evolved to solve problems—to take concrete actions to avoid the bad outcomes our minds can foresee. But when anxiety is approached in that entirely normal way, it becomes a signal of imminent bad outcomes—and anxiety is a normal response to imminent bad outcomes. In effect, we reach around our backs and squeeze our own throats without even realizing it. In the attempt to get free and breathe, anxiety becomes something to be anxious about.

In some ways, acceptance and commitment therapy was built on this paradox. Thirty years ago my own panic disorder threatened to take away everything I cared about. I struggled, making it worse and worse. Eventually, in my despair, accidents of history and learning led to something different. I began to abandon struggling with the hand on my throat. Life began to open up. That surprising outcome was replicated with my clients with early ACT methods. The power of acceptance, mindfulness, and values gradually became undeniable, personally, professionally, and scientifically.

Given that remote history, it is perhaps not surprising that there is a profound resonance between anxiety issues and ACT. You can see it clearly in this volume. John Forsyth and Georg Eifert are experts in developing and applying ACT methods. They are particularly well known for their work in anxiety disorders, and their professional book on that topic has already influenced thousands and thousands of clinicians. In this volume, they break down the ACT model, and in a simple, clear, step-by-step fashion they show how you can use it to find a life space where it is possible to live passionately and breathe freely … even when you are anxious! Never overwhelming, never forced, and paced beautifully, it lays down a reliable path you can follow. If you are struggling with anxiety, you will sense how well this model fits your situation.

It is especially gratifying to read such a well-crafted and helpful book by these two authors. As part of New Harbinger's commitment to publishing sound, scientifically-based, and helpful books, Georg,

John, and I oversee all prospective ACT books for the *Acceptance and Commitment Therapy Series* of professional and self-help books. As ACT Series editors, we review all ACT books published by New Harbinger, comment on proposals and offer guidance as needed, and use a gentle hand in making suggestions regarding content, depth, and scope of each book. We strive to ensure that any claims that are unsubstantiated or clearly ACT inconsistent are flagged for the authors so they can revise these sections to ensure that the work meets our criteria.

Books in the *Acceptance and Commitment Therapy Series*:

- Have an adequate scientific base

- Are theoretically coherent—they fit with the ACT model and underlying psychological principles as they have evolved at the time of writing.

- Avoid jargon and unnecessary entanglement with proprietary methods, leaving ACT work open and available

- Keep the focus always on what is good for you, the reader

- Support the further development of the field

- Provide information in a way that is of practical use

These guidelines reflect the values of the broader ACT community to ensure that people get information that can truly be helpful, and that can alleviate human suffering.

Sincerely,

Steven C. Hayes, Ph.D.

Acknowledgments

It wouldn't have been possible to write this book without the kind and generous support of many people, beginning with John's wife Celine and their three children, and Georg's wife Diana and their two children. They were there for us every step of the way as we wrote our first book for mental health professionals, *Acceptance and Commitment Therapy for Anxiety Disorders* (Eifert & Forsyth, 2005), and then a second book for people struggling with problem anger—*ACT on Life, Not on Anger* (Eifert, McKay, & Forsyth, 2005). And they stood by us every step of the way with the writing of this book too. They were willing to make personal sacrifices to see that this book would come to fruition. They saw us through the long hours and writing binges and they reminded us of the value of this work and its potential to help others. We are forever grateful for their loving support. We couldn't have done it without them.

The ideas and inspiration behind every keystroke in this book are not just ours. They belong to a broader group. Many people are working hard on how to best alleviate human suffering without trying to eliminate or disavow normal human pain and hardship. This collective body is the engine behind a new and rapidly growing "third wave" behavior therapy known as acceptance and commitment therapy (ACT). This group has touched and inspired us with their collective wisdom, practical know-how, compassion, generosity, kindness, and plain old hard work.

We are particularly grateful to Dr. Steven C. Hayes and the broader ACT community. Steve's personal and professional odyssey, coupled with his wit, wisdom, and energy, sparked the beginnings of ACT. And he, along with his colleagues Kirk Strosahl and Kelly Wilson, published in 1999 the first full-length book—*Acceptance and Commitment Therapy: An Experiential Approach to Behavior Change*. Several of the exercises we adapted for use with anxiety and problem anger first appeared in that book. Since then, ACT has mushroomed into a treatment with broad scope and solid research support.

We've also been touched and influenced by people outside the ACT community. Pema Chödrön, an American Buddhist nun, has written widely about the wisdom of meeting the strong energy of emotions, such as fear and anger, with patience, compassion, acceptance, and forgiveness. Her words—and those of Jon Kabat-Zinn, Jeffrey Brantley, Zindel Segal, and Wayne Dyer—are simple and clear, and they mirror the central message of this book. That message is one of practicing mindful acceptance, compassion, and patience when the flames of anxiety, fear, and panic are hot and of living a full, rich, and meaningful life. This message embodies the ACT approach that we'll be sharing with you here. We are forever grateful for their willingness to share their astute knowledge and practical wisdom.

Joseph Ciarrochi, David Mercer, and Sara Christian contributed the wonderful hand-drawn sketches that you'll see throughout the book. We would like to thank each of them for kindly giving us permission to reproduce their work.

We're also grateful to Kelly Wilson, Joanne Dahl, and Tobias Lundgren for sharing with us their work on values, which included assessment tools, illustrations, and useful activities, with additional thanks to our Swedish friends Joanne Dahl and Tobias Lundgren for providing inspiration for the Life Compass that we adapted from their work (Dahl & Lundgren, 2006). Thanks also to our British colleague Peter Thorne who shared with us the "Anxiety News Radio" and "Just So Radio" metaphors.

Thank you also to Ashleigh Louis for her editorial help, suggestions, and comments, and to Jackie Turner for her assistance in the recording of the audio exercises on the accompanying CD. Special thanks to Mariah Howard for her great voice. Special thanks also go out to the many professionals, students, and colleagues who have helped shape our thinking, and particularly to David Barlow for his groundbreaking and seminal contributions on the nature and treatment of anxiety disorders. All this generous sharing of ideas and materials by our ACT colleagues has occurred in the spirit of "spreading what is good and what works," which unfortunately is not the norm in the competitive world of science.

New Harbinger Publications is a major outlet for the dissemination of newer third-generation behavior therapies like acceptance and commitment therapy. We are grateful to Matthew McKay and all the New Harbinger staff for seeing the value of this work and its potential to alleviate a wide range of human suffering. We also owe a debt of gratitude and heartfelt appreciation to Catharine Sutker of New Harbinger for her tireless energy, encouragement, and kind support with this project, and to Jess Beebe and Elisabeth Beller for their masterful and diligent editing. And we'd also like to thank Troy DuFrene for his efforts with the mechanics of this project and in helping produce the book and CD companion.

Finally, we would like to thank the people who have sought us out because they believed that we could help them heal their anxious pain and reclaim their lives in a way that was dignified, whole, complete, and durable. These are the people, like you, suffering with anxiety problems. We have learned much from them, and the spirit of their journey out of suffering and into wholeness and a more vital life is everywhere in this book. This book is a testament to their courage.

We sincerely hope you'll benefit from reading this book as much as we have benefited from working on it. It has profoundly and deeply changed how we view and approach the emotional pain and suffering of the people we encounter (our clients, colleagues, family, and friends) and how we approach our own pain and suffering in ways that keep all of us moving in directions we value. We know that you can have that too.

—John P. Forsyth, Ph.D.   Georg H. Eifert, Ph.D.
University at Albany, SUNY   Chapman University
Albany, New York   Orange, California

August 2007

Introduction

You are suffering. Anxiety, fears, panic, unsettling thoughts, painful memories, and worry have brought ruin to you and your life. You may feel frustrated, broken, damaged, and at your wit's end. And you are looking for a way out. We can tell you this much: you are not alone. All of us experience worry, anxiety, and fear.

FREEDOM FROM ANXIETY MANAGEMENT

There's no way to escape the simple fact that anxiety is *part* of life. The emphasis here is on the word "part." Many people do live well, even with significant anxiety and often with the very same anxieties and fears you may be experiencing. You may wonder how they do that. You may wonder what little secret they have that you somehow lack. There's really nothing remarkable about what they do.

At a very simple level, they've learned to put anxiety and other unpleasant feelings and thoughts in their proper place—where they are just a part of life, but not the whole of life. At a deeper level, they've learned to free themselves from the pull of constant struggle with anxiety. In short, they don't let anxiety, fear, worry, panic, painful memories, and the like stand in the way of doing what they care deeply about.

The book you have in your hands will help you do this too. Anxiety need not continue to cause you to suffer by putting a choke hold on you and your life. There's another way—a set of skills that we'll help you learn so that you can devote more of your energies to aspects of your life that you care deeply about. This new approach, supported by research, will help you tip the scales back to where anxiety and fear become just a part of living well.

To get there you'll first need to face up to the fact that just about everything you've tried up to now hasn't really worked to keep anxiety and fear at bay. If you're like most people, then you know how difficult it is to get a handle on anxiety. And you've probably done many different things already to manage or reduce your panic, fears, worries, and tension. The activity below will help you get a better sense of this.

Here you'll find a list of some common things people do when they struggle with anxiety and fear. Look it over. Place a check mark (√) in the box next to the strategies that you've tried.

- ☑ Running away from situations that make me feel scared, anxious, or nervous

- ☐ Avoiding activities or situations that may bring on anxious thoughts, feelings, and memories (e.g., going outside, driving, working, being in a crowd, experiencing a new situation, eating certain foods, exercising)

- ☑ Suppressing or pushing out disturbing thoughts and feelings

- ☑ Distracting myself from anxiety, fear, and worrisome thoughts

- ☐ Changing how I think—replacing "bad" with "good" thoughts

- ☐ Talking myself out of anxiety, panic, fear, or worry

- ☐ Sticking close to "safe" people (e.g., friend or family member)

- ☐ Carrying objects or performing rituals (e.g., phoning, checking, counting, cleaning, washing)

- ☐ Talking or venting with a friend or family member about my anxiety

- ☐ Joining online support groups for persons with anxiety problems

- ☐ Educating myself by reading books written by experts on anxiety disorders

- ☐ Turning to self-help books offering "better" ways to control worry, anxiety, and fear

- ☑ Taking antianxiety medications, herbal supplements, or alcohol to dull the pain

- ☑ Going to psychotherapy

Here, we'll venture a guess that you checked at least one box but probably more than one. That's fine. Now we'd like you to consider the following question: how have these anxiety management techniques worked for you? These strategies may have bought you some short-term relief. But how have your coping strategies worked in the long run? Look deeply here. Have these strategies worked as you had hoped or intended, or have they cost you in some way?

Before going on, see if you can connect with at least one of the costs. What have you missed out on in an effort to avoid feeling anxious or afraid? Think about something you really care about, however small or big. Perhaps it's work, finances, or family? Maybe it's travel, exercise, a hobby, or your health? Or it may involve relationships, intimacy, your freedom, or spirituality. Take a moment and write that one important thing below. We'll come back to that later on in this book.

Because of my anxious thoughts and feelings, strong fear and panic, worry, or disturbing memories, I have missed out on or am unable to _____Fly_____.

Anxiety and fear are intense and action-oriented emotions that are hard to control and harder to cope with. Your experience up to this point tells you as much. Your experience is right on.

The truth is that anxiety may never go away entirely. You may never be able to reduce, let alone eliminate, the intense feelings of panic, the painful thoughts, or the bad memories. What you *can* do is learn how to not let anxiety take over and undermine the things you want to do, the things you care about doing. You can end your suffering. You can get out from under anxiety and fear. You can get your life back! We'll teach you how.

A NEW WAY OUT OF YOUR WORRIES, ANXIETIES, AND FEARS

This book will take you on a journey of sorts. We can't tell you for certain where you'll ultimately end up, but we can say that the journey will be quite unlike anything you've tried before. This is good.

We aren't about to take you down the same old path. We won't advocate strategies that keep fanning the flames of fear and anxiety and don't work in the long term. You won't find anything in this book about teaching you "more, better, different" anxiety management and control strategies. This book is much bigger than that. It's about your life!

We're going to take you down a path that will challenge you in many ways. We'll show you how to change your relationship with the thoughts, memories, and images that trigger anxiety, and with the feelings themselves. We'll teach you how to bring acceptance and compassion to your worries, anxieties, fears, painful memories, and thoughts. This will defuse the sting of these experiences. And it'll weaken their power to get you off track from the life you want.

Developing acceptance and compassion for the more painful parts of your inner emotional experiences will give you the space to discover, or perhaps rediscover, what you want to be about in this life and where you want to go. You'll learn to reduce the unnecessary suffering that anxiety has caused you and others by focusing your energies on people and experiences that matter most to you. This is the most critical and important aim of this book—helping you live a better life.

Nobody wants to be about anxiety and its management now and forever more. Yet this is what you can become so long as anxiety is met with negative energy. That negative energy is packaged in the form of active resistance, denial, struggle, suppression, avoidance, and escape. If you read the book and do the exercises, you'll learn why this is so. And as you learn how to meet your anxiety with acceptance and compassion, you'll find that the things you spend your time doing will change. New possibilities will emerge. You'll learn how to live out your dreams. You can have that without first winning the war with your anxiety monsters.

These ideas are not fluff. They're backed by a growing research base (Eifert & Forsyth, 2005; Eifert & Heffner, 2003; Hayes, 2004; Hayes, Follette, & Linehan, 2004; Hayes, Luoma, Bond, Masuda, & Lillis, 2006; Hayes, Strosahl, & Wilson, 1999; Salters-Pedneault, Tull, & Roemer, 2004) showing that anxiety management and control feeds anxiety and fear, shrinks lives, and promotes the suffering you know about firsthand. This is why everything in this book is about increasing your vitality and your ability to create the kind of life you want to live—a full life, free of the pain of ongoing struggle with anxiety.

And, as strange as it may sound now, you'll learn how to engage your life more fully and deeply with whatever your mind and body may dish out from time to time. When you do more of that, you can expect to think and feel better too. Acting to control your worries, anxieties, and fears is no way to live. Are you curious or suspicious? Good—read on.

HOW TO USE THIS BOOK

Many chapters include a number of exercises that provide you with new experiences. They are the most important parts of this book. The exercises bring to life in a personal way what you've learned. They'll help you make contact with what works and what doesn't work. Some of them help you feel worries, anxieties, and fears—and show you how you can experience all of them without acting on them. Understanding this logically is helpful, but only experiencing it for yourself will make a difference in your life. This book will help you and work for you—but only if you work *with* it. How can you do that?

Put Taking Care of Yourself on Your To-Do List

To benefit from this workbook, you'll need to intend to work with it. You'll need to consider whether you and your life are as important as the mundane tasks that you and everyone else place on to-do lists each day. We think you're important enough to be at the top of such a list. So put taking care of yourself on your to-do list every day. We know that this may sound silly, but when people do it, they get results.

Make Reading a Priority

Make reading a priority in your schedule. Commit to a reasonable amount of time you can set aside to read this book and practice the exercises. Be flexible. There's no right time to read. If you planned on reading in the morning and missed that reading time for whatever reason, allow yourself time to do it later on. The most important thing is that you do it.

Pace Yourself and Be Patient

Change takes time. You haven't arrived at this place overnight. And we understand that you might feel the urgency to fix things quickly, but getting a different outcome in your life can't be done overnight. We recommend that you not read several chapters of this book all at once. If you do that, it'll be hard to put the concepts into action. And you may end up feeling overwhelmed. You need time to think about the concepts—let them seep in. And you need to allow time to put the concepts into practice. So be patient with yourself.

We suggest that you pace your reading at a rate of one chapter per week. This is a great way to take care of yourself too. The same can be said of doing the exercises every day. Chapters in part 1 can be read more quickly, but when you get into parts 2 and 3, *slow things down!* We've structured the chapters to be read this way. It takes time to learn any new skill. And it takes time to counter the old habits that have kept you stuck and miserable. So take as much time as you need with the material in each chapter. Don't move on too quickly. Allow yourself time to put the concepts into action. Let your benchmark for moving on be this: Your ability to apply the concepts and new skills in your life.

Some Concepts Will Be Repeated for a Reason

Some themes will come up again and again. This repetition is deliberate. We understand that you may be going this alone, without the benefit of a therapist to guide you. If we could be with you in person as you use this workbook, then we'd naturally return to earlier themes and concepts over time. Core themes are just as important in the later sections of this book as they are in the beginning. So think "familiar-sounding themes are important themes." Integrate the familiar with the new material you come across in the workbook.

Use the Workbook CD Containing Forms and Audio Files of Exercises

Forms for some of the exercises are included on the CD in the back of the book. Use the CD to print out as many clean copies of a form as needed for your own personal use. These forms are clearly marked in the right-hand margins of this book with the CD icon shown here.

A few exercises are best listened to with your eyes closed. We know this from our own experience with the exercises. And we've also learned that from people just like you. Being able to listen can pull you more quickly into the spirit of the exercises and guide you in learning the skills. You'll see what we mean soon enough. These audio exercises are clearly marked in the right-hand margins of this book with the musical-note icon shown here.

Use the Workbook on Your Own or as Part of Your Therapy

This book was written as a stand-alone workbook to help anyone suffering from any of the anxiety disorders—which you'll learn more about in chapter 2. You might also find this book helpful if you happen to be working with a therapist for anxiety problems. Therapists with experience and training in newer cognitive behavioral therapies, such as acceptance and commitment therapy (ACT), will know the approach in this workbook inside and out. If you are currently seeing an ACT therapist, you may find that the chapters for each week roughly correspond to the material your therapist covers with you. If you are looking for an ACT therapist, you can find one at www.contextualpsychology.org.

OUR JOURNEY: WHY WE WROTE THIS BOOK

We wrote this book because we know that what it contains can be of enormous benefit. And we wrote it out of our sincere desire to help. Many paths led us to these goals. Here, we'd like to share with you a bit of ourselves and our journey.

We are trained as clinical psychologists and researchers, with most of that training in what's known as cognitive behavioral therapy (CBT). Our focus is on the causes and treatment of anxiety disorders, though our interests are more broadly about getting to the root of human suffering.

We used to teach anxiety sufferers state-of-the-art CBT techniques. We focused on helping people gain mastery and control over their unpleasant thoughts and feelings. Many of these techniques, in turn, are about teaching ways to change thoughts and feelings. For instance, it's quite common to teach someone with an anxiety problem to identify catastrophic negative thoughts, help them see that they are unrealistic, and then replace those thoughts with more realistic thoughts.

Another major part of all effective treatments for anxiety involves having anxious persons expose themselves to the things they most dread. Usually these are cues and triggers for anxiety and fear. Some triggers can be found in your mind and body, and many more lurk in the world around you. With exposure, exposure, and more exposure, people face their fears. And, with time, many get anxiety reduction. These and many other related techniques have strong research support. They work for some people, some of the time. Yet the treatments are far from being a cure.

In our own research and clinical work, we've been confronted time and time again with persons getting better—meaning less anxious—then coming back later for additional help. They come back because their anxiety and fears have returned. The techniques they learned to manage their anxiety lost some of their punch. This observation is not unique to us. Partial or full return of anxiety following traditional CBT is more common than many of us would like to believe.

Many people seeking help with anxiety problems have been through the mill of sensible strategies, often with limited results. Something here didn't seem right to us. And, as we stepped back, we began to wonder whether CBT was sending the wrong message. That message is this: anxious thoughts and feelings are the problem, and in order to have a better, richer, more meaningful life, anxious people like you need to learn ways to master and control upsetting thoughts, feelings, and memories. In short, CBT teaches that living well follows from thinking and feeling well. And CBT is about teaching better anxiety management too. The same message is supported by our culture—fix your pain and you will be happy and live well. This view didn't sit right with our own life experience. We know people, and you do too, who seem to challenge this basic rule. And both of us have had our fair share of life's ups and downs, significant hardships, and at times significant anxiety and pain.

We've gotten stuck now and then trying to get a handle on our mental and emotional hurts, only to find that our trusted bag of CBT strategies didn't seem to work well in the long term. Yes, even the two of us—the anxiety experts—can't get rid of our anxiety. And you know something? That's okay. Our collective personal and professional experience is telling us that anxiety management is not a prerequisite for, or a guarantee of, a vital life. Thinking and feeling well does not translate into living well, nor is it a path to happiness.

As CBT expanded, new ideas began to emerge. These ideas seemed to challenge just about everything we'd been taught and were trying to apply in our own lives. This newer work was suggesting that perhaps thoughts and feelings aren't the enemy. Perhaps they need not be managed to live a vital life. This new wave of CBT was even going so far as to suggest that the *struggle* with our minds and bodies is the root source of human suffering.

In place of anxiety management, this work pointed to something radical, fresh, new, and, yes, even counterintuitive. That idea was this: Perhaps the struggle is unnecessary and even part of the problem with anxiety. And if that's true, then we ought to be teaching people how to develop comfort in their own skins. And we ought to help people redirect their energies to managing things that they can control and ought to manage—their actions in the service of living well.

That new approach involved a very simple idea and a powerful set of research-supported strategies and skills to help people bring acceptance, compassion, and gentleness to their unpleasant thoughts, feelings, memories, and even sense of self. In short, stop struggling to feel and think better, and instead start living better with whatever you might be feeling or thinking.

This expanded view of wellness and suffering was building on several lines of research like those we outlined early on, showing that when you add management and struggle to normal human pain you often get more pain. You get suffering. You get pulled out of doing what most people consider important in this life.

ACT is part of this new approach. We've spent a good part of our careers expanding ACT to help people just like you. And we've been putting it into action in our daily lives—at work, with our kids, in our marriages and friendships, with our health, in our communities, and while doing things that are fun like music, exercise, or travel.

Using acceptance and mindfulness skills has put us in much fuller contact with ourselves and our world. And yes, sometimes we don't feel or think well, but we are kinder and gentler about that when it happens. And we're simply unwilling to let our emotional pain stand between us and where we want to go. Instead, we're able to focus our energies on doing what we care about—living well. And as we do more of that, we've noticed that we tend to think and feel better too. Our lives have been enriched in so many ways simply because we've learned how to put our energies to good use. We're less caught up in our painful heads and hearts and more engaged in doing what we care about. And we've seen this work with those who have sought us out for help.

Our intent is for you to make the most of your one precious life too. Everything that we know, we've crammed into this workbook to help you on the way. Now it's your turn. We hope that you make the most of it and see what this book can offer you. If you give it a real chance, we think you'll be pleasantly surprised. Your life will be better for it too.

BEGIN YOUR JOURNEY

This book is designed to help you get something different by doing something different! Reading this book—and internalizing what you learn—is part of this process. But there's no book on the planet, no pill, no person who can make you live your life in a certain way. It'll be up to you to put what you learn into action. You are the only person that can make the changes you need to make. In the end, you control the direction you want your life to take—that's your choice.

There is a Buddhist saying that the journey of a thousand miles begins with one step. By selecting and reading this book, you've taken that first step on your journey out of your anxiety and into a new life. Congratulations! Now comes the hard part: keeping yourself moving forward.

A life lived well is the end product of a number of small moments. It takes a lifetime to create a life. Living according to your values is something we will help you do more of, one step at a time. On your journey, you'll learn, progress, and see life in a way that you may never have experienced before.

This book is a travel guide of sorts. Use the information here to help you decide where you want to go. As you commit to putting your values into action, the quality of your life, and of those around you, will begin to improve.

PART 1

PREPARING THE WAY FOR SOMETHING NEW

Choose a New Approach to Get a Different Outcome

Your life is a sacred journey. And it is about change, growth, discovery, movement, transformation, continuously expanding your vision of what is possible, stretching your soul, learning to see clearly and deeply, listening to your intuition, taking courageous challenges at every step along the way. You are on the path . . . exactly where you are meant to be right now. . . . And from here, you can only go forward, shaping your life story into a magnificent tale of triumph, of healing, of courage, of beauty, of wisdom, of power, of dignity, and of love. —Caroline Adams

This chapter is about preparing the way for something new in your life. As much as we hate to admit it, we know that to get a different outcome we need to change what we are doing *now*. This is a good mantra we use in our own personal lives. The mantra (based on Hayes, Strosahl, & Wilson, 1999) goes something like this:

If I continue to do what I've always done, then I'm going to get what I've always got.

Write it down and keep it with you as you work with the material in this book.

YOU HAVE CHOICES

Here's the good news: you can choose a new approach to get a different outcome in your life. This new approach is what you'll get in this workbook. You'll see that the material in this book will help you act on your anxiety and your life differently by putting you in control of what you can control. Put simply, you *can* control and change how you *respond* to your anxiety-related feelings, thoughts, and worries:

- You can stop trying to cope with worries, anxieties, and fears (if coping and other management strategies have not worked in a lasting way).

- You can learn to leave worries, anxieties, and fears alone and simply experience them as thoughts, sensations, feelings, or painful memories.

- You don't have to act on your anxiety, and it doesn't need to drive what you do. As much as you feel like running from intense anxiety, you can learn to act differently. You can learn to watch anxious feelings and worrisome thoughts and *not* do what they tell you to do.

- You can learn to move with your anxious discomfort and do something that's potentially vital in your life.

you can control how you respond to your anxiety

We know from research and clinical experience that the solution to worry, anxiety, and fear is not more struggle. It's not about trying to bring them down when they rear their ugly heads. It's not about trying to get rid of them. It's also not about combating or replacing negative with positive thoughts. You know this battle firsthand, and so do we. You may think that you must win it—perhaps by trying harder, struggling more, learning better strategies, reading about anxiety problems, finding a new medication, venting, and so on.

The reality is this: this battle cannot be won. But here's more good news—you don't need to win this battle in order to begin living the life you want to lead. As you work with this book, we'll show you why this is a rigged game where the solutions to everyday sources of pain in the world around you are being applied in areas where they don't really work.

For now, we ask that you entertain the possibility that the solution to your anxiety problems is not to fight "better or harder." The solution is to change your relationship with, and your response to, your anxious thoughts and feelings. You can choose to stop fighting. To get there, you'll need to learn how to acknowledge anxious thoughts and feelings without "becoming" them, and without acting on them and doing what they say.

As we guide you in learning these skills, we'll help you develop compassion for yourself and for your anxiety and other painful experiences. You'll also rediscover what truly matters to you: you'll focus on what you want your life to stand for and then act in ways that move you forward in your life, even if that means bringing worries, anxieties, and fears, or other unwanted thoughts and feelings along for the ride.

This may not be the first book offering a new relationship with anxiety. But it's the first book that'll teach you how to cultivate that relationship with acceptance and compassion, and with both eyes focused squarely on helping you live your life with meaning and purpose.

Our sincere goal is to help you spend your precious time on this earth doing what you care deeply about rather than spending your time and energy trying to control anxiety. Keep this in mind as you work with the material in the book. The prize we're after is a life lived well—your life lived to its fullest!

WHAT IS ACT?

This workbook offers you a way out of your anxiety and fears and into your life, based on a revolutionary new approach called *acceptance and commitment therapy* (ACT, pronounced "act"). This pronunciation is important because it summarizes what ACT ultimately stands for: committed ACT*ion*.

Accept—Choose—Take Action

The easiest way to get the gist of ACT is to focus on what the three letters stand for: Accept—Choose—Take action. Put another way, ACT is about letting go, showing up to life, and getting yourself moving in directions you want to go. Don't worry if this strikes you as too general or idealistic. We'll get more specific as you move on and practice the exercises. For now, we'll unpack the ACT acronym just a bit to give you a sense of what's to come.

ACCEPT

This is the first step in ACT and a step that we'll help you nurture again and again in this workbook and, we hope, throughout your life. It involves active skills that'll help you to respond differently—with kindness, compassion, gentleness, less engagement—when anxieties, fears, worries, panic, and other sources of emotional and psychological pain show up. The idea is to accept what you're already having anyway. This skill disarms the struggle you're having with unwanted thoughts and feelings. As you learn to let go, your anxious suffering will go too. With that, the need to eliminate or change those thoughts and feelings washes away.

After you drop the rope in your tug-of-war with your anxiety monsters, you'll notice that your hands, feet, mind, and mouth will be freed up to be put to use for the things in your life you truly care about. In the process, your life will grow and develop in ways that may have seemed impossible up until now. Acceptance will help you make anxiety just a part of your larger life.

CHOOSE

The second step is about choosing a direction for your life. It involves identifying what you value in life and what you want your life to stand for. It's about helping you to discover what is truly important to you—what you value—and then making a choice. What kind of child, sister or brother, student, or friend do you want to be? What types of activities are meaningful to you? Answering these kinds of questions is about choice—choosing to go forward in directions that are uniquely yours *and* accepting what is inside you and what comes with you and accompanies you along the way. It's a step you'll make time and time again.

Here your life is asking you an important question: are you willing to contact and stay in touch with what your mind and body are doing anyway, fully and without avoiding or trying to escape from them? If the answer is no, you'll get smaller and your anxiety will grow larger. If the answer is "yes," you'll get bigger and your life will get bigger too. Living well will become your focus, not living to feel and think well.

TAKE ACTION

The third step involves taking steps toward realizing your valued life goals. It's about making a commitment to action and changing what you can change. This means learning to behave in ways that move you forward in the direction of your chosen values. As you work with the material, you'll begin to see that there's a difference between you as a person, your actions, and the thoughts and feelings you have about yourself. And you won't find us asking you to simply face your fears in the hope of a better life. Our goal is to foster your willingness to take your inner emotional discomfort along with you in the service of your life goals and dreams.

You may feel intimidated by these three big, bold steps. In fact, you may be quite scared. You may say, "This is too big—I can't do this." If you do feel this way or have other similar thoughts and feelings, that's fine. All we ask is that you hold your thoughts lightly. Just keep the book in your hands. Use your eye muscles to keep on reading. Let the thoughts be what they are and let them do what they do. Like other thoughts and feelings, it's okay if they come, it's okay if they stay, and it's okay if they go.

WHY ACT?

What we are about to share with you in this workbook is supported by research showing that anxiety management and control efforts are unnecessary. They can even be counterproductive and increase suffering because they restrict your life.

Recall the earlier list of anxiety management and control strategies. They may look different from one another, but they're all about one thing—reducing painful thoughts and feelings. They're about struggle. Here's a brief synopsis of what the research tells us about struggle with emotional and psychological pain:

- **Increases activity of the sympathetic branch of your nervous system.** This system is the engine that ignites when you feel anxious, angry, or when your life is in danger. It makes you feel ramped up and more uncomfortable.

- **Worsens memory for important life events.** This is because reducing or getting rid of unpleasant thoughts and emotions demands your attention. Focusing attention on your anxiety and hurt is pulling attention away from other more vital life areas.

- **Is effortful.** Another way to think about this is that it's hard work to push against unpleasant thoughts, feelings, and memories. Think of it as trying to use the palm of your hand to hold back water in a garden hose. You end up getting wet.

- **Works just well enough in the short term.** This is why people keep doing it—pushing against thoughts and feelings often will buy you some temporary relief. In the long term though, it doesn't work. People continue to suffer. And people pay a price for short-term relief too.

- **Doesn't change the quality of negative thoughts and feelings.** In fact, people tend to feel as bad or worse during and after fighting unpleasant thoughts and feelings.

- **Pulls you out of your life.** This is the most important finding. People who fight their thoughts and feelings on a regular basis report poorer quality of life, feel less authentic, have fewer close relationships, and generally feel limited in what they do. They feel stuck.

These and other findings point to one conclusion: trying to change anxious thoughts and feelings doesn't work. ACT capitalizes on this research by offering a way out of anxious suffering without more management, struggle, and control. That way out begins with doing something that goes against the grain of what you've been doing up until now. You do the opposite of anxiety management. You change your relationship with your anxious discomfort—especially how you act in the presence of it—by no longer fighting it.

These changes open doors. They'll give you wiggle room and energy to live your life more fully. This is what we mean when we say that ACT is all about allowing yourself to feel what hurts while doing what works and is important to you. In a nutshell, it is about acceptance *and* change at the same time. If you're 100 percent willing to give this a shot, then you'll learn to accept and live with your uncontrollable anxiety-related thoughts and feelings *and* take charge of what you can control: your behavior, or what you do.

WHY ACCEPTANCE AND ACTION ARE VITAL

Most people will gauge whether you're successful or not by what you spend your time doing, not by what you think or how you feel about it. This is another way of saying that your actions in life, however large or small, add up to what your life is about. It's only with your actions—what you do—that you move your life in the directions you want it to go.

When you act in ways contrary to your aspirations, you become emotionally and psychologically stuck. You may already know what that feels like—anxiety management versus life management. Using ACT, we'll teach you how to get unstuck and move forward by developing comfort in your own skin. You'll explore new ways of living *with* unpleasant thoughts and feelings rather than struggling *against* them.

Our goal is to help you develop skills to approach your anxious discomfort in a mindful, compassionate way while pursuing what really matters to you. We won't offer any cheap or quick fixes like the ones you hear every day from the media and our culture in general. You know the message—get rid of your pain and suffering, and then you'll be happy and have the life you want.

Being pain free is no guarantee of a vital life. Quite a few people seem to have no pain and hardly any worries, and yet they are unhappy with the life they lead. We also know that many people live with enormous pain and hardship and still manage to find meaning and dignity in their lives. They go about living each day as if it were their last. You can do this too. When you live each day as if it were your last, things that had seemed very important suddenly seem much less important—we have several exercises that build on this idea in the chapters to come.

We'll show you how to reduce your anxious and fearful suffering by increasing your vitality and ability to do what you want to do with your life. You'll learn skills that will help you stay with your unpleasant thoughts and feelings without acting on them or because of them. So instead of trying to replace anxious "negative" thoughts with less-anxious "positive" thoughts, you'll learn how to watch your thoughts, all of them, with gentle, dispassionate interest and without entanglement.

This skill set will also help you learn how not to let anxiety continue to be a monster that seems to have control over your life. It'll position you to break loose from anxiety by making space for it. As you do that, you'll be free to put your attention and energy into living a life that you care deeply about. As that happens, anxiety and fear will become just a part of your life, not the very fabric of your being.

You've probably heard the basic message of ACT in another form—the well-known serenity creed: *Accept with serenity what you cannot change, have the courage to change what you can, and develop the wisdom to know the difference.* Most people find that it is much easier to agree with the serenity creed than to do what it says. That's because many people simply don't know what they *can* and *cannot* change. Many more don't know how to accept and live with thoughts and feelings that hurt. Even then, few know how to apply this profound statement to their daily lives. We'll show you how to put the serenity creed into action.

When you read this book and do the exercises, you'll learn how to make the important distinction between what you can and cannot change. When you read and practice the mindfulness and acceptance exercises, you'll learn how to make space for all of your experiences—the good, bad, and ugly ones. And with acceptance and compassion, you'll learn how to refocus your precious time and energy on doing what matters to you. This will start you on a new path out of your worries, anxieties, and fears and into your life.

ACT CAN HELP YOU WITH YOUR ANXIETY AND IMPROVE YOUR LIFE

Anxiety and fear come in many shapes and guises. Many people with anxiety problems experience the powerful rush of panic: intense bodily changes (e.g., racing heart) together with thoughts that something terrible is about to happen, feelings of terror, and a sense of gloom and doom. For some, panic attacks seem to come out of the blue. Others find that panic-laced thoughts and feelings show up in specific situations (e.g., in social situations, in front of a group, on an airplane, at certain heights).

Some people with anxiety are haunted by memories of traumatic experiences they once endured. Still others are consumed with intrusive, obsessive, recurrent thoughts, impulses, or images that bring on overwhelming anxiety. To reduce their distress, some people engage in ritualistic acts like checking, counting, or hand washing. These acts buy people a short-term honeymoon from anxiety. And then there is the large group of anxious people who worry day in and day out about all sorts of things (their past, future, daily hassles) without being able to resolve any of them.

In the next chapter, we'll do our best to explain what we know about all these worries, anxieties, and fears, and how they're not as different from each other as they appear to be. If you have any of these experiences and are fed up with the toll they've been taking on your life, the ACT approach we describe in this book can help you get unstuck. Yet words are only words unless you get out there and put the words into action.

If you have any doubts about the importance of action, think about how you learn to ride a bike. You learn not by reading about bike riding or by watching a bicycle race. The only way to learn how to ride a bike is to get on one and start riding. You also need to be willing to fall once in a while, because you will. There's no other way to learn. It takes practice, commitment to learning how to do it, willingness to experience pain and falls, and recommitment to getting back on the bike after a fall. You just have to do it, and do it again and again.

In a similar way, learning about anxiety and fears with just your head, without taking steps to put your learning into action, is a dead end. You probably know this already from your own personal experience. Studies have shown that people learn best when they practice what they learn. In short, the best learning is active learning. So the challenge is to apply what you learn from this book in your daily life. This will take hard work on your part.

■ *How ACT Changed Mark's Life and His Experience with Panic*

Mark's story is typical. Panic disorder came from nowhere to haunt and limit him in his late twenties. At first, he tried to ignore it, suppress it, and push it away: "Of course, I don't suffer from this 'affliction'; that's for other people."

Mark tried several medications, some talk therapy, and a couple of self-help books. Nothing really worked. He remained unable to cross bridges, drive on highways, or ride in airplanes without extreme discomfort. As much as possible, he avoided these situations and many work and social events. Mark described his life as being consumed with "anxiety management." He was bitter, frustrated, and ready to give up.

He finally got help and found it in a place that he never thought to look before. He came face-to-face with the stark reality that living in the service of his panic was what he'd become and that this was no way to live. He learned skills emphasizing acceptance, mindfulness, and actions that would move him toward things that he cared about in his life. For Mark, this path was new and at times scary. It's also what changed his life.

As he worked with this new approach, Mark eventually changed jobs, got in shape, and began living a fuller life. For Mark, this life included accepting himself and his vulnerabilities without letting them run the show. This meant starting to do things he had stopped doing because of anxiety and instead being willing to be anxious while doing them.

When Mark was asked to pinpoint the one thing that changed, it was this: accepting panic for what it is. He learned that his greatest fear was not of the plane crashing, the car skidding off the bridge, or an accident on the highway. His greatest fear was of the panic itself.

Using mindfulness and other acceptance skills, Mark learned to recognize his beating heart and rapid breathing for what they truly were—physical sensations—rather than the terrible things his mind was telling him about them. He stopped struggling with what his body was doing and the negative news his mind was feeding him. He learned to sit still with the wild discomfort and kindly observe what was going on instead of acting on what his mind was telling him to do. Applying these new skills enabled him to do what mattered to him.

This acceptance had an odd effect—it made the feared symptoms less intense and less fearsome. Some of them were still there, but they'd lost much of their sting and edge.

Mark had learned a new way of relating with his body and judgmental mind by accepting the moments of manufactured terror and dread. This took time and effort, and it's not easy to do.

At times Mark still feels uncomfortable, but he no longer runs from his discomfort. He embraces those moments and the task at hand—in his words, "I have reclaimed what was always mine: a full life—not without worry—but one where worry and fear occupy a safe place that feels okay." He now flies, drives, and even engages in some public speaking.

Mark's journey out of anxiety and into his life can be yours too. We'll show you the way.

HOPE AND CHANGE: THE ACT WITH ANXIETY WAY

Before wrapping up this chapter, we'd like to pull together some key elements of this workbook to help you see what you are getting into and what you can expect. We'll do this with some cartoons and a few text prompts. Just imagine that you are the person illustrated in the cartoon.

This first image is about what most people want. Notice that you're moving toward the very things that you care most deeply about in this life. You are free, engaging life to its fullest.

And then as you do that, all kinds of things show up—sometimes unpleasant things.

And so you stop.

You think.

You fret, wallow, and stew.

And you do what seems to be the most sensible thing to do. You try to get the "bad" stuff out of the way because it seems to stand between you and your life.

As you're trying to get a handle on your discomfort, you turn around—turning your back on your life and where you wanted to go. And your life notices this too: "Huh . . . what about me?"

Your life waits as you pour your energies into getting a grip. You try many different ways of coping, but nothing seems to work.

On and on it goes—a scene that has played out countless times. All the while, time is ticking by . . . ticktock . . . ticktock. There you are struggling, and your life is waiting, just waiting. And your life becomes sad too, because it knows the outcome. And here it is: you pull out of life. Now look at your life—living is not getting done.

When you pull out, you never truly get away from your hurts. Notice that when you run, you take all those hurts with you too.

You're left feeling exhausted, frustrated, at your wit's end, head hung low.

And your mind is still at work—feeding you more negative news. Why can't I be normal? Why can't I get a handle on my anxiety and fears?

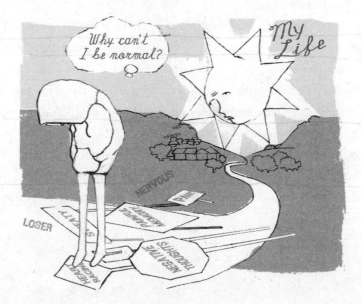

So there you are stuck, wallowing in this "out of my life" place with pain on top of pain. You feel bad, broken, like a loser, and without hope. You may even feel sad that you've once again missed out on important things in your life. You might feel cheated, even mad at yourself too. Notice that your life is sadder than before and is still waiting for you.

But then something changes.

Something profound and beautiful happens.

You see what's really going on.

You take stock.

You say enough is enough.

You open up to other possibilities.

Maybe, just maybe, your thoughts and feelings are not barriers at all. Maybe they're just part of you. Perhaps you can bring them along with you as you do what you care about.

Your life seems to like this idea.

So you take a step—a bold and courageous step forward in the direction you want to go. You bring compassion and kindness to whatever shows up inside your mind and body. You're moving. You're headed back into your life and doing what matters to you.

Your life notices right away. Others notice right away. You notice right away.

You commit to doing what you care about with whatever your mind or old history dishes out.

You run toward life. And as you do more of that, your life improves. Your life enjoys spending time with you!

This last illustration sums up the approach we take in this workbook. Elements in all the other scenes that precede it will be addressed too, except one: there's no way we know of to stop unpleasant thoughts and feelings from showing up from time to time (see the second cartoon on page 19 above). When you run toward your life, you're bound to get all sorts of thoughts, feelings, and bodily sensations. You can't have one (a life) without the other (a full range of thoughts and feelings).

But we can teach you how to keep your anxious mind and body from standing between you and your life. You'll learn to stop turning your back on your life in the service of anxiety management. You'll learn how to stop struggling with your emotional and psychological hurts. You'll develop skills to be kinder to yourself so that you don't wallow, beating yourself up with more negative judgments and blame. Most importantly, we'll show you how to win the war with your anxiety, not by defeating it, but by welcoming it as you engage your life one step at a time.

Living well is how you'll defeat anxiety. As with Mark's case, it starts by acting on your anxiety differently than you have done before.

YOUR COMMITMENT TO CHANGE

Commitment is a central component of any effort to change your life. Are you ready for that commitment with your worries, anxieties, and fears? Are you willing to learn another way to approach your worry, anxiety, and fear—and your life?

Answering yes means that you're one step closer to taking control over your actions and committing to move yourself in life directions you truly value. If you answered that way, great!

If you answered no, then stop. Ask yourself what is getting in your way. Write the barriers down in the space below.

_____

_____

Look at them. Take some time with them if you need to do that. We're not asking you to overcome any barriers. We're only asking if you're willing to learn a different way of relating with your anxieties, fears, and the like. Only you can decide whether the barriers are significant enough to stand between you and getting something different out of your life. When you're 100 percent willing to make this commitment, do so, and do it again and again with each new chapter.

Commitment doesn't mean you have to get everything right and that you'll never go back to your old ways. We know you'll sometimes go back to old patterns. Commitment only means that you're committed to do your very best at what you set out to do.

And if you end up breaking a commitment, it doesn't mean you've failed or, worse, that *you* are a failure. Give yourself a break. This is just your mind talking. Beating yourself up for being human is never helpful. In fact, it's a surefire way to feel worse.

Breaking a commitment simply means you've fallen off the bike, as we all do from time to time, particularly in the beginning when we're still learning to ride. When you realize you've "done it again," you can choose to recommit, mean it, and do what needs to be done the next time.

Here's why we think commitment is so important: Without commitment to action—if you don't complete the exercises—nothing much is going to change in your life. We've touched on this theme already in this chapter, but it's worth repeating the mantra. Steven Hayes and his colleagues put it this way: "If you always do what you always did, you will always get what you always got!" (Hayes, Strosahl, & Wilson, 1999, p. 235).

This means that to get a different outcome, you need to do something quite different than you've done before. Just reading this book without doing anything new is a surefire way to continue to get what you've always gotten.

THE TAKE-HOME MESSAGE

Change can be scary and vital at the same time. It involves some risk. Yet the risk of doing more of the same ought to be more frightening. To get something new, all of us need to do something new. It's that simple. And it starts with you making a choice and a commitment to do that. When you ACT on your anxiety differently, you have much to gain and nothing to lose.

Preparing Myself for Something New in My Life

Point to Ponder: To get something new, I must do something new.

Questions to Consider: Am I ready to choose a new approach with my anxieties, fears, and worries? If not, then what is getting in the way?

CHAPTER 2

You Are Not Alone: Understanding Anxiety and Its Disorders

The truth is that our finest moments are most likely to occur when we are feeling deeply uncomfortable, unhappy, or unfulfilled. For it is only in such moments, propelled by our discomfort, that we are likely to step out of our ruts and start searching for different ways or truer answers. —M. Scott Peck

YOU ARE NOT ALONE

You may have told yourself, "I feel so alone. My anxiety is so intense, and nobody understands what it's like." As you read through this chapter and discover some facts about anxiety, we hope you'll see that many other people share your fears, thoughts, feelings, and behavioral tendencies.

Many of the people we have helped feel a sense of relief when we present them with the facts you are about to learn. We hope you too will discover that your problem is indeed well recognized and understood. So please remember that you're not alone!

People with anxiety disorders are everywhere. They live in every town, state, and country. They belong to all ethnic groups. Anxiety disorders affect the rich and the poor alike. In fact, anxiety disorders are among the most common psychological disorders, affecting up to 30 percent of the general population at some point in their lifetimes (Kessler et al., 2005). This may seem like a small number to you, but in reality that number is enormous. In fact, if everyone with an anxiety disorder decided to wear a red hat, you'd be hard-pressed to go about your day without seeing someone wearing one.

Anxiety disorders also tend to be chronic. This means that without some changes on your part, the problems tend to stick around and may even get worse over time. Given that so many lives are affected by anxiety disorders, it's not surprising that anxiety disorders are associated with enormous personal, social, and economic costs.

One of our colleagues, the accomplished anxiety researcher Dr. David Barlow (2002), pointed out that the actual expenses dwarf even the most pessimistic estimates. Counting both the direct costs of services and lost work productivity, the total annual costs of anxiety disorders in the United States are estimated at approximately $45 billion, with only 25 percent of that amount stemming from psychological and psychiatric treatment. In fact, the bulk of the costs come from unnecessary use of health care services, lost productivity, and reduced life functioning.

WHAT IS THE NATURE OF ANXIETY AND FEAR?

All humans are born with the capacity to experience anxiety and fear. If you're reading this book, then you certainly have this capacity or, more likely, think you have "too much of it." And you've probably educated yourself a bit about the nature of anxiety and fear too.

Here, our intention is to add a bit to what you may know already. And we'd like to offer you a slightly different perspective on what you think you may know. As you read on, you'll see that this fresh perspective has to do with getting a sense of the difference between normal and "abnormal," or disordered, anxiety and fear.

Before you read on, take a moment to jot down what you think best describes three critical differences between normal and abnormal anxiety and fear. For instance, you might think that normal anxiety is *less extreme* compared with abnormal anxiety.

1. Normal anxiety/fear is ____less intense____ compared with abnormal anxiety/fear.

2. Normal anxiety/fear is ____less Frequent____ compared with abnormal anxiety/fear.

3. Normal anxiety/fear is _____ compared with abnormal anxiety/fear.

We're not going to spend much time with what you just wrote down. We only ask that you hold your ideas lightly as you read on, starting with the most basic and primitive of all emotions—fear.

Fear: The Present-Oriented Basic Emotion

Fear is an intensely felt alarm response that you must have to survive. It helps you take protective action when your safety or health is threatened. When you experience this emotion, your body will do a number of things to help you to get moving to take care of yourself. For instance, you may experience rapid heartbeat; breathlessness; smothering sensations; increased blood pressure; feel hot, sick to your stomach, or dizzy; or break out in a sweat. You may even feel as though you're about to pass out.

Your body and brain are also kicking into overdrive. A number of other bodily systems are activated. All of this activity may leave you with a feeling of heightened energy—the adrenaline rush. These bodily changes are necessary to help you take evasive action. They represent what we call a powerful action tendency to fight or flee from signs of threat or danger.

Fear also tends to heighten awareness of your surroundings so that you may quickly detect sources of danger. This heightened awareness helps you stay focused on whatever triggers the fear (Barlow, 2002). And it helps you to take quick action to protect yourself.

Anxiety: The Future-Oriented Emotion

Anxiety, by contrast, is a future-oriented mood state. People know anxiety by having anxious apprehension or a sense of foreboding, worry, and muscle tension. You still need the capacity to experience anxiety because it can help motivate you to get things done.

The bodily changes associated with anxiety are much less pronounced and dramatic than those associated with fear. At the same time, anxiety and worry can last much longer than acute fear, often ebbing and flowing for days, weeks, months, or even years. This is possible, in part, because anxiety tends to be fueled more by what your mind says than by real sources of danger or threat.

EXERCISE: CAN YOU TELL THE DIFFERENCE BETWEEN ANXIETY AND FEAR?

Below is a list of circumstances that may help you get a sense of the difference between anxiety and fear. Read each item and then circle (A) if you think the event would most likely cause anxiety or (F) if you think the event would bring on fear.

▪ Seeing a bear in the woods	A (F)	▪ Possibility of seeing a bear in the woods	(A) F
▪ Being mugged in the city	A (F)	▪ Chance of being mugged in the future	(A) F
▪ Car almost hitting you	A (F)	▪ Chance of getting hit by a car	(A) F
▪ Suffering a serious injury	A (F)	▪ Possibility of being seriously injured	(A) F
▪ Being in a house fire	A (F)	▪ Chance of your house burning down	(A) F

What you should notice from this activity is that all the situations in the left column are present oriented, whereas those in the right column are future oriented. So what you should end up with is all Fs in the left column and all As in the right column.

The point of this activity is to help you get a sense of one critical difference between fear and anxiety: the present versus future quality. People are typically anxious about something that may happen in the future. Fear is a reaction to what is or could be happening in the moment. As an example, you might experience anxiety about the possibility of living through an earthquake and its aftermath, but fear would be your experience when the earth is actually shaking.

Behaviors most closely linked with anxiety have to do with what you think and say to yourself (e.g., worrying, ruminating over something, even making plans), whereas behaviors most closely associated with fear involve overt behavioral actions (e.g., running, fighting, taking cover, freezing). If it helps, you can think of the differences this way: "Fear requires little thought; anxiety needs big thought."

Normal Fear and Anxiety Keep Us Out of Trouble

Experiencing fear and anxiety is healthy and adaptive. Both emotions serve the purpose of keeping you and everyone else out of trouble and alive.

For instance, fear is perfectly adaptive in situations where you might be faced with real danger or threat. In those circumstances, fear serves to motivate and mobilize you to take defensive action—get away or, if necessary, fight to defend yourself. Everything going on in your body and mind during fear is for one purpose: to help you to protect yourself, period.

Some of these actions are so automatic and hardwired that you don't need to learn them in order to respond. An example would be closing your eyes and turning your head to avoid a fast-moving object flying in the air toward you. We can also *learn* to respond with fear, often with the help of language. In fact, our capacity to use language makes it possible to run in fear in response to someone yelling "Get out—the building is on fire!"

Anxiety and worry often can be useful and adaptive too. In fact, it would be maladaptive not to worry about future events that could truly threaten your health and welfare. We know that a bout of anxiety and worry can help motivate people to take appropriate steps to plan for the future.

So you might put together an action plan to prepare yourself for potential threats to your health, employment, safety, or the welfare of your family. A good example would be a family coming up with an action plan in the event of a house fire. The plan may be simple or elaborate, but the goal is the same: to help you take effective action when faced with actual threat.

What About My Fear and Anxiety?

You may be wondering how your situation fits into this picture. Before we get into fear and anxiety as a problem, think of a recent example where you experienced intense fear and where it was very useful to have such fear.

By "useful" we mean a situation where you were suddenly faced with real danger—perhaps a car on the road that you didn't see or a person or animal that threatened to harm you. You can pick a recent example or one that happened a while ago and that you remember well because it was a "big deal"— where experiencing fear and doing something to save yourself (or someone else) made a real difference, perhaps even saved your or someone else's life.

EXERCISE: HAS RESPONDING WITH FEAR AND WORRY BEEN USEFUL TO ME?

On the lines below, briefly describe the threatening/dangerous event, your response, and how your response worked out. Doing this little exercise will also be useful later when we'll help you figure out when acting on fear and anxiety is helpful and when it is not useful and can make matters worse. We'll start with a situation where you felt strong fear and then move on to anxiety.

Threatening/dangerous event:

guy in car

Your response (thoughts, feelings, actions):

not look at him

How it was useful:

didn't engage him

Now think of a situation or event where being anxious and worrying about a possible negative event or outcome helped you make a plan and where having a plan and acting on it was somehow useful to you. On the lines below, briefly describe the event, your response, and how your response worked out.

Potential problem:

our # after death

Your response (thoughts, feelings, actions):

estate planning

How it was useful:

have thoughtful plan

This activity may have been hard for you to do because you probably see your anxiety and fear as unwelcome guests, not as real assets or "friends and allies." That's fine and totally expected from the vantage point of where you are now.

Still, we'd like you to see if you can dig deep here and give yourself some time to do this exercise. See if you can put the "Worrying, anxiety, and fear are bad" idea to the side for a moment as you think about at least one example from your life where fear and anxiety were helpful for you.

The reason this exercise is so important is that it ought to help you see that fear and worrying have served you well in the past and that you'll likely need to draw on your capacity to experience both in the future. We encourage you not to forget this fact as you go through this book. Write this down if it helps: _I need the capacity to experience worry, anxiety, and fear just like I need air to breathe, water to drink, and food to eat._

This doesn't mean that you ought to be anxious 24/7 either. In fact, we'd venture a guess that being anxious 24/7 might be typical of your experience without you trying to be that way. And it probably seems that more often than not, your worry, anxiety, and fear are more hurtful than helpful. They happen too often or too intensely. They happen when you're at no risk of being harmed. Your worries may seem to stretch to infinity. Your thoughts are too disturbing and next to impossible to turn off.

All of this and more has certainly interfered with you living your life the way you want to live it. In fact, interference with life is probably one of the chief reasons you picked up this book in the first place. It turns out that life interference is actually one of the key litmus tests that professionals, such as medical doctors and psychologists, use to determine when fear or anxiety move away from being adaptive and shift into the realm of an anxiety _disorder_.

Let's have a closer look at how this applies to you.

IDENTIFYING YOUR TYPE OF ANXIETY PROBLEM

Self-help books written for people with anxiety disorders typically spend too much time describing the various types of anxiety problems and helping people diagnose themselves. We don't want to lead you down this path because we don't think it'll be of much use to you.

Labeling yourself with a diagnosis or two will not make your life more livable or help you in other ways. For instance, a diagnostic label is not going to help you accept what needs to be accepted and change what can be changed. And the label can even become a self-fulfilling prophecy—something you become. It's hard to shake labels once they're applied.

I need the capacity to experience worry, anxiety and fear.

Your most important task here is this: to identify the root of what turns *your* fear, anxiety, worry, or obsession into the life-shattering problem or disorder *you* have been struggling with. The kind of anxiety problem you have is important for another reason. We've found that people do better with treatment when they focus their efforts on their most vexing concerns. We've also noticed that as they do that, other related or less pressing concerns tend to improve too.

In the following sections you'll find a description of each of the major anxiety disorders. We also present brief stories of real people who have struggled with each type of anxiety problem. We offer these stories to help you better appreciate key features of anxiety problems. As you read on, you'll notice that all the real-life examples are different from each other in many ways. Yet as you read through them, you may also detect some common features. See if you can find those.

Panic Attacks

A *panic attack* is a sudden rush of fear. It's accompanied by intense physical sensations, a strong urge to escape or get away from the situation or place where those sensations occur, and a sense of impending doom—the feeling that something really bad is happening.

Below is a list of experiences that the American Psychiatric Association (2000) uses to define a panic attack. Check (√) all items that you experience when you have a panic attack:

- ☑ Pounding or racing heart

- ☐ Chest pain or discomfort

- ☐ Shortness of breath or smothering sensations

- ☐ Trembling or shaking

- ☐ Feeling of choking

- ☐ Sweating

- ☐ Dizziness, unsteady feeling, or faintness

- ☐ Nausea or abdominal distress

- ☐ Feeling you or your surroundings are strange or unreal

- ☐ Numbness or tingling in face, hands, or legs

- ☑ Hot flashes or chills

- ☐ Fear of dying (e.g., fear of having a heart attack)

❑   Fear of going crazy

❑   Fear of doing something uncontrolled

Panic attacks often occur quite unexpectedly—"out of the blue"—without obvious sources of real danger or threat. They're also called "false alarms" for this reason. This makes the experience even more frightening because the panic attack makes no sense and doesn't seem to serve any purpose.

We know from large research studies that panic attacks are common: about ten to thirty-three people out of one hundred experience at least one panic attack (or false alarm) in a given year (Barlow, 2002). Having much stress in your life can certainly make panic attacks more likely, but panic attacks can happen during periods of calm too. They can even show up when you're asleep in bed at night.

Take the case of Brandon, a twenty-four-year-old college graduate. He experienced a panic attack as he was about to have a job interview.

■ Brandon's Story

I had to pull over on my way to a job interview. I felt dizzy and light-headed at first, and my heart felt like it was beating out of my chest. My head felt like a giant air balloon that was going to explode at any second. My hands were trembling, and my palms were sweating. My fingertips felt numb too. The pain in my chest was so bad I was sure I was about to have a heart attack, and the dizziness just got worse and worse. As hard as I tried, I couldn't catch my breath. My breathing was so out of control, I thought I was going to die. I tried to make it all go away. Nothing worked.

How Panic Attacks May Turn into Panic Disorder

Having many unexpected panic attacks without an obvious trigger or cause is *one* of the official standards used by mental health professionals when diagnosing panic disorder. Yet this isn't the whole story. Even if you've had many panic attacks and continue to have them as often as once a month, several times a week, or every day, it doesn't mean that you have *panic disorder*.

A diagnosis of panic disorder requires that you also worry about when the next attack will strike and the possible consequences of an attack. For instance, you might worry that you'll die, lose control, faint, go crazy, vomit, or have diarrhea. You may even think that you'll humiliate yourself, lose your job, or end up in the loony bin. All of these thoughts can certainly make things worse, but they are not the most important feature of panic disorder.

To get a sense of what we mean here, you can go ahead and tell yourself this: "I'm going nuts." This thought likely had little effect on you at the moment you just had it. During a panic attack, though, this thought and the strong urges that go along with the response can lead you to do things that make you withdraw from your life; this withdrawal, or pulling out, is key.

In fact, the critical feature of panic that makes it a problem is this: a change in your behavior in order to cope with the attacks or prevent them from happening. We've summarized some of the more common behavioral changes for you below (Antony & McCabe, 2004). As you'll see, the behaviors look different from one another, but underneath, they are really quite similar—they all serve to make people feel safe (or at least safer) from panic. As before, check (√) all behaviors in the list that you engage in to manage your panic:

- ☐ Sitting near exits when at the movies or in a restaurant

- ☐ Checking where the closest exit is when visiting a shopping mall

- ☑ Carrying medication, money, cell phone, pager, water, or other safety items

- ☐ Avoiding activities (like exercise, sex, or thriller movies) that might trigger physical arousal

- ☐ Drinking alcohol to combat feelings of panic

- ☑ Avoiding caffeine, alcohol, or other substances (for example, MSG or spicy foods)

- ☐ Frequently checking your pulse or blood pressure

- ☐ Distracting yourself from the panic experience (for instance, reading a book, watching TV)

- ☐ Insisting on being accompanied when leaving the house

- ☐ Always needing to know the whereabouts of your spouse, partner, or other "safe" person

Some people with panic disorder don't avoid situations where panic attacks may occur. With courage and determination they refuse to let panic attacks dictate where they go and don't go or what they do or don't do. Most people with panic disorder, however, develop some degree of *agoraphobia* over time. This simply means they avoid places or events where panic attacks might happen. These are often places from which a quick escape is difficult and where they might feel confined or trapped.

Some of the most common situations people avoid are listed below. Again, check (√) all situations in the list that you avoid so you won't have a panic attack:

- ☐ Crowded public places: supermarkets, theaters, malls, sports events

- ☐ Enclosed and confined places: tunnels, bridges, small rooms, elevators, airplanes, subways, buses, getting a haircut, and long lines

    ❑   Driving: especially on highways and bridges, in bad traffic, and over long distances

    ❑   Being away from home: some people have a safe distance around their home and find it difficult to travel beyond that distance; in rare cases, leaving the home may seem completely impossible

    ❑   Being alone: at home or in any of the situations listed above

Let's look at how some of this played out with Ruth, a thirty-two-year-old journalist. Her frequent panic attacks have morphed into panic disorder: she's worried about future attacks. And she's changed her behavior to avoid having them. Like many people with panic disorder, over time she's developed some *agoraphobic avoidance*: she avoids places where panic may attack.

■ *Ruth's Story*

I have problems just going outside my house. I get in such a state of panic that I make sure that I have an escape option in all situations. I always drive separately to functions so I can leave if the panic gets bad. I even drove six hours alone for a weekend getaway at a lake house with some people I work with because I thought that if I had a panic attack, I could just drive away from there. I always have to make up excuses why I have to drive separately. I have major stomach problems and panic when I even think that I have no control of a situation, like being in a boat and there's no bathroom on the boat. In fact, I've decided to avoid these situations in the future—just to be on the safe side. I often feel like I must be crazy, which makes me panic too. I can't handle these attacks anymore and hate feeling like I have no control all the time.

Specific Phobias

Just about everyone has something that they're afraid of. Specific phobias are defined by a strong fear and avoidance of a feared object or situation. Large surveys show that at least 10 percent of the general population will have a specific phobia during their lifetime (Kessler et al., 2005).

The reaction that phobia sufferers experience is virtually the same as a panic attack but with one difference: the alarm response in specific phobias shows up upon exposure to the feared object or situation, whereas in panic disorder, the alarm response happens unexpectedly with no clear trigger.

Persons with specific phobias also experience a strong urge to get away from the feared object or situation. Many make great efforts to avoid future encounters with the feared object too. Depending on their life circumstances, avoidance may or may not be life constricting.

For instance, a person with a specific phobia of snakes may be able to do just about everything they'd like to do so long as they live in midtown Manhattan where seeing a snake is highly unlikely. But don't ask this person to go to a national park, the zoo, or for a walk in the woods. They'll most likely tell you that they've got other plans.

People typically recognize that their fear is excessive or unreasonable. This knowledge, however, has no impact on the urge to run from and avoid feared objects. And it does little to help them control or minimize the unpleasant emotional discomfort that's triggered by the feared objects.

The most common specific phobias are (in descending order) fear of animals, heights, closed spaces, blood and injuries, storms and lightning, and flying. As you might guess, these phobias may not be life impairing so long as the feared object can be avoided without getting in the way of what a person needs to do. As soon as the avoidance gets in the way of what a person needs to do or would like to do, watch out—we have the seeds of a problem.

Take a look at the list below and check (√) all items that give you an intense panic-like response when you encounter them:

- ❑ Situations (e.g., heights, closed spaces, dentists, elevators, or airplanes/flying)

- ❑ Animals (e.g., snakes, rats, spiders, dogs)

- ❑ Natural environment (e.g., heights, storms, lightning, water)

- ❑ Illness or bodily harm (e.g., diseases, injuries)

- ❑ Sight of blood or needles

- ❑ Other (e.g., choking, eating certain foods, vomiting)

Most people with specific phobias never seek treatment. They simply avoid the feared object. This is fairly easy to do because the object of fear is clearly known. In other cases, contact with the feared object is so unlikely that it never gets in the way of what they need to do. So if you have a shark phobia and you live in Idaho, then it's highly unlikely that you'll have much difficulty with this phobia. There's no chance of running into a shark in Idaho (other than in movies or on TV).

At other times, "successful" avoidance may come at a high personal cost. For instance, we once worked with an Australian family that used to spend weekends visiting a beautiful island just three miles offshore. The island was a popular weekend getaway destination for the family and many people in the area. The family stopped going because the mother had a shark phobia. She couldn't stand the thought of sharks swimming underneath the ferryboat during the crossing.

The critical question this woman faced was this: what is more important—my family or my fear? Her answer made a real difference in her life. And finding that answer came down to a choice between two alternatives: spending time with her family in a beautiful setting and having fear while getting there, or staying at home without fear and missing out on fun time with her family.

Jane is a thirty-four-year-old mother of two children and she has a phobia of crickets. She was also facing some tough choices.

■ *Jane's Story*

Even though I know it's totally unreasonable, I'm terrified of crickets. My anxiety skyrockets when I'm outside because I feel like they're everywhere. Sometimes I can hear them at night through my window. To blot out the noise I turn the TV on and crank up the volume. I end up staying awake all night because of the noise. Just thinking about them gets my pulse racing. I can even feel my breathing become very shallow and strained. When I hear them, or even worse, see them, I hyperventilate to the point where I'm sure I'll pass out. It's gotten so bad. I can't even go to the park with my kids for fear that I'll see one. The kids don't understand what it's like for me, and I feel terrible that I can't overcome my fear for their sake.

Social Anxiety and Phobia

Social phobia is an intense fear of embarrassment or humiliation. Usually, this fear shows up in situations where you're exposed to the scrutiny of others or where you must perform. Typically, people fear that they'll say or do something that will lead others to judge them as incompetent, weak, or stupid. They also worry that others might detect their social discomfort.

Social phobia is very common. In fact, about 3 to 13 percent of the population will suffer from it at some point during their lives (Barlow 2002). This makes social phobia the most common anxiety disorder.

Below is a list of social situations that people are often afraid of and that they try to avoid. You'll see that fear of public speaking tops the list. It's the most common social phobia and the most common type of any phobia. As before, check (√) all social fears that apply to you:

- ❑ Fear of public speaking

- ❑ Fear of blushing in public

- ❑ Fear of choking on or spilling food while eating in public

- ❑ Fear of writing or signing documents when others are present (e.g., at grocery checkout)

- ❑ Fear of being watched at work

- ❑ Fear of crowds

- ❑ Fear of using public toilets

Some people with social phobia also experience panic attacks. Mostly, these panic attacks are related to a specific type of social situation or being embarrassed and humiliated rather than being confined or trapped.

To minimize or reduce their discomfort, people with social phobia typically stay away from social situations as much as they can. Such situations include public speaking, meeting or talking with persons of the opposite sex, group meetings, speaking on the telephone, social gatherings, and using public restrooms or public transportation. More than 90 percent of all persons diagnosed with social phobia fear and avoid more than one social activity (Barlow, 2002).

That said, an interesting subset of people with intense social anxiety don't avoid social situations. In fact, performers (such as stage actors) and people whose jobs require them to make presentations will perform and make their presentations day after day and take their anxiety along with them into these situations. How do they do that? We'll return to that question in chapter 5.

Let's take a look at Mike, a twenty-five-year-old speech pathology major struggling with social phobia. As you read through Mike's story, see whether you can detect how he's not only distressed in social situations—he also does whatever he can to avoid and get rid of that distress.

■ Mike's Story

I've been suffering from social anxiety for as long as I can remember. I was a loner as a child and never had any friends. Even when I'm not with people, I believe that they're thinking about me. I think that every time I say something or do something (or don't do something) they could suddenly not like me anymore. I feel very uncomfortable around people and fear that they can see my discomfort. Talking is an effort. I fear that people are judging me constantly. I feel like anything out of my mouth will make others think badly of me . . . that I'm stupid or selfish or lazy. I'm extremely negative and critical of myself. It's so frustrating. I work so hard to get through the day. I start student teaching in a little over a week. I'm terrified about that, but I'm trying not to be—trying to tell myself that I'll be fine. Last semester, when I did my clinical practice, was the worst time of my life. I cried and had panic attacks every day. I completely avoided my housemates. It was just so horrible. I couldn't eat much and lost fifteen pounds. I can't go through that again. It's really hard, and I'm really scared. I don't know what to do to make it better.

Obsessive-Compulsive Disorder

Being neat, tidy, orderly, organized, and following rules can be a blessing in many situations in life. But when these behaviors are carried to the extreme, they can become disruptive and take over a person's life. When they do, it's called *obsessive-compulsive disorder* (OCD).

Obsessions are recurring and persistent thoughts, impulses, or images that bring on intense anxiety. Examples include images or thoughts of harming someone, being contaminated with dirt or germs, or fearing you left your lights or stove on or your door unlocked. People typically experience these thoughts or images as intrusive (that is, happening despite efforts to resist them), unreasonable, and distressing. Obsessions can become so intense, so consuming, that some people spiral into a full-blown panic attack. This reaction is similar to that seen in panic disorder except that the phobic objects in OCD are thoughts or images rather than bodily sensations or changes.

Here's a list of some common obsessions. As before, check (√) all items that apply to you:

- ❑ Thoughts that you might harm self or others

- ❑ Violent or horrific images

- ❑ Fear of blurting out obscenities or insults

- ❑ Fear of acting on unwanted impulses (for example, to stab a friend)

- ❑ Fear of stealing things

- ❑ Fear of being responsible for something terrible happening (such as fire or burglary)

- ❑ Sexual thoughts, images, or urges

- ❑ Fear of acting on "forbidden" impulses (incest, homosexuality, aggressive sexual acts)

- ❑ Concern with sacrilege and blasphemy, right/wrong, or morality

- ❑ Concern that someone will have an accident unless things are in the right place

- ❑ Fear of saying certain things because they might come true

- ❑ Fear of losing things

- ❑ Intrusive (nonviolent) images, nonsense sounds, words, or music

- ❑ Concerns about dirt, germs, or bodily waste or secretions (urine, feces, saliva)

- ❑ Concern about getting ill from possible contaminants

- ❑ Concern about environmental contaminants (asbestos, radiation, toxic waste)

- ❑ Excessive concern with household items (cleansers, solvents)

- ❑ Excessive concern about animals (for example, insects)

Compulsions are repeated ritualistic behaviors (for example, checking, hand washing) or mental acts (such as counting, praying). The purpose of performing rituals is to reduce anxiety and suppress or neutralize the disturbing intrusive thoughts or images. Attending to obsessions and ritualizing is enormously time consuming. And it puts so many constraints on life that people literally run out of time to do what they need to do. This cycle interferes with daily routines and social functioning. In extreme cases, hospitalization may be needed to break the cycle.

Here's a partial list of common compulsions. As before, check (√) all behaviors that seem to apply to you:

- ❑ Excessive/ritualized cleaning (hand washing, bathing, toothbrushing, grooming, toilet routine)

- ❑ Excessive cleaning of household items or other inanimate objects

- ❑ Checking locks, stove, appliances, and so on

- ❑ Checking that you did not/will not harm others or yourself

- ❑ Checking that nothing terrible did/will happen

- ❑ Checking that you didn't make a mistake

- ❑ Needing to repeat routine activities (jogging, going in/out door or up/down from chair, rereading, rewriting)

- ❑ Compulsively collecting or not being able to get rid of useless objects (e.g., junk mail, old newspapers, garbage, and other useless objects such as Band-Aids, ear swabs, wrappers)

- ❑ Performing mental rituals (other than checking/counting)

- ❑ Excessive list making

- ❑ Needing to tell, ask, or confess, or touch, tap, or rub

- ❑ Ritualized blinking or staring

- ❑ Ritualized eating behaviors

- ❑ Engaging in superstitious behaviors

- ❑ Compulsive hair pulling (top of head, eyelashes, eyebrows)

Most people struggling with OCD realize that their rituals are excessive and unreasonable. Yet they continue to do them, chasing a sense of relief that comes about by struggling to neutralize unwanted thoughts and associated anxiety.

The problem is that rituals typically only reduce anxiety for a short while, and then anxiety and tension come right back. The same is true of the thoughts that trigger the anxiety in the first place. In fact, there's mounting research evidence that attempts to suppress unwanted thoughts and images can actually backfire, setting people up to have the unwanted thoughts with increasing frequency and intensity (Hayes, Wilson, Gifford, Follette, & Strosahl, 1996; Wegner, 1994). This process keeps the vicious cycle going with OCD.

Ray is a forty-year-old office clerk who feels completely controlled by the endless cycle of recurring obsessions, anxiety, and compulsive washing.

■ Ray's Story

For as long as I can remember I've been terrified of germs and the prospect of getting diseases. When I go to stores, I can't even open the door myself. I have to stand outside and wait for someone to go in or come out and then I try to catch the door with my elbow. I can't stand to even think about touching public property and wouldn't ever leave the house without antibacterial hand gel. I can't eat off plates or silverware at restaurants, so I never eat out with my friends. Even in my own house I eat off paper plates and use plastic silverware. My hands bleed because I wash them so much. I can't sleep if I feel like I might have germs on me, and so I have to shower ten times before falling asleep. As much as I want to enjoy normal activities like everyone else, I can't make the anxiety go away. My cleansing rituals are the only thing that helps, and then the anxiety comes right back again and again. Will it ever end?

Post-traumatic Stress Disorder

Post-traumatic stress disorder (PTSD) is a cluster of anxiety problems that can develop in the wake of a severe traumatic experience. Such experiences would produce intense fear, terror, and feelings of helplessness in anyone. Experiences like that include violent crimes against yourself or family members (such as rape and assault), combat situations (for instance, wounding of self and others, committing or witnessing atrocities), natural disasters (such as earthquakes or tornadoes), and accidents (such as car or plane crashes).

People suffering from PTSD may notice a number of changes after the traumatic event. Some changes affect how they experience their world. These altered experiences may take the form of seeing the world as a dangerous place, feeling emotionally numb, or feeling a sense of detachment from the self or surroundings—like an out-of-body experience. Other changes are more behavioral and may include being startled easily, scanning the environment for threat, and avoidance or escape. These changes tend to creep up on people over a period of several months after the traumatic event.

As you read through the items in the list below, check (√) all items that apply to you:

- ❏ Repetitive, intrusive or upsetting thoughts about a distressing event

- ❏ Nightmares related to the event

- ❏ Intense and vivid flashbacks, leaving you feeling or acting as if the trauma was happening again

- ❏ Attempts to avoid thoughts or feelings associated with the trauma

- ❏ Attempts to avoid activities or external situations associated with the trauma—such as driving after you have been in a car accident

- ❏ Emotional numbness—being out of touch with feelings

- ❏ Feelings of detachment or estrangement from others

- ❏ Losing interest in activities that used to give you pleasure

- ❏ Always feeling on edge—difficulty falling or staying asleep, difficulty concentrating, startling easily, scanning the environment for signs of danger or threat, and irritability and outbursts of anger

- ❏ Elevated bodily arousal that can spiral up into a full-blown panic attack

Many people with PTSD are chronically anxious and depressed even if they are not acutely experiencing any of the behaviors on the above list. The trauma seems to be there as "background noise" all the time. Regardless of the type of trauma, persons suffering from PTSD often go to great lengths to avoid thinking about the traumatic event. They also avoid any cues or situations that may remind them of the event.

The central purpose of avoidance is to prevent reexperiencing the emotions and psychological pain associated with the trauma. As with other anxiety disorders, when this avoidance becomes extensive, it can restrict life functioning to such a degree that PTSD sufferers no longer engage in routine activities.

It's important to remember that experiencing a traumatic event doesn't mean that you or anyone else is destined to develop PTSD. In fact, research conducted with World Trade Center survivors shows that "only" about 25 percent of those who were caught in the buildings after the 9/11 attack developed PTSD.

Mary, a thirty-eight-year-old secretary, is a good example of someone who's exhausted by her unsuccessful struggle with PTSD. Her story shows how PTSD can interfere with just about all aspects of a person's life.

■ *Mary's Story*

Less than two years ago I was attacked and mugged outside my car one night after work. Since then I've been in a constant state of extreme anxiety and panic whenever I walk alone, day or night. I can't sleep without having intense nightmares of the attack, and often I wake up soaked in sweat with my heart pounding out of my chest. Even during the daytime my mind will often wander off and I'll have vivid flashbacks of the event: I can't seem to stop my mind from replaying the event over and over again. Lately, I've been trying to avoid these memories by taking up new activities so that I'm constantly busy, but I can't find anything I'm interested in, and it doesn't seem to make a difference anyway. No matter what I do, I can't control the flashbacks when they come. Simple tasks like going to the grocery store are unbelievably difficult. Harder things like work have become nearly impossible. All of my limited energy goes into trying to make the memories stop, but they keep coming. I'm completely exhausted.

Generalized Anxiety Disorder

Generalized anxiety disorder (GAD) is characterized by excessive worry about a number of events and activities. People commonly report that they feel "stressed" and overwhelmed by everyday life experiences, or "daily hassles." Worrying typically occurs more days than not and causes significant distress or impairs functioning either at work, at home, or both.

Approximately 5 percent of the general population will suffer from GAD at some point in their lives (Barlow, 2002). GAD typically develops slowly over time, often beginning at an earlier age than other anxiety disorders. Because of this, many GAD sufferers think that they "have always been a worrier" and "an anxious person." Worry and anxiety tend to be more intense during periods of life stress and less intense during periods of low stress.

As you read through the items in the list below, check (√) all that apply to you:

- ☐ Attempts to stop or control worrying and to reduce anxiety by means of worrying

- ☐ Can't stop worrying even if it doesn't seem to solve anything and is unproductive

- ☑ Restlessness—feeling keyed up

- ☐ Muscle tension

- ☐ Being easily fatigued

- ☐ Difficulty concentrating

□   Irritability

□   Difficulties with sleep

People with GAD often have a pervasive feeling that they can do little to predict and control stressful events in their lives, so they end up worrying about them. There's now convincing research evidence that people engage in worry as a way to avoid this unpleasant imagery and the physical tension associated with anxiety (Borkovec, Alcaine, & Behar, 2004).

This avoidance works in the short run—it buys the person some relief. Yet in the long run it doesn't work. People get caught in a loop. They tend to experience even more intense anxiety followed by efforts to reduce anxiety by engaging in more worrying. All the while, they are unable to work through their problems and arrive at active solutions. This is what we mean by the worrying being unproductive. The following two cases show this vicious circle.

Larry is a thirty-three-year-old risk analyst working for a bank—a job that feeds right into his anxiety problem. He cannot remember a time without GAD. Jenny is a twenty-eight-year-old legal assistant. She feels her mind has gone on "worry autopilot" in recent years.

■ *Larry's Story*

The constant fear and worry is ruining my life because I don't know what it's like to have normal, secure relationships with people or really to just have fun and enjoy life. I can't really imagine what it would be like to live and not have anxiety all the time. I avoid all sorts of situations. And I often worry about things that are so unlikely and aren't all that important. I shouldn't be thinking about them at all. Just yesterday I couldn't go out with friends because I couldn't shake the fear that we would be hit by a car or mugged. I worry about people and pets dying, friends deserting me because I'm crazy, getting an illness or disease. . . . Basically, I worry about everything. I have a lot of trouble falling asleep at night because I can't shut my mind off. I just wish I could control what I was thinking so I could live a normal life.

■ *Jenny's Story*

My anxiety has been getting progressively worse over the last few years. I feel like my mind is always wired. I'm constantly obsessing over things that I don't think other people worry about. My brain is always working overtime, thinking about situations that make me really nervous and tense. It gets so bad sometimes that I throw up because of it. Lately my jaw has been really sore from clenching it so tightly during most of the day and night. The only time I feel like myself is the first few seconds after I wake up in the middle of the night. During those times I'm too disoriented to be worried.

ANXIETY DISORDERS HAVE MUCH IN COMMON

This overview has, to some extent, emphasized the differences among the anxiety disorders. OCD, for instance, differs from panic or PTSD much like an apple differs from an orange. To be sure, anxiety disorders do differ in some ways. Yet now more than ever before, we're coming to terms with the fact that anxiety disorders are more similar than we've made them out to be. And it turns out that the similarities are much more important than the minor variations when it comes to helping people like you. Have a look at the list below to get a sense of what we mean.

- **Anxiety and fear are triggered by something.** There are an infinite number of possible triggers for anxiety and fear, including stress. The triggers can spring forth from within you (thoughts, images, memories, or bodily sensations), from the world around you, or some combination of both. For some types of anxiety disorders we can pinpoint what actually brings on fear and anxiety. And when the source of fear and anxiety is known, you can anticipate it reasonably well. Examples of anxiety problems with obvious triggers include specific phobias, social phobia, and PTSD. With panic disorder, OCD, and even GAD, the triggers tend to be more subtle. And they can be difficult to detect. Yet not having a clear idea about your triggers doesn't mean that your anxiety and fear aren't triggered. The triggers are there and simply need to be revealed.

- **Duration and intensity of anxiety and fear ebb and flow over time.** Our bodies cannot sustain anxiety and fear 24/7. In panic disorder, specific phobias, and social phobia, the fear and accompanying physical changes people experience are intense but relatively short-lived—typically no more than half an hour and rarely beyond one hour. People who experience such difficulties may report the feelings lasting longer, but this has more to do with our minds than our bodies. Our bodies cannot keep up panic or extreme anxiety for long periods of time. In GAD, the anxiety and related physical reactions are less intense, and they persist over much longer periods of time than fear. In OCD and PTSD, anxiety and tension may vary greatly in intensity and duration over time. None of it lasts forever.

- **Fear is fear, and anxiety is anxiety.** It turns out that the experience of fear and anxiety doesn't differ in form or substance across the anxiety disorders. Fear is fear. Anxiety is anxiety. Both emotions characterize all anxiety disorders. And, at a basic level, the nature of fear and anxiety that people with anxiety disorders talk about is identical to fear and anxiety experienced from time to time by people without anxiety disorders.

- **Similar treatments work well for all anxiety problems.** If anxiety problems were truly different in kind and substance, then you'd expect that we'd have special treatments matched to each unique anxiety problem. This turns out not to be the case. Research shows that similar treatment strategies work for all anxiety disorders. In fact, most effective treatments for anxiety problems share a small set of common exercises and skill-building tools. We've wrapped those effective elements into this book. This is good news for you.

This list highlights what we've learned from research in recent years. It shows that anxiety disorders share some striking commonalities. Yet the most important commonality of all is not on that list. We left it out. It's time to state it boldly: *people with anxiety disorders struggle with, avoid, and run away from their fear and anxiety*. This tendency defines the actions of just about every person with an anxiety disorder. And struggle turns out to be the most important toxic element that constricts lives and transforms anxiety from being a normal human experience into a life-shattering problem. You got a glimpse of where avoidance can take you with the cartoons in chapter 1. We'll focus more on this critical issue in the next chapter.

> *People with anxiety disorders struggle with, avoid, and run away from their fear and anxiety.*

OTHER PROBLEMS WITH ANXIETY DISORDERS

Studies from the United States and various parts of the world (Craske, 2003) show that more than half of the people who are struggling with an anxiety disorder also have other significant emotional and behavioral problems such as depression and drug abuse. We cover these below because there's a good chance that they might apply to you.

Depression

Depression is a persistent mood state where people feel very sad, "down and empty," worthless, and hopeless about the future. Some people say that depression feels like a black curtain of despair has come down over their lives. And just about everything they do is cast in darkness by this curtain. Many question whether their life situation will ever improve.

Lack of energy and fatigue are common complaints, and many report difficulties concentrating, remembering, and making decisions. Many also have sleep difficulties. Others feel irritable and restless all the time for no apparent reason. They often lose interest in hobbies and activities that they once enjoyed, including sex.

Depression is by far the most common emotional problem that people with anxiety disorders experience. In fact, about half of all people with an anxiety disorder will also experience significant depression at some point (Barlow, 2002). At times depression may develop before an anxiety disorder, but it's more common for depression to creep up on people after they've been suffering from an anxiety disorder for a while.

Given the way anxiety and fear can get in the way of meaningful life activities, it's not surprising that people start to think and feel that life is no longer enjoyable or worth living.

Alcohol Abuse

One of the common features that virtually all people with anxiety problems share is that they engage in similar strategies to cope with their anxiety—strategies that have not worked very well or at all. For instance, men in particular have been found to "self-medicate" their anxiety problem with alcohol to make their life situation more bearable (Barlow, 2002). This is a self-defeating strategy chosen by at least one in every four people with an anxiety disorder.

As with avoidance, this tactic blunts the emotional and psychological pain for a short while, but over time it comes right back (often worse than before), and now the person has two problems—a more entrenched anxiety disorder and budding alcoholism.

Medical Conditions

Many medical conditions can mimic signs and sensations associated with anxiety and fear. This makes it hard to distinguish a medical problem from an anxiety disorder on your own. This determination is best left for a trained professional.

For this reason, it is important to rule out any medical conditions or possible drug-related factors that may be contributing to your anxiety and related difficulties. Examples of medical disorders that can trigger symptoms of panic or anxiety include thyroid problems, balance disorders (e.g., inner-ear disturbances), seizure disorders, asthma, and other respiratory or heart conditions. Use of stimulant substances (like cocaine, caffeine, diet pills, and certain other medications), withdrawal from alcohol, and use of other drugs (like marijuana) can also trigger panic-like feelings.

So before assuming that you have an anxiety disorder, it's important to talk with your doctor and have a full medical workup. This will help determine whether there's a physical cause for your problems. You can also think of this as a good way to take care of yourself. Once physical causes are ruled out, you can be much more confident when using the strategies described in this book.

TAKING STOCK: A LOOK AT YOUR ANXIETY PROBLEMS

At this point, it might be helpful to go back over some of the checklists in this chapter. Going over those checklists and reading the various anxiety disorder summaries serves an important purpose that we'll describe in a moment.

You may find that you fit neatly into one particular anxiety subtype. Although that's possible, it tends to be somewhat rare. Research studies and our clinical experience have taught us that most people do not fit neatly into one category. What they do have is some kind of mix of anxiety problems. More than half of the people who are diagnosed with one anxiety disorder also suffer from another anxiety disorder (Barlow, 2002).

You may notice that some of the problems described in the depression section apply to you too—perhaps not all of them, but some of them—even if just to a mild degree. You also may have started to engage in behaviors to give yourself relief from anxiety (for instance, excessive use of alcohol or other drugs).

The problem is that alcohol and other strategies to reduce anxious discomfort may provide some anxiety relief in the short run but cause bigger problems in the long run. As you read on, you'll see that much of what feeds and perpetuates your suffering with anxiety and fear has to do with buying into what your "critical mind" says about your anxiety and also buying into what you have learned from our culture about what can and should be done about anxiety.

THE SHINING LIGHT AT THE END OF THE TUNNEL

The good news is that it doesn't really matter whether you meet all the defining features of one or more anxiety disorders, if you have a unique mix, or if you have anxiety with or without some depression. To help you get unstuck from your current situation, it is much more important that you do this: identify what is feeding your anxiety and keeping you stuck. You don't need to figure out what your "correct" anxiety disorder diagnosis may be before you can do that.

The key is to start with the most problematic aspects of your anxiety problem. In fact, research shows that you are more likely to benefit from this treatment when you focus on your most problematic anxiety area, whether that be panic, fears of an object or social encounters, PTSD, or obsessions and compulsions. And when you do this, other areas where anxiety has been a problem will likely improve too.

For the purpose of working with this book, it is important to ask yourself this question: "What are the most disturbing and interfering aspects of my problem with anxiety?" To answer this question, go over the checklists and then write down what stands out to you. Think about problems that lead you to pull out of your life in a flash, where you'll try like crazy to avoid the anxiety and fear. Refer to your own experiences with anxiety and fear here; you can also revisit the case examples. This will give you a clear focus when it comes to choosing events, situations, and behaviors later on for the exercises.

fear of flying / closed places / elevators
fear of anxiety / panic
fear of illness / death

THE TAKE-HOME MESSAGE

Fear and anxiety are two unpleasant emotions that can be healthy and adaptive. Both emotions propel us into action and serve the purpose of keeping us out of trouble and alive. Labeling yourself with a diagnosis for your anxiety problem will not make your life more livable or help you in other ways. Instead of the label game, we're going to help you identify the root of the most problematic aspects of your anxiety problem. In short, we'll help you identify and change the things that turn your fears, anxieties, worries, or obsessions into the life-crushing problem or disorder *you* have been struggling with. Facing this squarely is the key to making changes that will move you in directions that are truly important to you.

Discovering the Differences Between Normal and "Disordered" Anxiety

Points to Ponder: Finding the "correct" professional diagnosis won't help me get my life back. What I need to do is look into how the drama of managing and avoiding anxiety plays out in my life so that I can start taking steps to do something about that.

Questions to Consider: What exactly are my problems with anxiety? What are the most disturbing and interfering aspects of my problem with anxiety?

CHAPTER 3

Confronting the Core Problem: Living to Avoid Fear and Anxiety

*Problems cannot be solved by thinking within the framework
in which they were created.* —Albert Einstein

Thoughts and feelings of panic and anxiety are unpleasant, intense, overwhelming at times, and even terrifying. But they aren't the real enemy. The real enemy is rigid avoidance of fear and anxiety.

In fact, as we touched on earlier, the weight of research shows that excessive avoidance is the most important toxic element responsible for turning worries, anxieties, and fears into potentially life-shattering problems and psychiatric disorders. Remember the image in chapter 1 of the person turning their back on life and struggling with their discomfort. That is the problem as far as your life is concerned.

As you saw from the case examples in the last chapter, toxic avoidance of anxiety and fear takes many forms, such as avoiding people, places, activities, and situations that might lead to anxious and fearful feelings, using substances to minimize the occurrence of such feelings, and running away from situations where you experience unpleasant emotional states.

A life lived in the service of not having anxiety and fear is quite limiting and may have come to define how you live your life—an issue that we'll explore more in chapter 6 and throughout this book.

For now, though, the key thing to remember is that avoidance, particularly when rigidly and inflexibly applied, gets in the way of the things you want to do and the directions you want to go. There's no way to embrace a vital life while avoiding emotional and psychological pain.

AVOIDING ANXIOUS DISCOMFORT IS THE PROBLEM

Discomfort avoidance is the common thread that binds all anxiety problems together. How people avoid anxiety and fear may differ from person to person and across anxiety disorders, but avoidance is avoidance no matter how it's done.

For instance, people with panic disorder, specific phobia, and social phobia avoid the situations, objects, and events that could bring on fear—particularly situations where they have experienced intense anxiety in the past. People with PTSD avoid painful memories and people and places that may remind them of past trauma. People with OCD may avoid contact with germs or dirt so as not to experience the unpleasant feelings that may arise by touching objects that have germs on them.

So you might avoid people or situations where there's a chance of thinking distressing thoughts and feeling anxious or afraid. You may avoid things like sex, exercise, certain movies, unfamiliar or new activities, or foods that activate your internal triggers. And when you find yourself in a hot-button situation, you may do many things to cope as a way to keep anxiety and fear in check.

Now, if and when all of this fails, you can cut and run too—pulling out of situations after anxiety and fear kicks in and threatens to overwhelm you. And in the aftermath of the storm, you'll likely say and do things to regain a foothold—repeating positive things to yourself, lying down, taking medications, breathing, thinking pleasant thoughts, and on and on.

> *The basic purpose of all these behaviors is the same: to make fear and anxiety go away.*

Let's take a closer look at how this plays out with the people we talked about in chapter 2.

Panic Disorder

> *Trying to beat and overcome anxiety is part of the problem. Remember avoidance!*

Ruth's experience gives us an important insight into what people with panic disorder fear most: they are afraid of fear itself. People are not so much afraid of particular places, spaces, or events as they are afraid of having a panic attack in those places or situations. And all the safety behaviors they engage in have one central purpose: to minimize the likelihood of experiencing a panic attack—and if they cannot avoid having a panic attack, they hope that their strategies will minimize the impact of panic and make it go away as quickly as possible.

Specific Phobias

As in the other case stories, Jane's example shows how her cricket phobia changed her behavior and restricted her life. Recall that she couldn't go to the park and was deeply concerned about how her fear was impacting her kids, and her ability to be a good mom. Jane also was aware that the crickets weren't the real problem: what she really dreaded most was the panic and terror she experienced—the discomfort when encountering a cricket or when just thinking about one.

At first glance, it seems like the purpose of not going to the park was to avoid a cricket encounter. Yet the deeper and more critical issue for Jane was this: she didn't want to experience the panic she knew would come if and when she saw a cricket. By avoiding crickets, what she was really avoiding was the possibility of fear itself—just like someone with panic disorder.

Social Anxiety

Mike's story shows that the problems with social anxiety go well beyond a fear of specific social situations or public events. The central issue is being afraid of experiencing fear and anxious discomfort in those contexts or of somehow failing in front of others. The avoidance is of the discomfort of being vulnerable to scrutiny, humiliated, or embarrassed in social situations.

Obsessive-Compulsive Disorder

Here again, the most problematic features of OCD—the compulsions—are actions designed to reduce or minimize anxiety, tension, and other discomfort related to unwanted thoughts and images. Compulsions are avoidance. As you saw with Ray, compulsions pull people out of their lives in a flash—consuming enormous amounts of time, energy, and resources. Absent the compulsions, you're left with emotional discomfort and unpleasant thoughts. And without engaging in the compulsions, you'd be free to engage in other potentially more vital behavioral options too.

Post-traumatic Stress Disorder

The trauma is past, but the pain remains, often resurging at times when it's most unwelcome. It's what people do about the memories of the trauma—and when they encounter current painful reminders along with unpleasant physical sensations—that accounts for much of the suffering with PTSD. Mary's story tells us as much. As painful as these memories and flashbacks undoubtedly are, they're not the real problem. The real problem with PTSD is the avoidance of emotional and psychological pain related to memories of past traumatic events.

THERE IS HOPE—YOUR LIFE CAN BE DIFFERENT!

In chapter 6 we'll help you figure out what solutions to your specific anxiety problem haven't worked for you and why they haven't worked. This is the first step toward making room for a completely new approach—one that is radically different from anything you've done before.

There's an impressive and growing research base (see Hayes et al., 2006) that points to one conclusion: even the most sophisticated attempts to control, reduce, or somehow "manage" anxiety often don't work and can even make things worse. You might be frightened by this prospect because if that's really the case, then you may think there's no hope your life will ever get any better. But this conclusion can be liberating, too, for it points to a more hopeful solution. The next metaphor hints at that.

Poison Ivy and the Anxiety Itch

Poison ivy is a plant that produces a strong skin irritant. Most people avoid touching the plant because they know what they'll get: a nasty, red, blistering rash that itches like hell. If you've been unlucky enough to have been exposed, then you know what this is like. You've got the strong urge to scratch. And when you do that, you make matters worse. You end up with open sores on your skin. And if you haven't washed the plant oils from your hands and exposed areas, you may spread the allergic reaction to other parts of your body. No amount of scratching will cure the inflammation. You need to stop the scratching and allow your body to heal itself.

The anxiety itch is like this too. The discomfort rages through your head and body, and you have a strong urge to get relief. So you avoid. You struggle. The problem is that you can't avoid exposure to anxiety in the same way you can avoid a poison ivy plant. Anxiety can show up anytime or anywhere. When you scratch your anxiety itch with avoidance or struggle, it makes the anxiety worse—the anxiety grows and spreads to infect most of your life. And all that avoidance scratching pulls you out of your life too.

This reflection on the perils of poison ivy and anxiety points to hope and liberation too. Nobody asks for poison ivy. No amount of blame and struggle will make it go away. The same can be said for anxiety and fear. So take heart. You aren't to blame for your anxiety troubles. The moral isn't that if you'd only tried harder, then you could've overcome your anxiety by now. The message is that you've done what you thought was best. Now you need to stop scratching.

One thing we've noticed again and again in working with people struggling with anxiety and fear-related problems is this: they constantly beat up on themselves. They feel that they're not good enough; they're too weak; they just haven't got what it takes to lead a more fulfilled life. They're somehow broken. No book lists this type of self-denigration as a feature of an anxiety disorder—and yet it's there anyway.

This judgmental virus of the human mind is active all the time. It can poison many aspects of your life if you let it. The antidote to this mind virus is compassion and learning skills that will help you look at and relate to your mind, body, and life in a different way—a way that won't get you tangled up in what your mind is throwing at you all the time.

As we teach you to do that, you'll slowly discover that your life can be different. Your life need not be determined by how much or little anxiety you have. You don't have to be one of those people who live out that one sobering conclusion we mentioned early on—continuing down the dark path of more anxiety management and control when we know it doesn't really work. The skills you'll learn in this book will show you another way, another path. That path will weaken the powerful hold that anxiety and fear have over you. You can learn how to ACT on your anxiety differently! This is the kind of hope and liberation we're after in this book.

Don't Believe Us or Your Mind—Trust Your Experience

So if managing anxiety doesn't work, what else can you do? As we suggested in chapter 1, the way to get back into your life is to go into your anxiety and let it be—no more running. Instead, you choose to experience anxiety for what it is and start doing what you care about doing. The skills we'll teach you in this book will help you observe anxiety and relate to it in kinder, gentler, less-engaged ways. This will position you to make more vital life choices. We know this may sound strange. And yes, some of what you read in this book is going to sound odd at first, even silly and bizarre.

You don't need to believe what we say. And you don't need to understand it all right away either. We guarantee that your mind will throw many arguments at you as to why this or that sounds impossible, is too difficult, or doesn't make any sense—"This book is rubbish; just put it down" or "You can't do it; this is all far too difficult." When such thoughts show up, thank your mind for each of them. Then move on.

You need not argue with your mind. Don't get stuck trying to convince yourself of anything. The only thing we ask is that you stay open as you learn new ways of relating to your anxieties and worries, that you do the exercises and check out whether, over time, they start working for you. Then trust that experience and let your mind do its thing.

You have little to lose and much to gain by approaching your problems with anxiety in a radically different way. We'll show you the way. Just keep on reading and begin to do the exercises starting with the one in the next chapter—and then trust that experience.

THE TAKE-HOME MESSAGE

The most critical element that separates normal from problematic anxiety and fear is this: avoidance, avoidance, and more avoidance. It's the common tie that binds all anxiety disorders together. Avoidance of fear and anxiety feeds anxiety and fear, and it shrinks lives. It's toxic for this reason. This is why we're going to help you cut it out with actions that are kinder, gentler, and more compassionate. These powerful skills are the salve that will cut avoidance off at its root and allow your life to grow.

Discovering the Toxic Root of "Disordered" Anxiety

Points to Ponder: Avoidance can turn normal anxiety and fear into a life-shattering problem. Attempting to control and run from my anxious discomfort may be the real problem I need to face and do something about.

Questions to Consider: How do I avoid my emotional and psychological discomfort? Am I willing to meet my anxious discomfort with actions that are kinder, gentler, and more compassionate so I can lead a better life?

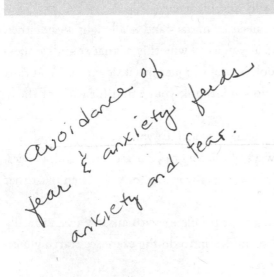

avoidance of
fear & anxiety feeds
anxiety and fear.

CHAPTER 4

Myths About Anxiety
and Its Disorders

*Life is a process of becoming, a combination of states we have to
go through. Where people fail is that they wish to elect a state
and remain in it. This is a kind of death.* —Anaïs Nin

A good deal of what you just read in the previous three chapters ought to have resonated with you. There's comfort in being able to put a label to your suffering. Yet do you really want to be known as "a social phobic," "a panicker," "a worrier," "someone with PTSD," "an agoraphobic," or "an obsessive-compulsive" now and for the rest of your life?

Labeling is seductive. It implies that knowing more about your problems will lead to knowing a solution or way out. You might pause here to ask if this is true of your experience.

Has knowing more about anxiety and its disorders really helped you move forward in vital and lasting ways? Has learning about how others cope with anxiety or staying on top of the latest research, self-help techniques, and so on really helped? These activities may make you feel good temporarily and will, over time, make you more of an anxiety expert. Yet that expertise and fleeting sense of comfort won't get your life back on track.

Once you buy into the label of "your disorder," you can quite literally become it—thinking and behaving like someone with an anxiety disorder. This kind of information is next to useless as far as your life is concerned. Labels are a ruse that can keep you stuck and wallowing in worry, anxiety, and fear. You're enough of an expert about your anxiety and your life already. Maybe what needs to happen is for you to do something radically different than you've done before.

David Allen (2002), in his book *Getting Things Done*, tells us that useful knowledge helps you achieve practical results. That kind of knowledge points you toward actions that make a difference in your life. And it's by your actions—what you spend your time doing—that you create your life one step at a time. This is what others will see about you too. This is the kind of change we'll be emphasizing in this book. So let's start by focusing on actions that are potentially vital and different from what you've done before.

> *If I continue to do what I've always done, then I'm going to get what I've always got.*

You can start by allowing yourself to let go of the label. Entertain the possibility that you are much more than an anxiety disorder—the label isn't you. This chapter will start you down a new road, beginning by dispelling some common myths about anxiety and fear.

COMMON MYTHS ABOUT ANXIETY AND FEAR

It seems like every day we're learning something new about anxiety and its disorders. In fact, much of what we've learned in recent years serves as the foundation for this book. This practical know-how is based on laboratory and treatment research on what turns anxiety and fear into life-shattering problems and, most importantly, what you can do about it.

You probably know quite a bit about anxiety and its disorders already. Some of this you know from your own experience. You may have picked up other pearls of wisdom from newspaper and magazine articles, books on the topic, TV, the Internet, conversations with family members and others, or from what your doctor has told you. You may have heard that anxiety disorders are a disease, just like diabetes or cancer, or that some people inherit anxiety disorders.

You may have heard that anxiety disorders can be treated with herbal remedies or by changing your diet. You may have learned from TV commercials and other sources that anxiety disorders are caused by your brain's neurochemicals run amok, and so you need medications to repair your faulty brain.

In fact, just recently we learned of a new study claiming that injections of a natural hormone known as cortisol can block intense fear reactions and that antihypertensives can weaken how your brain forms and stores emotional memories following exposure to traumatic events. Still others are promoting untested practices, such as magnets, aromatherapy, Bach Flower Therapy, biofeedback gadgets, brain wave synchronizers, thought field therapy, hypnosis, homeopathy, passionflower tea, or special diets as ways to cure anxiety and panic.

The message behind many of these sound bites is that it's abnormal to experience intense fear and anxiety. You may even think so too. And you might think that this means you are weak, broken, or on the verge of losing it and going crazy. Perhaps you've heard that learning better ways to manage and control your thoughts and feelings is a way out of your anxiety. This is another pervasive message promoted by our culture.

These are all common experiences and beliefs about anxiety, and even some mental health professionals accept them. Yet none of them are true. Each is a myth or at best a part truth. They are unhelpful because they keep you and others like you stuck in old patterns that don't work. They leave you wanting, waiting, and struggling to get a foothold. They feed thinking patterns that set you up as being unlike most people that seemingly glide through life happy and carefree. This isn't so. So let's take a look at the myths and reveal them for what they are.

Myth #1: Anxiety Problems Are Biological and Hereditary

Are you born a phobic, a worrier, a panicker, or someone destined to be trapped in obsessional thoughts and ritualistic acts? The medical establishment and the popular media would lead you to think so. You may even think so yourself. For a time, many leading researchers studying anxiety disorders thought so too. The intense physical sensations that accompany anxiety and fear lead, in part, to the idea that heredity and biology are at the core of anxiety disorders. Now we're learning that genes and even biology are only a small part of the story.

Our best available research suggests that people are not born with anxiety disorders. In fact, current estimates place the genetic contribution to anxiety disorders at about 30 to 40 percent (Leonardo & Hen, 2006). This means your genes may make you more vulnerable to an anxiety problem, but inheriting an anxious *predisposition* isn't the same as inheriting an anxiety *disorder*.

The bulk of what makes anxiety a psychiatric problem has nothing to do with your biology or genetics. That other 60 to 70 percent has to do with how you relate with your anxiety and fear—what you do about your anxious thoughts and feelings. This is the more important part because it's something you can control and change. You cannot change your genes or biology in any permanent sense, even by resorting to medications. But you can change your life (and even your biology) by changing what you do. This is why we'll focus on helping you work on what you can control and change in this book—your actions, or what you do when you have anxious feelings.

> People don't inherit anxiety disorders.

The bulk of what makes anxiety a psychiatric problem has nothing to do with your biology or genetics.

The other 60 to 70 % has to do with how you relate with your anxiety and fear – what you do about your anxious thoughts and feelings.

Myth #2: Intense Anxiety Is Abnormal

One of the main reasons people seek help for anxiety is this: they do not like how they think or feel. The anxiety and fear seem overwhelming, the painful memories too much to bear, the thoughts and worries paralyzing or next to impossible to turn off. In a word, anxiety is too intense.

It's certainly true that intense anxiety tends to go hand in hand with all anxiety disorders. It's also true that intense anxiety doesn't make an anxiety disorder. We need the capacity to feel intense emotions like anxiety and fear. Even newborn babies have this experience. Most children and adults report strongly felt anxiety at some point in any given year, often more than once, and even in situations where there's no risk of being harmed. All humans are wired to experience a range of emotions at varying levels of intensity. It would be abnormal for this not to be so.

As you saw in chapter 2, intense fear and anxiety has one purpose—to ready you for action when faced with real danger or risk of harm. Life-threatening events such as combat, sexual assault, abuse, accidents, natural disasters, and the like fall into this category. In these situations, most people will experience intense anxiety and fear. And without the capacity to feel such emotions intensely, we wouldn't have survived as a species. These reactions are 100 percent normal.

Your mind might be saying, "Yes, but I experience anxiety and fear in situations where I'm not at risk of being harmed. . . . Surely *that's* a problem." And when that happens, you likely do what most people would do when at risk of being harmed or even killed: you freeze, drop what you were doing or were going to do, and then attempt to run away. Here you ought to notice where your intense anxiety and fear go when you do that. They go with you, right? You can't run away from them. They're a part of you. You can't run from you.

Take stock of what else happens when you act in ways to avoid or run from anxiety. You likely feel better temporarily, but in the meantime, you're not doing the things that you care about. Over time, your life space shrinks and you get stuck. Intense anxiety may seem like a barrier that stands between you and your life. And it will remain a barrier as long as you continue to buy into the myth that strongly felt anxiety is a problem.

The short of it is this: Intense anxiety is not in itself a problem. Many people experience intense anxiety, even panic attacks, in their daily lives *and* continue to do what's important to them. Intensely felt emotions need not be a barrier to the life you want to lead. They can be welcomed in as a vital *part* of you. This is why we are going to help you to learn new ways of relating with your anxious thoughts and feelings and then how to take them with you. If you're willing, this approach will get you unstuck and back on track toward the life you want.

Myth #3: Anxiety Is a Sign of Weakness

Anxiety isn't a sign of weakness, personality defect, poor character, laziness, or lack of motivation. Anyone can get stuck and off track because of their emotional or psychological pain. All human beings have pain. Having pain is built into the human condition.

You may buy into the idea that anxiety is a sign of weakness because other people in your life seem so well put together. You see others making it, doing things that you'd like to do, and they seem to do it without the shadow of anxiety hanging over their heads. This is a great illusion.

The illusion is fueled by two sources. The first one is the tendency for our minds to make inferences based on very limited information. When you see and interact with others, you may not see them as anxious or actively suffering. You may then think, "Why can't I be that way?" And your mind may then take you to the next step: "Something must be wrong with me."

What is needed here is some perspective. Imagine that you're able to shadow one person who you think has it all together. You can watch their every move 24/7, and you can hear what they're thinking and feel what they're feeling at any time. If you were able to do this, you'd have a hard time ignoring this simple fact: that person is not so different from you.

As you open up to their humanity, you'd see a person who experiences a whole range of thoughts and feelings just like you—pleasant, unpleasant, and everything in between. They need to eat, drink, sleep, and use the bathroom, just like you. They, like you, will at times feel frustrated, be worried about this or that, or experience sadness, loneliness, regret, and anger. And at times they'll also be anxious or afraid.

Anxiety isn't a sign of weakness.

The second source that fuels the weakness myth is social comparison. When you narrowly view your life as full of anxiety and emotional pain and see others as dancing through the lily fields of life, happy and carefree, you'll naturally feel that something is wrong with you. You'll think that you're missing something they have. As long as you believe your anxiety problems flow from some inherent weakness or character flaw, you'll be stuck wanting and waiting for a fix that may never come. You'll become a victim.

The truth is that you have everything you need. You aren't broken. The capacity for change lies within you. You and only you are responsible for what you do with your precious time and energy. This is why we'll be nurturing your capacity for responsibility. With that, you'll create change in your life by refocusing time, energy, and resources in those areas that you can control and change—the things you do with your hands, feet, and mouth.

Myth #4: Anxiety Can and Must Be Managed to Live a Vital Life

Of all the myths, this one is the most damaging. It's fueled by social conventions or what we call the *culture of feel-goodism*. These conventions set up emotional and physical pain as barriers to a life lived well. The message is this: *In order to live better, I must first think and feel better. And once I start thinking and feeling better, my life will improve for the better.* This is a trap.

The bait for the trap is the emotional and psychological pain you experience with anxiety, panic, worries, unwanted thoughts, or memories. In your mind, this pain isn't just pain. It's *bad* pain. Your mind has judged it as unacceptable and has linked it with not being able to do what you care about. When anxiety pain shows up, you go after it to make it go away or to weaken it. You also do this or that to prevent that *bad* pain from showing up in the future, and on and on it goes.

EXERCISE: DON'T THINK ABOUT A PINK ELEPHANT OR WORSE

This brief exercise will help you see what trying to suppress and control unwanted thoughts gets you. Go ahead and get in a comfortable position. Now, when you're ready, we'd like you to close your eyes and try this: Don't think about a PINK ELEPHANT! Go ahead. Try hard. Give yourself a few minutes to really work at it. After you've given it a go, open your eyes and read on.

If you're like most people, you'll find this task difficult or next to impossible. The reason is that you cannot do what the instruction says without thinking of the thing you aren't supposed to think about. Put another way, the thought "Don't think about a PINK ELEPHANT" is itself a thought about pink elephants. So there you are, stuck with the very thing you don't want.

Your mind may have come up with other clever tactics to accomplish the goal of not thinking about a pink elephant. You might have tried thinking about something else. This seems reasonable. Yet how did your mind do that? How did you know that the other thought was not a pink elephant? In order to think of something that is clearly not a pink elephant you need to compare it to a pink elephant. So there you are, back with the thought of a pink elephant again.

Your mental programming has lots of links with things like pink elephants. Most of these will come to you quickly because you've learned them. They're automatic in this sense. Here are a few. Go ahead and complete the blanks without giving them much thought.

Twinkle, twinkle, little	_____	Practice makes	_____
Don't spill the	_____	Actions speak louder than	_____
Look before you	_____	The early bird gets the	_____

Now, we'd like you to pick one of these statements and read it slowly, but don't think about the word that completes the phrase. For instance, read "Twinkle, twinkle, little" but don't think _____ ("star"). What happened? Could you do it? Let's take this a step further.

Imagine that "star" is one of those really distressing thoughts, bodily sensations, feelings, or memories that you struggle with and wish not to have. You're now in a situation where your automatic programming kicks in. Here it comes—"Twinkle, twinkle, little _____"—but you can't have what comes next. What do you suppose will happen here? You end up with more of the thing you don't want to experience. And you'll probably do this or that to avoid it in the future.

When you take the bait, look at what happens to the pain and your life. You're devoting enormous time, energy, and resources to keeping the anxiety and panic at bay. You keep doing this because it has often bought you some temporary relief. You also do it because this is what you've been taught to do in our culture, whether or not it actually works for you in the long haul.

If you suffer from panic disorder, then you may know what this is like. Having a panic attack at the grocery store or elsewhere is a highly unpleasant experience. And it may lead you to do this or that to prevent it from happening again. So you may stop shopping, shop with a "safe" person, only go to the store late in the evening when few people are around should the attack happen again, and so on. All the while, you may be concentrating on relaxing as you also watch for signs of a possible panic attack.

> Anxiety management and avoidance leave you feeling safe and less anxious in the short term and greatly limit what you can do. This inaction is a problem.

Similar tactics might be used by people with social anxiety. They'll take many steps to minimize or avoid altogether having anxiety in social encounters. This is a hard thing to do in a highly social world like ours and so can be quite crippling. Imagine going about your day without interacting with people for fear that you might panic in front of them, or humiliate or embarrass yourself. It's harder still knowing that none of us can control how other people respond to us.

In fact, we'd venture a guess that these strategies haven't worked particularly well for you. Your anxiety comes back, perhaps even stronger the next time. Worse, time spent trying to manage and control anxiety is time and energy away from doing things that you care deeply about.

So anxiety management and control actually double your pain: on top of the pain of more anxiety, you also get the pain of loss or regret. You get this other pain when you fail to do something that really matters to you. Both forms of pain are a natural consequence of fighting a battle with your unpleasant thoughts and feelings.

Research studies have shown as much too: when you don't want anxious thoughts and feelings, you'll get more of them. And the more you don't want them, the more you're stuck with them. We'll show you more about how this works in a moment. For now, the important thing to remember is that these actions fuel your anxiety and slam the trapdoor shut on your life.

The exercises in this book are designed to help you recognize the anxiety management and control myth for what it is—a rigged, no-win game that has brought much unnecessary suffering to your life. You can avoid getting sucked into the anxiety trap by learning not to take the bait. You can learn to live better without first having to think and feel better. You can learn to bring comfort to the unpleasant experiences your mind and body are serving up and do what matters to you. Again, our intention in this book is to help you do just that.

WHERE THE MYTHS WILL TAKE YOU IF YOU LET THEM

Each of the myths feed anxiety and can keep you stuck and cut off from the life you want to lead. The myths are, in a sense, like a sticky spiderweb. When you get caught up in the web, the natural reaction is to struggle to get out. And the more you struggle, the more tangled up you become. On and on it goes; eventually you become the anxiety management expert, searching, hoping, perhaps praying, for that magic cure or new solution.

The hard truth is you won't find a cure for anxiety in a pill, an online support group, or even in some solid psychotherapies known for offering "new, better, different" strategies for getting control over your anxious thoughts and feelings.

Whenever your mind tells you otherwise, look at your experience. Have these and other options worked in the long term? Does your experience tell you that they will work if you work harder, longer, or better at them? Do you want to be about dealing with anxiety for the rest of your life? Haven't you worked hard enough?

■ *Sharon's Story*

Sharon, one of our recent clients, shared a story with us that illustrates where the myths can take you if you let them. She came to us at the age of forty-five after twenty years of crippling struggle with anxiety, panic, and depression. She struggled with thoughts of meaninglessness in life. She believed that something was biologically wrong with her. She thought of herself as the kind of person who had been dealt a bad hand—a life filled with too much emotional pain and anguish. Her runaway mind was constantly feeding her doom and gloom, self-blame, and negativity. Sharon didn't think she had much of a chance for a bright future.

She feared having a nervous breakdown if she ever found herself stuck, away from home, and isolated from family and friends. She feared the dark, being out alone, and driving at night. She saw her life ticking by, feared being put in a hospital, medicated, doped up, and cut off from her children and her life. When she wasn't seeing herself carted away to the hospital or waiting for hospice, she imagined being isolated and alone, unemployed, and with her kids in an orphanage.

Sharon had been on and off antidepressant and antianxiety medication and in and out of cognitive behavioral therapy, often finding that such treatments left her with a renewed sense of hope, a honeymoon from the crippling panic, wrenching anxiety, agoraphobia, and disturbing thoughts. She bought a sun lamp to stave off the depression. She invested hundreds of dollars in professional and self-help books about anxiety disorders, belonged to many online support groups, and even attended seminars.

For about two years, Sharon was living better and seemed to feel better too. Armed with a formidable set of tools to keep her anxiety and fear at bay, she was able to readily challenge her negative thoughts, relax away the tension, dismiss the worry, and breathe herself out of panic. And she had the sun lamp and the books to read when she found herself in a pinch. These strategies seemed to work, but she never fully escaped the lurking sense that someday, somewhere, the strategies wouldn't work and then what—the shadow of anxiety and depression would return and take over. And that's exactly what happened and what ultimately led Sharon to us.

Sharon's question became "Can I learn to live with feelings and thoughts that I don't like and not allow them to control me and what I do?" You'll learn more about her in the next chapter.

THE TAKE-HOME MESSAGE

All of the myths about anxiety are set up and fed by Western notions of psychological health and well-being. The message is that happiness is normal. But what if happiness isn't normal? What if it was impossible for you or anyone to create a vital life, free of significant psychological and emotional pain? When you look more closely at people's lives, you'll find that significant pain and struggle are companions that we all must take along on the road to a vital life.

Your anxiety problems may have something to do with you buying into the "happiness or bust" message. You might think that your worries, anxieties, and fears must go away first so you can start doing what matters to you. But perhaps the solution is to do something radically different than what you've been doing. Are you willing to take that step?

The Myths Feed Anxiety and Keep Me Stuck

Point to Ponder: All the myths of anxiety send the message that my anxiety and fear are unacceptable and a barrier between me and my life.

Questions to Consider: What myths of anxiety have I bought into? Have I let anxiety control my life? Am I willing to take responsibility for what I do about my worries, anxieties, and fears? Will I let go of the myths?

CHAPTER 5

Letting Go of Old Myths Opens Up New Opportunities

How exactly does one become a butterfly? You must want to fly so badly that you are willing to give up being a caterpillar. —Trina Paulus

Dr. Seuss wrote a wonderful children's story called *Oh, the Places You'll Go*. The story speaks volumes about what it takes to create a life that is meaningful. We encourage you to get a copy of it on the Web or at your local library and then find a quiet place to read and reflect on it, slowly. Put yourself in the story. See if you can connect with the message and allow yourself to think and feel whatever may show up. Imagine that Dr. Seuss is speaking directly to you.

This is a story for the young and old for it speaks to life, pain, and joy—and what it takes to live out the life you want to lead. And as much as your mind might be telling you otherwise, you don't need to continue to do what you've always done. As Dr. Seuss tells us, you don't need to be one of those people standing in line waiting, just waiting, because of _____ [insert one of your big anxieties and fears here], waiting for your life to begin.

THE PLACES YOU'LL GO WHEN YOU LET GO OF THE MYTHS

As Sharon worked with the material in this book, she began to let go of the myths. She stopped playing the waiting game. She stopped feeding her negative thoughts and instead learned to watch them, with kindness, curiosity, and at times with humor. She began to see what buying into the myths about anxiety had cost her. She stopped trying to manage and control her anxiety and depression and would no longer allow them to stand between her and her life.

Sharon learned that she could live better when she stopped trying to conquer her anxiety and depression. And when she started living better, she began to feel and think better too. For Sharon, this didn't mean being free from anxiety and fear, worries, or negative thoughts. No—she still had these experiences. Yet when they showed up, she chose not to feed them. She was unwilling to dignify her anxieties, fears, and worries with more struggles. Instead, she met them with compassion and gentleness. She learned that she could start living her life without winning a war with her pain.

Some of the old habits remained. In fact, Sharon recently took a trip out of town with her husband and kids for a family vacation to the beach, something she'd never considered doing before. While packing for the trip, Sharon had stuffed a duffle bag full of her old safety myths: vitamins for her anxiety, her iPod loaded with ten gigabytes of relaxation tracks and self-help lectures, earplugs to blot out the noise of her kids screaming while they played in the hotel room, a sun lamp to ward off depression, and a dozen or so books on anxiety and its disorders. The weight of her baggage was enormous, literally and emotionally.

It turned out that all this antianxiety gear was unnecessary and next to useless. Over the weekend, Sharon didn't open her duffle bag once. With a chuckle, she said, "Sheesh. . . . I had times over the weekend when I felt anxious and had anxious thoughts. And then I reminded myself that I didn't want to be about what was in the duffle bag."

For Sharon, being about the contents of her duffle bag meant being holed up in her hotel room, alone, popping vitamins, with her iPod cranked up, while reading the book *Anxiety and Its Disorders* in front of her sun lamp. Instead, she spent her time outside, playing with her husband and children on the beach, going for sunset walks, searching for seashells, and reading a fun book. She went out to dinner and took the kids to a Sunday matinee. She even had a chance to share quiet conversation with her husband over a nice glass of wine on the balcony of her hotel room after the kids went to bed. These are the things that Sharon cared deeply about.

At times she felt really good while doing all these things. And at other times she was quite anxious about the possibility of having a panic attack. She even worried whether the good feelings would last. And no matter what happened, she remained steadfast in one choice she'd made: she was unwilling to spend time struggling with her anxiety, panic, and the negative news that her mind fed her from time to time. She kept on going and gave herself some space to have all those experiences without attempting to resolve them. Her weekend at the beach left her feeling alive!

— allowed herself to have anxiety, panic, fear without trying to resolve them.

Sharon's story is typical in many ways. Your story may be different. What may not be different is what has happened to your life. If you feel your life has shrunk to the size of a postage stamp, then you may be just as stuck as Sharon was. So ask yourself: Has buying into the myths taken you out of your life and left you stuck and trapped in your anxiety? Is it possible that, just like Sharon, you don't need to think and feel better in order to live better?

Sharon found her answers not by blindly trusting what we said. In fact, she had serious doubts about what our treatment program could offer her. The ideas were new, sounded a bit strange, and cut against the grain of just about everything she believed could and ought to be done about her anxiety and her life.

We didn't ask Sharon to get rid of or resolve her doubts. And we won't ask you to do that either. All that we ask is that you soften to the possibility that your old ideas about the solutions to your anxiety problems may not be serving you well and may be doing you more harm than good.

As Sharon began doing the exercises in this book, she learned to stop buying into and feeding her judgmental mind, to trust her experience, and to act in ways that mattered to her. She began spending more of her time doing the things she cared about—sometimes with and sometimes without anxiety— and less time with her anxious thoughts and feelings, including other sources of emotional pain that left her feeling hopeless and depressed. Sharon learned that things could be different when she approached her anxiety and her life in a new way. You have these options too.

F-E-A-R FUELS THE MYTHS AND KEEPS THEM ALIVE

Steven Hayes and his colleagues (1999) came up with a simple acronym that describes four key factors that fuel the myths about anxiety, turn anxiety into a problem, and keep you stuck. That acronym is F-E-A-R. Let's briefly have a look at each factor.

Fusion with Your Thoughts, Images, and Memories: The Mind Trap — *you have the capacity to become fused or tangled up with your Thoughts.*

Like every human being, you have the capacity to become fused or tangled up with your thoughts. When you fuse with your thoughts, you'll tend to treat them "as if" they were the same thing as the experiences or events they describe. Dr. Wayne Dyer, in his book *The Power of Intention* (2005), has a beautiful version of the F-E-A-R acronym to describe the fusion process: False Evidence Appearing Real. Keep this one in mind as you read on.

For instance, the word "panic" may conjure up all sorts of associations. These associations may include images of having a heart attack, dying, fainting, going crazy, losing it, or being carted off to the funny farm. Your mind will also throw evaluations into these associations, such as bad, dangerous, weak, stupid, humiliated, and so on. All of these judgmental labels have their own associations too, many of them quite negative.

What's important to see here is that the word "panic" is not a real panic attack nor is it the same as the associations and evaluations linked with the word. The word "panic" is just a word. The evaluation "bad" is just a word. You could choose to treat them just as words. Or you could respond to the word, associations, and evaluations as if they are more than that.

When you go beyond seeing words as words, you're buying into the illusion your mind creates. The thoughts shift from being thoughts to being something dangerously serious. And when that happens, you'll often find yourself trapped in old behavior patterns that are neither helpful nor in your best interest. We call this a *mind trap*.

Consider this: what would happen if you responded to the word "panic" and its associations as if the word and its associations were the real thing? You might lie down, take a tranquilizer pill, listen to soothing music, call your doctor or a friend or relative, or go to the emergency room. In short, you'd respond to the word and its associations with behavior. This is what we mean by *fusion*: responding to words, images, memories, or evaluations with actions—with things you do—as if the products of your mind are the same thing as the actual life events they represent or are related with.

Fusion can be a hard concept to explain let alone understand intellectually. This is why we're going to help you connect with it more experientially throughout the book. For now, all we ask is that you play with the idea that your anxious suffering is set into motion when you feed your unpleasant thoughts and feelings by getting tangled up and fused with them.

Your judgmental mind is at work here, and it's not your best friend at those times. When you allow your mind to take you down the fusion road unchecked, you'll naturally tend to react strongly to that sticky negative news between your ears and give thoughts more importance than they deserve. This can keep you stuck.

— give thoughts more importance than they deserve.

EXERCISE: GETTING TANGLED UP WITH ANXIETY

To get a sense of this process, take a moment to complete the following exercise. Select a thought, worry, emotional experience, or memory that's particularly upsetting for you. Once you have that in mind, jot down events or experiences that tend to go along with it. Here's an example of how Sally did it.

My Experience

Panic/strong anxiety

What Comes to Mind

1. *Jittery and shaky*
2. *Can't think clearly*
3. *Heart races, sweaty*
4. *Can't be in a crowd, drive a car, go near heights*
5. *Think I might be going crazy*

Sally noticed a couple of things here. When she bought into her anxious thoughts and feelings and tried to eliminate them, she also bought herself everything else on her list and then some. She felt more anxious. (Remember the pink elephant.) Worse, she now became the very thing she wished not to be by fusing her sense of being with her anxiety, as in, "I'm anxious."

In fact, Sally told us, "I'm Ms. PAT (Panic-Anxiety-Terror)." Once she fed that thought, she became a person who was not only anxious, but also incapable of being in a crowd, driving a car, and going to work on the fifth story of her office building. And she didn't like herself very much anymore either. No surprise, given that she had fused with the very things she most disliked.

My Experience	What Comes to Mind
_____	1. _____
(an unpleasant thought/feeling/memory)	2. _____
	3. _____
	4. _____
	5. _____

If you're like Sally, then you give a whole lot of importance to anxiety-provoking thoughts or feelings. That's because you've learned to buy into what your mind tells you about your experience. The more you do that, the more you become fused with the label and evaluations and trapped by your mind.

You might be thinking here, "Are they telling me that my fear and anxiety are not real?" Absolutely not. The bodily sensations, the thoughts, and the images are all there and are real, in the sense of being parts of your experience.

What we're asking is for you to look closely at what you're responding to. Are you responding to the images as images, thoughts as thoughts, sensations as sensations, and memories as memories, *as they are*, unedited and untainted by negative evaluations? Or are your actions steered by judgments and evaluations of these experiences—the stuff your mind feeds you about them?

The critical question here is this: must you respond to them as if they are what they say they are ("The racing heart is a heart attack and not simply a fast heartbeat") or can you just treat them as actual sensations, as thoughts consisting of words, or as fleeting memories or images of the past?

Perhaps you also feel like Ms. or Mr. PAT (or like Dr. Worry, the expert on worrying). And you may have had times when you've said, "I'm weak," "I'm depressed," "I'm a loser," or "I'm going crazy." Each of these statements may seem like they are who you are.

Now think for a moment what would happen if all of a sudden you had the thought "I am a banana." To find out, close your eyes for ten seconds

> *Your anxious thoughts and feelings are part of you—not you.*

What is my mind feeding me?

and keep thinking that thought: "I am a banana." What happened? Perhaps you saw a yellow curved object in your mind. You may even have imagined the taste of a banana. Did having that thought turn you into a banana? Is that thought any more true or false than any other thought your mind might throw at you now and then?

Intuitively, you may already know that your thoughts are different than the events they describe. As we teach you how to step back and defuse or disentangle a bit, you'll see that the thoughts are simply thoughts, sensations are sensations, memories are memories, and feelings are feelings—nothing more, nothing less. We'll teach you skills so that you don't "become" them.

Incidentally, this could be one of those moments where you might feel a bit confused. If that's the case, be patient and skeptical about what your mind may be telling you now, and keep on reading to discover for yourself what this might all mean and how it can help you.

Evaluating Your Experiences

Just about everything human beings experience and do is tagged with some sort of evaluation or judgment: good versus bad, right versus wrong, happy versus sad. Media and marketing are built around helping you experience a positive evaluation of products so that you go out and buy them. Similarly, models of health and wellness are built around the idea that emotional and psychological pain is not simply pain, but "bad" pain. You can apply this habit of evaluation as readily to yourself and your private experiences as you can to most events in your world.

There's nothing wrong with evaluating your experience provided that you recognize it for what it is: an evaluation of reality, not reality itself. To put it another way, you might call a duckling "ugly" or "cute" but that doesn't change the fact that the duckling is a duck. This is an important point that we'll revisit throughout this book.

Evaluations of your experience rarely add anything to the experience itself. When you buy into and feed your negative evaluations unnecessarily, you'll often fuel your suffering unnecessarily. It just plain hurts when we evaluate ourselves and our experiences negatively—as ugly, broken, screwed up, weak, worthless, stupid, crazy, foolish, and the like.

You may not be able to control the stream of evaluations, but you can choose to feed them or not. Here's a short story to give you a sense of what we mean by feeding your mind.

Feeding a Painful Wolf or a Compassionate Heart

A Native American grandfather was talking to his grandson about how he felt. He said, "I feel as if I have two wolves fighting in my heart. One wolf is the vengeful, angry, violent one. The other wolf is the loving, compassionate one." The grandson asked him, "Which wolf will win the fight in your heart?" The grandfather answered, "The one I feed."

In chapter 2 we talked about anxiety and fear as being a loose collection of bodily sensations, thoughts, and behavioral predispositions, all of which may tend to hang together with other events and situations you've experienced. Go back and review what you wrote down about these areas as they apply to your experience with anxiety and fear.

With these thoughts, bodily sensations, feelings, and behaviors in mind, take a moment to write down words that best describe your evaluation of them. You may think of these as bad, unwanted, unpleasant, nasty, aversive, painful, screwed up, awful, annoying, or wrenching, or you may have other words that you routinely apply to them.

scarey , overwhelming endless , trapped , painful , physical ,

Take a moment to look at what you tend to respond to more: your experiences as they are—unedited—or your judgments and negative labels of those experiences. When you buy into the negative evaluations, you are left with only one sensible option—to do what you can to rid yourself of the bad and potentially damaging experience. You feed the anxious wolf.

Buying into judgmental labels also leads to inevitable actions. Suppose one of your judgmental thoughts was "My panic attacks are so bad that they're eventually going to kill me." If you completely believe this thought and only react to what it seems to say, then you are left with few options. The thought says that your life is in the balance and so you *must* do something to alter that state of affairs—perhaps you won't leave the house or you'll take an antianxiety pill every few hours. The same principles are at work with obsessional thoughts that you might think will come true if you don't do something about them, like, "I might harm my children" or "I may have come in contact with germs."

The bottom line is this: nothing else makes sense except acting on the thought. As soon as you do that, you'll find yourself caught in the mind trap one more time.

Avoiding Your Experiences

Avoiding or escaping from experiences that bring on the "bad" thoughts and feelings may leave you with a brief honeymoon from the pain and its source. In fact, this is exactly what keeps avoidance and escape behavior going. When you avoid or run from bad emotional experiences, you'll tend to buy yourself temporary relief. Countless studies have shown that this temporary relief makes it likely that you'll use the same strategy the next time the "bad" anxiety or fear rears its "ugly" head (another evaluation).

This would be a sensible strategy if the situations could harm or kill you, or if you could truly live your life while avoiding unpleasant psychological and emotional experiences. What may be difficult to see is that avoidance is unnecessary and is, in fact, enormously costly. We'll walk you through some of the costs in the next chapter.

For now, we'd like you to consider the possibility that the pain that lies beneath your "bad" anxiety and fear may not be so bad after all. It may actually serve a purpose and be a type of "growing pain." You may need it to get you moving toward the life that you so desperately want. Below is a simple story that illustrates this point.

What Avoiding Pain Cost the Emperor Moth

A man found a cocoon of an emperor moth. He took it home so that he could watch the moth come out of the cocoon.

On the day a small opening appeared, he sat and watched the moth for several hours, just watching as the moth struggled to force its body through that little hole. Then it seemed to stop making any progress. It appeared to have gotten as far as it could. It just seemed stuck.

Then the man, in his kindness, decided to help the moth. So he took a pair of scissors and snipped off the remaining bit of the cocoon. The moth emerged easily, but it had a swollen body and small shriveled wings. The man continued to watch. He expected that, at any moment, the wings would enlarge and open out to be able to support the body. Neither happened! The little moth spent the rest of its life crawling around with a swollen body and shriveled wings. It never was able to fly.

What the man in his kindness and haste didn't understand was this: In order for the moth to fly, it needed to experience the restricting cocoon and the painful struggle as it emerged through the tiny opening. This was a necessary part of a process to force fluid from the body and into the wings so that the moth would be ready for flight once it achieved freedom from the cocoon. Freedom and flight would only come after allowing painful struggle. By depriving the moth of struggle, the man deprived the moth of health.

You may see a bit of yourself in this story. You wish to move on with your life without the pain of having anxiety and fear as a part of that movement. The story also hints at another possibility that may seem a bit wacky at first: Could it be that your worries, anxieties, and fears aren't your enemy? Is it possible that you need anxiety to "force fluid from your body into your wings" in order to have the kind of life that you so desperately want?

We're not suggesting that you just take off and fly into a happy life. All we're asking is that you open up to the possibility that your anxious thoughts, images, and feelings may serve an important purpose in your life. You may not see this purpose from where you are right now. In fact, it is next to impossible to see any important purpose behind anxiety and fear when you're focused on getting yourself out of your anxiety cocoon.

This is why we're going to teach you skills that will help you learn to be with your anxiety, without being consumed by it. As you learn these skills, you'll learn how anxiety is necessary for you to take flight in life directions that are vital and meaningful for you.

Reason Giving for Your Behavior

By now, you've probably come up with several reasonable-sounding reasons why you can't do this or that because of your worries, anxieties, and fears (WAFs). These WAFs are barking at you much like a dog might do: WAF . . . WAF . . . WAF! And when others ask you why you can't do this or that, you may respond with lots of reasons that take the form of "WAF . . . WAF . . . WAF!"

With your WAFs in mind, we'd like you to go back and recall what you wrote down on page 3 when we asked you this:

Because of my anxious thoughts and feelings, strong fear and panic, worry, or disturbing memories, I have missed out on or am unable to _____fly_____.

We can turn this around in the form of a question and a response. We might ask you, "Why can't you do that one important thing in your life?" You might say, "Because I might panic or get too anxious, faint, lose control, or act on my nonsensical thoughts" (WAF, WAF, WAF!).

In fact, it's common for people struggling with anxiety disorders to give themselves, or others, reasons that point to anxious thoughts and feelings. And many people will go along with what you say out of sympathy or to be kind and supportive. This only solidifies the link between your WAFs and your inability to take action.

The problem here is that you can start believing your reasons—your own stories: "I can't do _____ because of _____ [my WAFs]." Look at what happens. Like a big, fierce-looking dog, your WAFs have now turned into a barrier that stands in the way of going forward in your life.

Reasons that bind with anxiety and fear are now the causes of you being stuck. And when you buy into this story line, which is very difficult not to do in our culture, you'll be left thinking that the only way to go forward is to take care of the causes: "I must get rid of my WAFs."

We've already given you a taste of what happens when you buy into thoughts like "Don't be anxious!" We aren't about to snip off the opening of your life cocoon either. In the next chapter we'll help you get a better sense of what the struggle to control anxiety and fear has cost you and then help you develop skills to move with your anxiety and fear as a necessary part of a vital life.

WAF
WORRIES
ANXIETIES
FEARS

LEARNING TO OBSERVE VERSUS REACTING WITH F-E-A-R

One of the most courageous things you can do when your WAFs show up is to sit still with them and not do as they say. It's courageous because the impulse to cut and run is so great and so automatic. Doing nothing about them is the more difficult path. It's important to learn this skill because the urge to act on and through your WAFs with F-E-A-R greatly diminishes your life. Practicing mind watching will teach you to become a true observer of your mind rather than taking and swallowing whatever nasty-looking stuff your mind dishes up for you.

Mind Watching

We know observing F-E-A-R isn't easy. Your mind will be screaming at you to respond as you've done in the past. Through persistent practice, it'll get easier over time to observe and take note of thoughts, images, and urges rather than doing as they say. Here's how you get started.

NET

EXERCISE: MIND WATCHING

Get in a comfortable place where you won't be disturbed. Begin by taking a series of slow, deep breaths. Keep this up throughout the entire exercise. Imagine your mind is a medium-sized white room with two doors. Thoughts come in through the front door and leave out the back door. Pay close attention to each thought as it enters. Now label the thought as either a judging thought or a nonjudgmental thought.

Watch the thought until it leaves. Don't try to analyze or hold on to it. Don't believe or disbelieve it. Just acknowledge having the thought. It's just a moment in your mind, a brief visitor in the white room. If you find that you're judging yourself for having the thought, then just notice that. Don't argue with your mind's judgment. Just notice it for what it is and label it: "Judging—there's judging." The key to this exercise is to notice the judgmental thoughts rather than getting caught up in them. You'll know if you're getting caught up in them by your emotional reactions and by how long you keep each thought in the room.

Keep breathing. Keep watching. Keep labeling. A thought is just a thought. Each thought doesn't require you to react; it doesn't make you do anything; it doesn't mean you're less of a person. Observe your thoughts as if they were visitors passing in and out of the white room. Let them have their brief moment on the stage. They're fine the way they are—including the judging thoughts and all the other uninvited visitors. The important thing is to let them leave when they're ready to go and then greet and label the next thought . . . and the next.

Continue this exercise until you sense a real emotional distance from your thoughts. Wait until even the judgments are just a moment in the room—no longer important, no longer requiring action. Practice this exercise at least once a day.

F.E.A.R. False Evidence Appearing Real

Take Your Mind and Body for a Walk

Another way to learn to be a skillful observer of your thoughts and feelings is to practice moving with them instead of because of them. One way to practice doing that is to think of taking your mind and body for a walk. Start your practice by literally going outside for a walk—for fifteen minutes or longer. Do it without bringing along a radio or an iPod.

EXERCISE: MINDFUL WALKING

As you walk, you'll notice that you don't need to think much about what your legs and body do while walking. They seem to go on autopilot. As you begin this activity, focus on your breathing—deeply in and out, deeply in and out. Focus on the rhythm of your steps and how your body feels as it moves. If your mind wanders to other things, just notice that. Then, gently bring your attention back to the experience of walking. Notice the feel of your feet as they meet the ground with each step. Move your awareness to your hip area—experience how your hips move with each stride. What sensations are there? Then, move further up to your midsection, and allow yourself to feel all the movements there too. See how your body is in perfect rhythm and flow. Notice how you're moving with your thoughts and feelings too—all of them going forward. Sense the vitality in this movement. Reflect on this mantra silently to yourself: *My life is moving with my experiences.*

As with any other skill, learning to be an observer of automatic thoughts and feelings takes practice. The more you practice, the better at it you'll become. After a week or two of practicing mind watching and mindful walking, you'll be positioned to extend the practice wherever you are and whenever you remember it. This might include using the skills with other forms of exercise or activity too. And it can be done in your home, while shopping, or with any activity that requires movement, including mindful engagement in household chores like cooking, vacuuming, doing the dishes, cleaning laundry, or with hobbies. The point here is to practice being mindful of the experience of movement with your thoughts, feelings, and sensations. In fact, you can put a note in your pocket or purse or set a wrist alarm to beep every hour as a practice reminder to simply notice your experience just as it is.

THE TAKE-HOME MESSAGE

Recognizing how mind traps keep you stuck is an important skill. It's a critical step out of the struggle and avoidance trap. You can get something different out of your life if you're willing to learn to relate with your mind, body, and feelings in a different way. This is a choice only you can make. We hope that you make it now and act on that intention as you start working with the material in this book.

Mind Traps Keep Me Stuck in F-E-A-R

Point to Ponder: Recognizing the mind traps that keep me stuck and feed my struggle with anxiety is a way out of the anxiety trap and into my life.

Questions to Consider: Can I recognize F-E-A-R for what it is? Am I willing to face what buying into my raucous and judgmental mind has cost me?

PART 2

STARTING A NEW JOURNEY

CHAPTER 6

Facing the Costs to Take Charge of Your Life

For a long time it had seemed to me that life was about to begin—real life. But there was always some obstacle in the way, something to be gotten through first, some unfinished business, time still to be served, a debt to be paid. Then life would begin. At last it dawned on me that these obstacles were my life. —Alfred D. Souza

This chapter is about taking stock of where you've been and where you want to go. This is an important moment. We all have a finite amount of time on this earth. And many of us plow through each day on autopilot, never stopping to take a good, hard look at what we're spending our time doing or asking: "Is this truly what I want to be about?"

Alfred D. Souza learned that he had wasted precious moments of his life in the service of removing obstacles. You've got plenty of WAF obstacles too. His awakening only came after he became willing to face what he was doing and what he had become. Now is the time to wake up to what your struggle with anxiety has cost you before it's too late.

Here we'll be asking you to face squarely the costs of your battles with anxiety. Some of this may be painful for you to do. Yet it's vitally important that you do it.

So long as you hold on to old ways of solving your anxiety problems, you'll end up exactly where you are now. And if you continue to treat your WAFs as obstacles standing between you and your life, you'll naturally spend your time and energy trying to figure out ways to conquer them. In short, you'll continue to get what you've always gotten. WAF struggles will be your life!

As you fully, openly, and honestly engage this process, you'll see how attaching importance to activities and experiences that don't serve you well keeps you stuck. This may be painful, but there's a sober vitality—or a wakefulness—to this kind of pain that you may not have experienced before.

Roger von Oech (1998), in his wonderful little book called *A Whack on the Side of the Head*, compares the pain of wading through old patterns of behavior on the path of growth and creative change as being similar to a visit to a junkyard. As you know, a junkyard is a place for junk. Yet, everything in that junkyard was once something precious to someone. Looked at in this way, a visit to a junkyard can be a sobering experience because it's there that we see the final destination of almost everything we once desired.

You've certainly had precious things that have long since gone into the dumpster. You also have ideas about what needs to be done to get you out from under your WAFs. And you've probably attached a great deal of importance to overcoming your WAFs so that your life can truly begin. These strategies are, in a sense, precious and valuable to you. After all, your life seems to depend on finding a solution— and each new strategy seems to promise a solution. In this chapter you'll get to find out whether your WAF strategies are serving you well or perhaps ought to be left for the junkyard.

You've reached this moment—reading this book—because you want to be about more than your WAFs. What needs to happen now is for you to wake up to what you and your life have become because of your battles with anxiety. Then you can take a stand and decide that you no longer want to be about that. This is a choice only you can make. We hope that when you reach the end of this chapter, you will be willing to make that choice.

COSTS OF ANXIETY MANAGEMENT

Struggle with anxiety has cost you—in the coin of energy, time, deep and painful regret, missed opportunities, lost moments, financial burden, restricted freedom, relationships that might have been, and damaged or strained relationships with those with whom you have the closest bonds. And you've got a sinking sense that your best efforts at anxiety control haven't worked as intended. This failure at control has left a deep mark on you.

This is a good starting point. The difficult work is facing how you've struggled with anxiety and how that struggle has cost you in the various areas of your life. Remember the sobering process of wading through a junkyard.

Have you experienced broken and strained relationships, sickness and poor health, excessive stress, difficulties at school or work, poor concentration, or problems with alcohol or other substances? Or, in a more general way, do you feel that you may be unable to do what you care about because the WAFs seem to stand in the way? There may also be other less obvious costs too or those you prefer not to think about.

The following Costs of Anxiety Management exercise can help you get a better sense of the costs linked with your WAF struggles. This will also give you a clear idea of what you've missed out on by responding to your WAFs with struggle and avoidance behavior.

You'll see that we're asking you to look at your personal experience with worry, anxiety, and fear across various life areas. Nobody is a better expert about your experience than you. So as you wade through this exercise, gently remind yourself of this fact.

If your mind wanders, you can return to the spirit of the exercise by asking yourself this: What does my experience tell me about the costs of WAF struggle?

Are you willing to get started? If so, then use the lines below to address some of the questions in each life area. An example of how Susan did the exercise follows.

EXERCISE: COSTS OF ANXIETY MANAGEMENT

1. *Interpersonal costs*

   Summarize the effects of struggling with your WAFs on your relationships. Have friendships changed or been lost? Have family members been alienated? Do they avoid you, or do you avoid them? Have you lost a marriage or romantic relationship due to worry, anxiety, or fear? Or have you missed out on new social bonds because of fear, dread, or an unwillingness to trust because of past trauma? Are you unable to engage your roles as a spouse, partner, or parent because of those pesky WAFs?

   _____

   _____

   _____

2. *Career costs*

   Summarize the effects of struggling with anxiety on your career. Have you ever quit or been fired from a job because of attempts to get a handle on your anxiety and fear? This includes being late, being less productive, missing days of work, being unable to travel, avoiding tasks where WAFs might show up, skipping out on business and social interactions with colleagues and customers, or procrastination. Has a boss or have coworkers commented on your poor performance because of your anxiety management efforts? Have those efforts affected your school career (relationships with teachers, administrators)? Have they resulted in unemployment or being on disability or welfare?

_____

_____

_____

3. *Health costs*

    Describe the effects of managing your worry, anxiety, and fear on your health. Do you tend to get sick often? Do you have difficulties falling asleep and staying asleep? Do you sometimes ruminate and stew over anxiety and worry to the point of feeling sick or keyed up? Do you avoid taking care of your health because of your WAFs (e.g., avoid going to the doctor, having tests done, visiting a dentist)? Do you avoid exercise because it might bring on your WAFs? Have you spent quite a bit of time in the doctor's office or emergency room for your WAFs?

    _____

    _____

    _____

4. *Energy costs*

    Outline how managing your anxiety has affected your energy. Do those efforts sometimes exhaust you? Have you put time and energy into disappointing efforts at WAF control? Are you often engaged in mental planning and fact-finding in an effort to ward off or minimize your WAFs? Do you waste mental energy on worry, stress, fretting over distractions, checking, and negative thinking? Have you experienced difficulties with memory or concentration? Have your attempts to manage anxiety left you feeling discouraged, fatigued, or worn out?

    _____

    _____

    _____

5. *Emotional costs*

    What have efforts to get a handle on anxiety cost you emotionally? Do you feel sad or depressed about your WAFs? Have you tended to be on edge, perhaps exploding in anger in times of stress? Do you carry regrets and guilt because of what you have done or failed to do because of your WAFs? How do regrets about your WAF episodes affect you emotionally? Do you feel depressed or hopeless when your efforts to control anxiety aren't working? Do you feel as though life is passing you by?

_____

_____

_____

6. *Financial costs*

How much money have you spent on managing your WAFs? Consider money you've spent on psychotherapy for your WAFs and related difficulties (e.g., depression, anger, alcoholism). How about medications, money spent on doctor's visits, or the costs for anxiety books, tapes, DVDs, or seminars? See if you can come up with a reasonable estimate of these monetary costs. You can include costs due to disability, lost wages, and missed work because of your WAFs too.

_____

_____

_____

7. *Costs to freedom*

How have your efforts to control WAFs limited your ability to do what you want to do? Can you drive near and far, with or without others? Can you shop, take a train or plane, or go for a walk in your neighborhood, the park, a mall, or a forest? Do the WAFs keep you from trying new foods, new activities, new forms of recreation, experiencing your dreams, and doing what you care about? Consider also whether your WAF management strategies keep you from doing what you already enjoy doing.

_____

_____

_____

The Example of Susan

Here's how Susan, an office assistant, completed her Costs of Anxiety Management exercise:

1. *Interpersonal costs*

   Few friends. Avoid making eye contact. I'd like to enjoy stimulating conversation but find myself too busy worrying about how awkward I am. I've avoided being intimate. I don't go to parties, large gatherings, and haven't been to the beach or a movie in some time. Always make up excuses about why I can't do something fun with people. I am a people pleaser . . . always putting the needs of others before my own. I feel like I'm living in a shell. I'm turning into a real loner.

2. Career costs

Dropped out of college because I couldn't get my anxiety under control. Lost my previous job because I wouldn't drive long distances for business. My current work is only fifteen minutes from my house, but it takes me almost an hour to get there because I can't take the bridge. Just called in sick again because I'm having a shitty start to my day. Attending staff meetings is difficult, and I make up excuses for not going. Can't seem to get things done on time because I'm a perfectionist and worry that my work is not up to snuff. My boss has warned me about this.

3. Health costs

Constant tension. Getting sick a lot. I've been to several doctors and the emergency room, had EKGs, hormonal tests, chest X-rays, and saw a GI specialist. I've started to drink more booze to get my mind off my anxiety and panic, and to the point of getting sick. Now my panic seems worse. I wonder if I have a drinking problem. The dentist is one of my big anxiety/panic buttons too—haven't been in for a checkup in ten years. I don't sleep well or digest food well—upset stomach, feeling bloated. I've stopped exercising—the physical sensations are too much. Getting fatter too.

4. Energy costs

Getting a handle on anxiety is one big, constant challenge. I'm exhausted all the time—not just at night but also in the morning—must be all that tension. I try to stay busy to keep my mind from wondering when I'll have another panic attack. I can't seem to get a handle on my anxiety and I kick myself for being so out of control. I'm tired of not being able to enjoy life.

5. Emotional costs

Loneliness—my few friends have told me that I'm the biggest glass-half-empty person that they know. Depression, disappointment, things aren't turning out, and all that shit. It feels like I have a noose around my neck, or like I'm about to pop. Not going places because I feel "shaky," leaving food untouched in a restaurant because my stomach is upset from feeling shaky, lying to people about what's wrong because I'm afraid that the few people who love me will finally leave me and go find someone who isn't "broken." Feel like an angry nag—arguing more with my husband and yelling at my kids over little things . . . . Fear screwing up my kids and marriage.

6. Financial costs

I've been on a half-dozen anxiety medications (and still am on a few) . . . about a year of psychotherapy . . . and have bought a number of books. Bought several herbal remedies too. None of this has really worked. Counting all the tests and doctor and emergency room visits, I've probably spent close to $10,000 trying to kick this. This doesn't even include missed days at work, lost college tuition, and sick leave . . . . Shit, if I add all that in, then the figure is more like $20,000. Sad really. I could think of so many other ways to spend that kind of money.

7. Costs to freedom

Basically anxiety is completely controlling me. I feel like I have no life—like I'm disabled. My battle with anxiety and panic attacks has become a daily challenge. I can't go out to restaurants or to movies. Because I can't wait in lines at the grocery store, I have to shop really early in the morning or late in the evening. I *"rush" through the grocery store, and I REFUSE to go to the mall. I pretty much stay in my comfort zone, only going to the places "I know." I can't go to church or watch my children in their school plays. Missed my oldest daughter's graduation from college. I'd like to socialize at work but just can't do it. I'm just barely holding it together at my current job. I can't even take a family vacation beyond my backyard. Unfamiliar or new situations are out of the picture. Flying, buses, and trains are out too. I feel stuck—like I'm trapped in a time warp doing the same old things over and over. My kids are suffering too, and this really hurts me.*

Completing your Costs of Anxiety Management exercise is a crucial first step in honestly facing how your WAFs have damaged your life and continue to do so. But it has a further purpose. It's important that you recognize and actually feel the effects of your WAFs despite all your efforts to change. When you do that, you position yourself to do something differently. So let's start there.

WHAT HAVE YOU BEEN DOING ABOUT YOUR WAFs?

In the previous exercise you faced the costs associated with managing your WAFs in some important areas of your life. We've hinted at what makes the costs costly for you. Now we'd like to come out and say it more boldly. The costs have little to do with your WAFs. The costs have everything to do with what you're doing *about* your WAFs.

Anxiety Manager at WAFs "R" Us

You may feel like you've been forced into a new job for WAFs "R" Us. You don't necessarily want this job, but there you are—promoted—the new anxiety manager. This job, of course, is a full-time position, meaning 24/7 with no breaks.

The position requires that you engage your life fully while keeping your WAFs at bay. Sounds simple, right? You've got the tools at your disposal—your mind and your capacity to avoid. You're pretty good at figuring out when and where you might have the WAFs—your mind has this down—and so you plan, strategize, and the like to avoid these situations.

Sometimes you get caught off guard too, but then you know that you can opt for other tools, perhaps distraction, being with safe others, breathing your way out of it, medications, disputing those unsettling thoughts, or the tried-and-true cut-and-run response—escape.

You're doing reasonably well at your job as far as the WAFs are concerned. True, they still show up and bite you now and then, but you're able to quell the storm enough so that you don't lose your job. The problem though is that you aren't fulfilling the other more critical aspect of your job description—engaging your life fully.

You aren't able to do that because the other part of your job at WAFs "R" Us takes so much time and effort. Every time you try to do something you care about, you risk the old WAFs showing up. And your experience probably tells you that many things that you do care about in life are linked with the WAFs. So when you stop doing what you care about so as to get a handle on the WAFs, you aren't doing what you care about. This leaves you stuck in a funk.

Here's another way to look at your situation. Your employer at WAFs "R" Us is your mind, and it isn't serving you well. It's given you a job description—just avoid your WAFs at all costs—that cannot be carried out without major costs in other areas of your life. In fact, there's no way to avoid your WAFs without also avoiding what you care about. So you get the pain of the WAFs now and then, and on top of that, your life is shrinking around you—and this shrinkage just adds more pain.

There's another option. This option involves a change in emphasis and a choice. Taking this route means that you choose to do what you care about, even if that means that you're guaranteed to experience WAFs now and then. There will probably be some pain. And with that pain you'll get vitality that comes with being liberated from your WAFs. You'll be living.

Right now, you don't need to decide whether any of this makes sense. In fact, we're pretty certain that your mind is dishing out all kinds of reasons why this stuff doesn't apply to you. Don't argue with your mind now, and instead ponder two questions:

1. Have your WAF management strategies made you less anxious *and* happier with life?

2. Has being an anxiety manager moved you in directions you want your life to take?

Below, we're going to help you make contact with what you've done about your WAFs and how well the struggle for control has worked for you. You need to feel this in your heart and not just understand it in your mind.

Why might this be? The simple and honest answer is that we don't want you to go about doing more of the same, especially when old WAF management strategies haven't worked for you. Successful anxiety transformation begins with facing—openly and honestly—each WAF management attempt, each past strategy, and then looking to see how it has worked and what it has cost you. This isn't easy, which is why we have designed an exercise to help you identify clearly what hasn't worked.

Taking Stock of Your Anxiety Management History

Right now, we'd like you to look back over the last month at your past attempts to manage and control your WAFs. The following exercise will help you organize your memories across different situations and relationships.

EXERCISE: WHAT HAVE I GIVEN UP FOR ANXIETY IN THE LAST MONTH?

The purpose of completing this anxiety management exercise is to let you examine how costly managing your anxiety is for you. Think about your life—all the things (big and small) you care about and want to do.

As you go through this exercise, ask yourself what you have given up in order to manage, reduce, and avoid your WAFs in the past month. What opportunities to do things that you like or that matter to you have you traded in to control and manage anxiety? Over the past month, what have you missed out on in the service of WAF management and control?

In the first column, record each situation or event that triggered your anxiety, panic, concerns, or worries. In the second column, write down your anxiety, bodily sensations, thoughts, concerns, or worries. In the third, record what you did to manage your anxiety—your coping or management strategy. In the fourth column, record what effect your efforts to control or reduce your anxiety had on you. For instance, how did you feel afterward? In the fifth and final column, write down the consequences and costs associated with your efforts to manage your anxiety. What did you give up or miss out on?

Situation/Event	Anxiety/Concern	Anxiety Coping Behavior	Effect on You	Costs
Example: *was invited to go out with some friends*	Example: *was afraid of having a panic attack*	Example: *stayed at home and watched TV*	Example: *felt safer for a bit, but then lonely, sad, and angry with myself for being so weak*	Example: *lost out on good time with my friends; missed an opportunity to deepen friendships*
working 2 days	having too too intense + too much anxiety	limit session	felt more secure not taking on too much	$ costs - Kasi might not be happy

Taking Stock of Your Coping Strategies

After completing this exercise, we'd like you to take stock of what you've learned. Have your efforts to control your WAFs worked? Have they increased your vitality and ability to engage life to the fullest? Have your efforts to keep anxious thoughts and feelings down actually kept them down? Or have your WAFs simply returned again and again, crippling your life, and leaving you feeling stuck and hopeless?

If you're like a lot of people with anxiety problems, nothing you've done to control anxiety has really worked. You keep doing things you regret. You keep missing out on potentially vital life experiences. And you keep trading in more and more of your life flexibility in an effort to get a foothold. All the while, your life is slowly ticking by. What does your heart, your gut, tell you about your history with anxiety? What does your experience tell you about your response to your WAFs? Take a moment to take stock.

Anxiety and fear are powerful feelings that can sweep away your strongest resolve. Despite your best efforts to manage and control your WAFs, you still have the costs. You keep feeling bad about yourself and those thoughts and situations that trigger your anxiety. You want to change, but no amount of remorse or trying seems to stem the force of the WAFs when they show up.

You may wonder if you've got what it takes. You may think that you just have to try harder and apply more willpower. Check your experience for the answer. Haven't you gone down that road—perhaps even more than once? We suspect you have. And if this is true of your experience, then spending more of your time on Try-Harder Street, Effort Lane, or at the corner of Coping Avenue and More Willpower Boulevard isn't the solution.

How Have Your Coping Strategies Worked?

Each second you engage your WAFs is a moment taken away from something you want in your life. Much of what keeps this going and why it doesn't work has been covered in the earlier chapters and will be discussed further in those to come. For now, we can say this much: it all boils down to avoidance of your WAFs. Avoidance buys you short-term emotional relief but at significant costs to your life and freedom.

EXERCISE: SHORT- AND LONG-TERM COSTS AND BENEFITS OF ANXIETY MANAGEMENT

This brief exercise will help you connect with some of the short- and long-term benefits and costs of your WAF management efforts. To do this exercise, go back to the previous one and list each of your coping strategies. Note that some of them might also include less obvious ones, like therapy, use of alcohol, self-help, and anything you might think of that seems to be focused on avoiding, reducing, or getting away from your WAFs. Take your time with this.

As you do the exercise, watch for strategies that don't work long term and that tend to get in the way of you doing what matters to you in the short term. Don't be concerned about strategies that seem to work or that don't interfere with your life. Be mindful of this too: making the distinction between what works and what doesn't work can be difficult to do. Here's why: your mind may tell you the strategy works and doesn't interfere with your life. Yet, after thanking your mind for that thought, you ought to follow it with this question: What would I be doing with my mental and physical energy if I weren't spending it on coping with my WAFs? If you answer this question openly and honestly, then you'll likely come up with other activities that are new or potentially more important and interesting to you than successful WAF management.

Here's how Alice, a twenty-four-year-old college student, completed some of her cost-benefit analysis. We include her responses below as an example for you when doing the remaining parts.

WAF Coping Strategy	Costs		Benefits	
	Short-Term	Long-Term	Short-Term	Long-Term
Avoiding crowds	Can't go clothes shopping at the mall; feel bad about that	Keeps me out of many fun activities, like music, social events, movies; feel like a loser	I feel less anxious.	Nothing comes to mind.
Distraction	Can't focus on much else; tend to miss important details	Becoming more forgetful; others describe me as distant, like I'm in another world	Keeps my mind off my anxiety; anxiety tends to go down, but not always	Nothing

91

When Alice was finished, she noticed that most of the benefits she experienced had nothing to do with things she cared about in her life. They were all about buying some relief from her WAFs. And most of this relief was only fleeting.

She also spotted many costs and no long-term benefits to her anxiety management efforts. In fact, she suggested that we consider deleting the long-term benefits column. We haven't done so because we believe that you need to find out for yourself whether anxiety management and control buys you anything good in the long term. Go ahead and find out.

THE TAKE-HOME MESSAGE

You likely opened this book with the hope of finding a better way to manage and control your WAFs so that you can get on with living your life the way you wish. This makes sense so long as you, just like so many anxiety sufferers, continue to see your WAFs as *the problem*.

Our intention in this chapter was to help you connect with another possibility, however hard that may be for you to wrap your head around at the moment. That possibility is this: Everything you've done and continue to do about your WAFs has cost you much more than the WAFs themselves. The struggle itself is a trap. We'll show you a way out.

Assessing the Costs of My WAF Struggles to Take Back My Life

Points to Ponder: Life is a journey, not a destination. It is built one small step at a time by what I do. Managing anxiety has cost me dearly.

Questions to Consider: What have I given up as a consequence of managing my WAFs? What would I do with my time and energy if it were not spent trying to manage anxiety, fear, unsettling thoughts, memories, and the like?

CHAPTER 7

What Matters More to You: Managing Your Anxiety or Living a Good Life?

We look for happiness in all the wrong places. Like a moth flying into the flame, we destroy ourselves in order to find temporary relief. Because we often find such relief, we continue to reinforce old patterns of suffering and strengthen dysfunctional patterns in the process. —Pema Chödrön

What matters to you? This is one of the most profound questions we'll ask you to consider and reconsider throughout this book and for the rest of your life. Most people don't think about it until it's too late to do something about it. We don't want to see that happen to you.

Here we're going to walk you through two exercises that'll help you connect with what you want to be about in this life: a funeral meditation (adapted from Hayes et al., 1999) and writing your own epitaph. These exercises are very powerful and even a bit frightening. The payoff for doing them is a clearer vision of what you want your life to stand for. The exercises also reveal what struggling with WAFs has cost you.

We all know that death is inevitable. Sometimes we can delay death, but we can't avoid it. Although we can't control when or how we'll die, we can control how we live from this day forward. We know from testimonies that something profound happens when people have been near the precipice between life and death and have survived to live another day. Their lives change in dramatic ways.

Facing death forces people to take stock. And when they do that, many people end up radically changing what they've been doing and begin spending more time doing things they really care about. Old habits and activities that once seemed so important become trivial.

In short, contacting the precipice between life and death wakes people up. Something clicks. People change what they do and how they live in ways that are richer and more vital and meaningful than before. They make a choice to spend their remaining time on this planet doing things that matter. These activities are what they (and you) will be remembered for. The following exercise will help you make contact with this simple truth in a deeper way.

EXERCISE: FUNERAL MEDITATION

Go ahead and get comfortable. Imagine that you're observing your own funeral. Visualize yourself in a casket. Smell the fresh flowers. Hear the soft music in the background. Look around the room. Who do you see?

Perhaps you can see your loved ones, family, friends, relatives, coworkers, and people you've met at one time or another. Listen closely to the conversations and what they're saying about you. What's your partner saying . . . your kids . . . your best friend . . . your colleagues . . . your neighbor?

Listen carefully to each of them as they say the words that, in your heart, you most want to hear about yourself. This is how you want the people that you care about to remember you. Your wisdom will let you pick and choose exactly what you want and need to hear from them.

Now just pause for a moment and keep imagining this situation. Go ahead, sit back, and close your eyes. Stay with this image for a few minutes. Then come back to reading.

Remember the comments you heard. In your heart of hearts, what did you want to hear about your life? Take a moment and jot down what you heard and wanted to hear said about you in the lines below.

What I heard people say about me was . . .

a good person, followed my own path, kind, fun, loving

What I wanted to hear people say about me was . . .

this is fine

There's something critically important in what you heard and wrote down a moment ago: each utterance reflects your values, what you really want your life to be about. And what you heard others say about you was based on what they see you doing.

Some of what you heard may have left you feeling disappointed. Perhaps one person said, "He was always so anxious and uptight. . . . I wish he'd done more with his life" or "She had a tough life . . . never getting past her fears and worries."

The good news about this exercise is that your life isn't over yet. Your eulogies haven't been written. You still have time to do things to be the type of person you want to be. You can start living the way you want to be remembered later on.

There's another reason for doing this exercise. This reason is more practical and has to do with gaining perspective on your life and your actions. You won't be able to see the costs of the anxiety struggle in your life unless you can see what you want to be about. Anxiety is costly precisely because it gets in the way of what you want to do. If this weren't so, you wouldn't be reading this book. You'd be just like the millions of other people who have their share of WAFs, among other sources of hardship and pain, and yet march on doing what matters to them.

The next exercise builds on the previous one. It'll help you to connect with what you truly care about in life and where you'd go if your WAFs weren't ruling the roost.

This may seem like another strange and somewhat scary exercise. If you stick with it and complete it and feel a bit upset, then you'll get in touch with what you want your life to stand for. So don't rush. Find a quiet place to reflect, openly and honestly, about what it is that makes your life worthwhile. If you need to do this exercise in several sittings, then do that.

EXERCISE: WRITE YOUR ANXIETY MANAGEMENT EPITAPH

Your task in this exercise is to write your epitaph (the inscription on your gravestone) as it would be written if you were to die today. What would it say if it was about what you've been doing with your anxiety management? What have you become by living in the service of your WAFs? Bring to mind all of your WAF coping-and-management strategies and be mindful of how they've gotten in the way of what you want to do. Think of everything you say aloud, think to yourself, or do with your hands or feet before, during, or after the WAFs show up to keep them at bay. List them all.

Here is what Joan, a woman with a fifteen-year history of struggle with panic, wrote for her Anxiety Management Epitaph.

Joan's Epitaph
Here Lies Joan—A Long-Time Panic Sufferer

She spent the last eight years of her life homebound for fear of panic. She visited her doctor dozens of times and refilled countless prescriptions. She was unable to work and had few friends outside her immediate family. She avoided crowds, unfamiliar places, driving, and long-distance travel. She hadn't gone to the beach or watched a sunset from a mountaintop since high school. She spent her evenings surfing the Web for information about anxiety and reading books about her anxiety problem. Her husband was her safety net and pacifier—without him she wasn't able to do anything. Her life was about not having panic, and she left this earth enslaved by this goal and never having conquered it.

Now, when you're ready, go ahead and write your Anxiety Management Epitaph. Print a copy of the blank tombstone from the CD and work off that.

The exercises up until now were probably difficult to do, and it should be that way. We asked you to face squarely what your life has become in the service of anxiety and its management. The next exercise ought to be more uplifting.

We'd like you to do another epitaph-writing exercise, but with a twist. This time, we'd like you to write your epitaph as you'd really like it to read, without the stains of anxiety and fear and its management. You can think of this epitaph as representing the things you truly care about and wish to be known for. Rather than your anxiety epitaph, this is your Valued Life Epitaph!

EXERCISE: MY VALUED LIFE EPITAPH

Imagine that you could live your life free of any worry, anxiety, or fear. Wouldn't that be something? As you connect with this, imagine that one day the headstone in the drawing below will be the headstone on your grave. Notice that the headstone is blank. Your epitaph (words describing your life) hasn't been written. What inscription would you like to see on your headstone?

Think of a phrase or series of brief statements that would capture the essence of the life you want to lead. What is it you want to be remembered for? If you could somehow live your life without WAFs looming over your head, then what would you be doing with your time and energy?

Give yourself some time to think about these really important questions. If you find an answer—or more than one—just write them down on the lines on "your" headstone. Think big. There are no limits to what you can be remembered for.

HERE LIES

She overcame all her obstacles and lived a full, rich life of her own choosing.

This isn't a hypothetical exercise. What you'll be remembered for, what defines your life, is up to you. It depends on what you do now. It depends on the actions you take. This is how you determine the wording of your epitaph.

Now, we make no promises that people will build a Lincoln-type memorial for you at the end of your life. Yet if you persistently move in your valued directions, chances are that people will write things on your tombstone other than "Here lies Tom: he managed his anxiety better than his life" or "Here lies Mary: she spent most of her life struggling with panic."

When you're finished, compare your Valued Life Epitaph with your Anxiety Management Epitaph. If you need to, print copies of the forms for both exercises from the CD and then transcribe what you wrote for each exercise. Next, place each epitaph side by side in front of you and look at them. As you read each of them again, ask yourself the following questions (in no particular order):

- What epitaph do you want to be known for?

- Which one is more vital to you?

- What epitaph best fits your life now?

- Is your life about anxiety management or life management?

- Are your WAF monsters ruling the roost? And is this what you want to be about?
  have for the past 4 months.
- What have you become in the service of your WAFs?
  compromised
- Are you living better?

- Must you be free of WAFs?
  I suppose not - but I'd like to be.

We understand that getting a handle on anxiety is important to you. Then again, would you really like your tombstone to read, "Here lies Harry: he finally got rid of his anxiety disorder"? If that inscription doesn't excite you, we can tell you that you're not alone. We've done this exercise with many people just like you. And we've never seen anyone write something like that.

> *People will know you by what they see you do, not by what you think and feel about what you do.*

What does it mean that people never mention WAFs in eulogies and on tombstones? Perhaps getting rid of your WAFs—a goal you've been working so hard to achieve—isn't going to matter much in the grand scheme of things. Think of it this way: every sixty seconds you spend trying to get a handle on your WAFs is a minute away from doing something that matters to you.

In short, the WAF struggle pulls you out of your life. If you're not doing things to be the type of person you want to be, *now* is the time to live the life you want and do the things that are most important to you. To start doing that, you'll need to have a serious look at what you've done about your anxiety and how those actions have cost you. Then, and only then, can you make a choice to do something radically different than you've been doing up until now.

I'M STUCK AND AT MY WIT'S END—NOW WHAT?

This is an important moment. There's a lesson here that can change your life. Knowing in your mind and heart—with absolute certainty—that the things you've done because of anxiety don't work is the first step on a new road.

Admitting and accepting that your WAFs are stronger than your efforts to stop them creates a paradoxical new freedom. You can do something new—because all the old, tried-and-true ways to cope aren't working and will not work.

This is a watershed moment. It starts with acknowledging that your experience is your best guide. What does your experience with your WAFs tell you? Go ahead and look back at your responses to the earlier exercises. The situation probably looks hopeless, and it is. The old ways are hopeless. Something radically new is hopeful. For in doing something new, you risk getting something new.

To get that kind of hope, you must first *give up on and stop all the old WAF management-and-control efforts*. They haven't worked and will not work. They've kept you trapped with a false belief that control was possible, that anxiety management was possible, and perhaps that if you work harder at it or trade in a little more of your life, things will get better. Your experience tells you this isn't so—so long as you keep trying, you keep failing.

Everything you will learn here rests on this understanding: All the old strategies for *managing* worry, anxiety, and fear lead to a dead end. They hurt you. This is why you need to stop them. Your mind will tell you otherwise, but look to your experience here. It's time to let go of old unworkable strategies. We know this sounds easier said than done. So we'll talk more about that right at the beginning of the next chapter.

EXERCISE: LIFE ENHANCEMENT AND THE LIFE FORM

We've said that this book is about something much bigger than your WAFs. That "something" is your life and nurturing your capacity to live it, each and every day, without getting bogged down in the snares of your judgmental mind and the needless struggle with your emotional mind and body.

To help you, you'll need to learn how to see the struggle and its costs as they unfold, moment to moment, day in and day out, in real time. This is a skill that you can learn, and we've created a simple worksheet—Living in Full Experience (LIFE)—to help you do that.

The acronym LIFE is not accidental; it's our deliberate intention to frame this exercise in terms of what really counts: you living your life. A blank copy of the worksheet is at the end of this chapter. You'll also find it on the CD at the back of this book, so you can print out additional copies. Be sure to print or make several copies of the form for this week and carry them with you. You'll need them.

without getting bogged down in the snares of your judgmental mind and the needless struggle with your emotional mind and body.

99

The purpose of the LIFE Form is to help you get a better sense of where and when WAFs show up and, most importantly, what you do about them when they show up. You'll see that the LIFE Form can be used to monitor and track situations where your WAFs show up, related experiences you might have (thoughts, physical sensations, and behaviors), your willingness to have those experiences, and how your reactions to them get in the way of, or diminish, your capacity to engage in activities and experiences that you care about.

This form should be completed shortly after each episode in which unwanted WAFs show up. Don't put it off until much later or the next day. If you do that, then you'll almost guarantee yourself inaccurate information. And if your life depended on getting accurate information about your experience—and, in a sense, it really does here—then you ought to do the exercise as intended. Inaccurate information won't help you.

The LIFE Form is short. It asks you to fill in the date and time of an unwanted WAF episode and then provides you with a series of check boxes listing several sensations you may have experienced during an episode. After that, you're asked to check whether the emotion was more like fear, anxiety, depression, or some other feeling, and to rate how intensely you felt that emotion.

The next question asks you about your willingness to have what you were having without acting on your WAF experiences in any way. "Willingness" is a topic that we haven't covered in much detail yet, but will shortly. For now, you can think of willingness as allowing your WAF thoughts and feelings to be just as they are rather than struggling with them. The more you struggle and try to get rid of your WAFs, the lower your willingness level would be.

The remaining fill-in questions are fairly straightforward. You'll see that several of them get at some of the issues that we've covered in this chapter, such as the things you care about doing. Take your time with them because they'll come up again as you move through this workbook. They'll also give you a clearer sense of what you're trading in, each moment of every day, in the service of controlling your WAFs.

Completing the LIFE forms throughout this week is a commitment. Don't do the forms because we said they're a good idea. Do them because you want a different outcome in your life. Make it a choice. Are you willing to do that?

If so, then start each day with the intention to complete the LIFE forms, as necessary, throughout the day. When you do that, you'll be doing something new and different.

Here's how Jennifer, a stay-at-home mom and mother of three, completed one of her many LIFE forms for the week. She's been struggling with anxiety and worry for several years.

LIVING IN FULL EXPERIENCE—THE LIFE FORM
A Life Enhancement Exercise

Date: _1/15/07_ Time: _9:30_ A.M./(P.M.)

Check off any sensations you experienced just now:

☐ Dizziness	☐ Breathlessness	☐ Fast heartbeat	☐ Blurred vision
☐ Tingling/numbness	☐ Unreality	☑ Sweatiness	☐ Hot/cold flashes
☑ Chest tightness/pain	☐ Trembling/shaking	☐ Feeling of choking	☐ Nausea
☑ Neck/muscle tension	☐ Detached from self		

Check what emotion best describes your experience of these sensations (pick one):

☐ Fear   ☑ Anxiety   ☐ Depression   ☐ Other: _____

Now rate how strongly you felt this emotion/feeling (circle number):

0 ------ 1 ------ 2 ------ 3 ------ 4 ------ 5 ------ (6) ------ 7 ------ 8

Mild/Weak   Moderate   Extremely Intense

Now rate how willing you were to have these sensations/feelings without acting on them (e.g., to manage them, get rid of them, suppress them, run from them):

0 ------ 1 ------ 2 ------ 3 ------ 4 ------ 5 ------ 6 ------ (7) ------ 8

Extremely Willing   Moderate   Completely Unwilling

Describe **where you were** when these sensations occurred: _I was at home alone and had just gotten the kids on the bus for school._

Describe **what you were doing** when these sensations occurred: _I was planning on making a list of the things that I needed to get done for the day before the kids and my husband would get home._

Describe **what your mind was telling you** about the sensations/feelings: _I have so much to do and can't even think straight. My head is spinning. I need to focus. Feel tired._

Describe **what you did** (if anything) about the thoughts/sensations/feelings: _I tried to take some deep breaths. Thought about taking a shower. Tried to get my mind off the worry and tension so that I could think. Turned on the TV._

If you did anything about the thoughts/sensations or feelings, **did it get in the way of anything** you really value or care about? If so, describe what that was here: _Didn't get my to-do list done. Ended up jumping around from one task to the next, never really finishing anything. Forgot about my ob-gyn appointment that morning. And didn't get the groceries I needed for dinner and the kids' lunches the next day._

THE TAKE-HOME MESSAGE

Every strategy, every failed attempt, each plan or effort at WAF control has gotten in the way of what you want to do with your time and energy. You're living your Anxiety Management Epitaph more than your Valued Life Epitaph. This needs to change. You can liberate yourself from the struggle. The answer lies in a place you've never looked before. It will be difficult, it will feel backwards, it will mean heading *toward* what you instinctively rush away from. All that said, we promise that you can do it. What you learn in this workbook will work as long as you're willing to be open to what you experience rather than fight it. And this new path will give you relief from the struggle, the losses, and the failures. All you need to do now is to keep reading . . . *and* do the work.

What Matters Is Living a Full Life

Points to Ponder: My life is created by what I spend my time doing. I can choose to live my Anxiety Management Epitaph or my Valued Life Epitaph.

Questions to Consider: Have I (and others) suffered enough from the effects of controlling my anxiety? Do I want my life to be about much more than getting rid of my WAFs? Am I willing to give up being an anxiety manager and go down a different path?

my life is created by what I spend my time doing.

LIVING IN FULL EXPERIENCE—THE LIFE FORM
A Life Enhancement Exercise

Date: _____ Time: _____ A.M./P.M.

Check off any sensations you experienced just now:

- ❑ Dizziness
- ❑ Breathlessness
- ❑ Fast heartbeat
- ❑ Blurred vision
- ❑ Tingling/numbness
- ❑ Unreality
- ❑ Sweatiness
- ❑ Hot/cold flashes
- ❑ Chest tightness/pain
- ❑ Trembling/shaking
- ❑ Feeling of choking
- ❑ Nausea
- ❑ Neck/muscle tension
- ❑ Detached from self

Check what emotion best describes your experience of these sensations (pick one):

❑ Fear   ❑ Anxiety   ❑ Depression   ❑ Other: _____

Now rate how strongly you felt this emotion/feeling (circle number):

0 ------ 1 ------ 2 ------ 3 ------ 4 ------ 5 ------ 6 ------ 7 ------ 8

Mild/Weak   Moderate   Extremely Intense

Now rate how willing you were to have these sensations/feelings without acting on them (e.g., to manage them, get rid of them, suppress them, run from them):

0 ------ 1 ------ 2 ------ 3 ------ 4 ------ 5 ------ 6 ------ 7 ------ 8

Extremely Willing   Moderate   Completely Unwilling

Describe **where you were** when these sensations occurred: _____

_____

Describe **what you were doing** when these sensations occurred: _____

_____

Describe **what your mind was telling you** about the sensations/feelings: _____

_____

Describe **what you did** (if anything) about the thoughts/sensations/feelings: _____

_____

If you did anything about the thoughts/sensations or feelings, **did it get in the way of anything** you really value or care about? If so, describe what that was here: _____

_____

CHAPTER 8

Ending Your Struggle with Anxiety Is the Solution

Experience has shown that, ironically, it is often our very attempts to solve the problem that, in fact, maintain it. The attempted solutions become the true problem. —Giorgio Nardone and Paul Watzlawick

It is often our very attempts to solve the problem that, in fact, maintain it.

The exercises in the previous two chapters have shown you that all your attempts to fix your anxiety problem haven't solved anything. Each so-called solution—each attempt to stop or at least stem the tide of your WAFs—has gotten you to this place. And your WAFs still feel out of control.

We know that most seemingly sensible solutions to anxiety problems are really about control. Remember the myths we talked about in chapter 4? The voice in your head tells you to get a handle on your WAFs: "Breathe slowly," "Take a pill," "Watch TV," "Go to bed early," "Take it easy," and so on. This voice comes from the belief, established and recycled over generations, that WAFs are dangerous, that it's impossible to feel anxiety and still live a good life, that managing and controlling anxiety is the way out of misery and into happiness.

The voice is fooling you. Controlling anxiety doesn't work in the same way that control works in other areas of life. In this chapter you'll learn why. You'll also learn to recognize when and where control works well. And you'll learn how to start letting go of the anxiety management agenda and get on with your life management agenda.

ENDING THE TUG-OF-WAR WITH ANXIETY

You've already taken the first step toward understanding the struggle. You've examined the costs. You've faced all your past attempts to manage and control intense physical sensations, nervousness, worries, disturbing thoughts and images, urges, and other unwanted thoughts and feelings.

And, if you're still reading, then you've faced the difficult truth that nothing has really worked. No matter how hard you've tried, no strategy to manage anxiety has helped long term. On top of that, the costs of the struggle are still there.

So what can you do instead—must you go on fighting the good fight until you win (or the WAFs win!)? The good news is that there's another way: you could give up the struggle with anxiety—and you could surrender.

We can almost guarantee that your mind is feeding you all kinds of messages right now. The alternative we just suggested cuts against all the old programming about what your mind has told you needs and ought to be done as far as your WAFs are concerned. So take a moment to observe what your mind is doing, without getting into an argument with yourself, and then read on.

Here's what letting go of the struggle agenda is about. It means allowing yourself to feel anxiety just as it is, just as it comes, instead of trying not to feel anxiety. You can learn to have those unpleasant thoughts and feelings *and* learn how to distance yourself from them just enough so that you can keep doing whatever you want to do—go to a party, meet new people, drive on the highway, take an elevator, see a movie, and so on.

The list of vital life-affirming actions has no limits, no borders—that is, so long as you let go of the struggle and stop fighting against yourself. When you lay down your arms, you are in a sense admitting defeat. This is a smart and enormously vital move on your part. It makes no sense to continue fighting an adversary that cannot and need not be defeated in order for you to have what you want in life.

By surrendering, you're really doing three things: First, you're acknowledging the struggle itself. Next, you're allowing yourself to experience how futile and exhausting that struggle has been. And lastly, you're facing how the struggle has kept you stuck in the same place with nowhere to go. Let's have a closer look at this process.

You could give up the struggle with anxiety—and you could surrender.

It means allowing yourself to feel anxiety, just as it ~~is~~ is, just as it comes, instead of trying not to feel anxiety.

The Exhausting Fight with WAF Monsters

It may seem like you've been fighting a tug-of-war with a team of WAF monsters pulling at one end of the rope and you pulling at the other end. Yet no matter how hard you've pulled to defeat the WAF monsters, they've always come back stronger, pulling harder.

It may look like there's nothing else you can do while you're engaged in this sort of battle. You've got both hands firmly clenching the rope, and your feet are dug in, stuck in the same position. Back and forth it goes.

And as this battle plays out, you're getting more and more worked up too—your chest tightens, your breathing becomes shallow, your teeth are clenched, your face red with pearls of sweat welling up on your brow and forehead, and you can see the whites of your knuckles. You're stuck in an endless and exhausting fight for your life, or so it seems.

Your options may appear limited in this situation. Yet you do have other options. What else could you do in this situation? Take a moment to jot down a few possibilities that come to mind.

_____

_____

You may have come up with only a few options here. That's okay. Your mind may have suggested that you pull harder, try harder, or dig in more. Maybe your mind suggested that there's a better medication or a new coping strategy that'll give you the strength to win. Yet isn't all of this more of the same—old wine, new label?

Here's another option—you don't need to win this fight. This may seem like another wacky idea— *and* it's a potentially vital idea too. It'll allow you to consider this: what would happen if you decided to stop fighting? Think about that.

Suppose you just decided to surrender and drop the rope. As you connect with this possibility, notice what happens to your hands and feet. They're free, right? And you've regained some space and options that were impossible while you were in the middle of the battle: you're now positioned to use your hands, feet, and mind for something other than fighting.

To help you see how you might play out this new option in your life, imagine that something or someone you care deeply about was on the sidelines next to the battle, watching and waiting for you and the fight to finish. Suppose it was your child waiting for a hug or a friend wanting to spend time with you. Or perhaps it was a project, a vacation, or something spiritually uplifting. See if you can visualize that important thing in your life that is just waiting . . . waiting for you to finish fighting.

Now, let's have a closer look at what happens when you drop the rope. The WAF monsters haven't gone away just because you've stopped fighting. They're still there, taunting you with the rope, hoping that you take the bait and grab hold for another round. And you certainly could do that. Or you could decide to keep your hands and feet free so that you can use them to do something you care about—those watching and waiting things on the sidelines.

> **I can drop the rope and end the fight with myself.**

Dropping the rope and ending the struggle creates a window. If you aren't consumed with reducing and controlling anxiety, avoiding the next panic attack, stemming the tide of another painful memory, or putting out disturbing thoughts or worry, then you create a window of opportunity. You create space to move toward the life you've put on hold. One of our clients captured this moment very well when he told us, "When I drop the rope, I'm free."

Remember, your epitaph is written based on what you spend your time doing. If you need to, go back to chapter 7 and remind yourself of what you want your life to stand for.

WHERE ARE YOU IN CONTROL?

So why are so many people reluctant to drop the rope? Why do we keep struggling with anxiety, hurt, and pain when it hasn't really worked well and has cost us so much? The answer has to do with what we've learned about struggling for control.

Below is a little story about two mice who both got caught in difficult and quite frightening situations. Have a look at their different responses.

The Struggle of the Two Mice

Two little mice were happily scurrying around a farmer's kitchen and pantry, looking for tasty snacks. The first mouse was on the kitchen floor sniffing for scraps from that night's dinner. All of a sudden the farm's tomcat entered the kitchen. When he saw the little mouse, he immediately went after it, and the little mouse ran for her life. She frantically ran around the kitchen floor looking for places to hide but couldn't find any at first. The cat's pursuit was relentless and he had come awfully close to pouncing on the little mouse when she finally discovered a small hole in the floorboard. The mouse slipped into it and was safe. The cat was still trying to get her with his paws but he couldn't. The hole was too small. The little mouse had saved her life through her persistent efforts.

Meanwhile a second little mouse in the pantry next door was looking for snacks up high on the countertop. Her eyes were fixed on a bread crumb at the edge of the counter, and so she went over to have a look. As she approached the bread crumb, she lost her footing and fell right into a bucket of cream on the floor below. At first, she struggled frantically to get out. Around and around she went, looking for a way out. The situation looked quite hopeless, and the little mouse was growing tired. Every minute of struggling sucked more energy out of her. Deep down inside she knew she would end up completely exhausted and drown if she continued like this. So she did something counterintuitive and courageous. She decided to slow down and take a closer look around at where she actually was and what was happening to her. That's when she realized, "I am in a bucket filled with tasty cream." She started to take a few sips and continued to move around just fast enough to stay afloat—all the while taking sips of cream. This went on for quite a while. The little mouse wasn't happy to be caught in a bucket. At the same time, she noticed that if she didn't do too much and just kept on sipping away at the cream, she might eventually be fine. She wouldn't run out of energy, and sooner or later the cream would be gone—no more danger of drowning.

We're all just like the first little mouse in many ways. We've learned that effort and struggle *is* the way out of life's hardships. And there's some truth to this too. Human beings and animals will quite literally fight for their lives when faced with *real* danger in the world around them. In these situations, you ought to exert effort and struggle because both help to keep you safe from harm, or even death.

And you don't need to have experienced a life-threatening situation, either, to pick up on this idea. From a very early age, you've learned that success and happiness never come easily, and never come at all for those who wait, give in, or do nothing. This basic idea has been recycled and repackaged over generations.

Under most circumstances, this is a highly adaptive and workable strategy. It often produces desired outcomes. For instance, if you can do something to reduce the chance of real pain and suffering, then it makes sense to do so. Your experience with the world tells you as much, and a sizable psychological literature supports exercising effortful control for better psychological health and physical well-being. There's comfort in knowing this and acting in kind. Life may not always be fair, but we can and should do something to make things right.

As a person suffering from anxiety, you're all too familiar with the mantras of struggle and effortful control: *Pull yourself together, Where there is a will, there is a way,* or *Try harder.* Yet some of the exercises in the previous chapters show that these strategies don't work when it comes to anxiety.

Like the second mouse in the story, you're still stuck in a bucket. Your bucket is not filled with something that can actually hurt or kill you; your bucket is filled with WAFs, and you're desperately swimming around trying to find a way out. The struggle, in short, is with you. Your WAFs may not taste like cream, but if you slow down, look, and listen, you may notice that you can move and swim with them. You will only run out of energy and feel like drowning in your WAFs if you keep struggling with them. If you stay with the energy your WAFs provide, you might even be able to use that energy in a way that is helpful to you.

The key point here is that the same effort you might exert to keep yourself safe and protected from danger in the outside world can be overextended and applied to your inner painful thoughts and feelings where it doesn't work and actually hurts you. You'll only end up feeling exhausted and drained of energy.

Go back to the costs of anxiety management you worked up in chapter 6 and see if all the effort and struggle you've put into getting out or away from your anxiety has made you safer and moved you closer to the life you want. What does your experience tell you? The long-term answer ought to be a resounding "no!"

Here's a thought: It may be possible to have anxiety and not be drowned by it if and when you decide to willingly experience anxiety just as it is and if you give up your struggle with it. For now, hold this idea lightly because we'll expand on it in the chapters to come.

You may wonder why control can work so well with the demands and strains of the world and yet be so ineffective with anxiety and other forms of emotional pain. The answer is that anxiety differs in important ways from other problems in life that can be controlled quite effectively. Being able to see this difference is critical, and it's a skill you can learn. You'll find exercises in this chapter and the next to help you discover when and where control works, when it doesn't work, and how to tell the difference.

When Control Works

Control works well when you apply it to your actions—what you do with your hands and feet. Action is a great litmus test for knowing when control may work. You just need to ask if you or others could see what you're doing and the results of what you do. For instance, if you'd like to clean up your yard, you can go and get a rake and get started. Here are some other examples of situations where control works:

- If you want to change the color of the walls in a room in your home, you can go out and buy new paint and then paint the walls.

- If you no longer like some of your clothes, you can simply throw them away or pass them on to someone who may actually wear them.

- If you're in a job you don't like, then you can quit that job, seek out a new employer, and work there instead.

- You may decide to reconnect with an old friend by picking up the phone and calling or sending an e-mail.

- If you want to perform an act of kindness, then you can give a person a gift, a compliment, or a hug.

- You can exercise regularly and watch what you eat and drink to promote your health and well-being.

The common thread in these life examples is this: they all involve behavior—things you do with your hands, feet, and, at times, your mouth. Another commonality that makes these situations controllable is that they tend to involve objects or situations in the world outside your skin. Changing things in the world around you often *is* possible and works well.

This strategy works so well in so many life areas that it only makes sense to want to apply it to manage emotional and physical pain. And, at times, control does work to manage pain. For instance, you may take an aspirin for a headache, see a doctor for an illness or injury, take time to relax so as to feel more energized, or exercise regularly to maintain emotional balance.

I can control what I do with my hands and feet.

You can also avoid or manage situations that may result in physical injury or death by acting to escape from them when and if they occur. We talked about these kinds of extreme situations a bit in chapter 2, mostly in the context of traumatic events. And you need the capacity for this kind of control in less extreme circumstances too.

As an example, suppose you're unlucky enough to be walking across the road and suddenly you see a car dart out from nowhere and approach at a high rate of speed. In this situation, the obvious response would be to run or jump out of the way. If you didn't act, you'd end up dead or severely injured. This type of fear-motivated behavior is highly adaptive and often works to everyone's advantage. There's nothing problematic about this form of control.

The problem is that what works well in the external world just doesn't work well when applied to things going on inside you. You may try to deal with your thoughts and feelings in the same way you deal with clothes you don't like. Now look at your experience to see what happens when you do that. Can you give away or throw out your unpleasant thoughts and feelings—has that ever worked for you? Can you replace an old painful memory or a reminder of your past with a new one—have you ever been able to do that?

Remember the exercise in chapter 4 where we asked you *not* to think of _____ [what was it?]. This is pretty much impossible, because the thought "Don't think about the PINK ELEPHANT!" is itself, obviously, a thought about a pink elephant. The more you try not to have this thought, the more of this thought you'll have. The same is true of unpleasant thoughts, feelings, and bodily sensations.

The take-home message here is this: you can't win a fight against yourself. And, as much as you may want to throw out your WAFs, there's simply no way to take them in your hands and out of the room to the dumpster. Your WAFs can't be removed in the same way that you can swap out a chair you don't like in your living room. Your WAFs follow you wherever you go.

If you can allow yourself to come to terms with this basic truth, then you'll be faced with the stark and sobering reality that more effort and muscle power isn't going to help you one iota. In fact, if you look back and review chapters 6 and 7, then your experience ought to be screaming this message loudly at you.

Let's examine more closely when control doesn't work and why this is so.

When Control Doesn't Work

Anxiety is, in many respects, an unpleasant emotional state. So it's understandable when you say, "I don't like anxiety" or "I want to get rid of it." Most people without anxiety problems don't like anxiety either. Yet you'll recall that not liking anxiety doesn't make it a problem. If that were true, then most people on this planet would suffer from anxiety disorders.

Problems arise when "not liking" gets mixed with control strategies that are taken to the extreme—when they become overly intense and rigid and when they're applied in situations where they're unnecessary and don't work. In short, the strategies don't produce the anxiety reduction you were hoping for, or if they do, the temporary relief they offer restricts your life.

Consider Beth and Roger's stories.

■ Beth's Story

Beth had a full-blown panic attack in her car while making a right-hand turn. To control having more panic attacks, she started avoiding making right-hand turns while driving. Although this tended to reduce Beth's anxiety somewhat, she paid a huge price for that brief period of comfort. Even short trips to work or to run errands became convoluted, time-consuming, difficult excursions requiring a map, careful planning beforehand, and constant vigilance. Spontaneous drives on unfamiliar routes were out of the question. When possible, she stayed at home for fear of having more panic attacks if she stepped outside. It seemed that controlling anxiety—maximizing feeling good while minimizing emotional pain and suffering—had become the focus and purpose of Beth's life. Yet this strategy didn't leave her panic free or feeling good—far from it. Beth lived her life in the service of controlling panic, and her life became more restricted as a result.

■ Roger's Story

Roger had been battling social anxiety for as long as he could remember. Much of his anxiety and panic centered around his job. He worked hard to prevent his anxiety and panic at work. Situations where he had to talk in front of small groups of businesspeople were downright nasty for him. Nothing seemed to work. This led Roger to quit his well-paying and interesting job. He ended up taking a back-office job where he didn't have to interact with other people. He also earned much less money and felt bored and isolated.

In these two examples and in many others we've seen, control efforts are life constricting, not life expanding. You probably feel this way too. You may even beat yourself up for not being able to control unpleasant thoughts and feelings. You're not alone. From an early age onward most of us are taught that we *should* be able to control them.

One problem with control strategies is this: they often work just enough to keep your WAFs at bay, but in the long run you're left feeling more anxious, anticipating and preparing for the next WAF attack. As Beth and Roger learned, once this cycle of struggle and control is set into motion, it can take over and become your life.

> *I cannot and need not control my WAFs. Instead, I can drop the rope to have my life back.*

Anxiety Is Not a Hot Stove: Even When You Pull Away, You Still Get Burned

Life has taught you how well control works. As a child you probably avoided touching a red-hot stove because it hurt to touch it. You may have learned this the hard way or by listening to your parents or caregivers warning you about the consequences: "Don't touch _____ because you'll get hurt." Keeping your hand away from hot things kept you safe and prevented injury.

This sensible avoidance strategy has repeated itself in both obvious and subtle ways in your life—because it often works to keep you alive and unharmed. Take a moment to think about a situation or two where this has been true in your experience and write them below.

_____   _____

What you've learned over and over again is that control works to help you avoid and reduce external sources of pain and harm. Naturally then, it would seem that these strategies ought to work when you apply them to internal sources of pain and hurt. It's vitally important that you begin to understand this external versus internal distinction.

People get into trouble when they act to avoid their emotional pain and hurt (inside) in the same way that they would act to avoid sources of real harm and danger in the world around them (outside). Look at your experience here—you've been down this road too.

You've treated your WAFs, and responded to them, much like when faced with a red-hot stove. You try to pull away, get away, and avoid them because anxiety, like the hot stove, seems dangerous. When WAFs show up, you feel you must do something. And yet you keep getting burned.

Anxiety is one type of emotional pain. When people act to get rid of emotional and psychological pain, they end up, instead, with more of it. All of what we know about emotional pain boils down to this simple fact: you can't keep your unpleasant thoughts and emotions from burning you the way that you can pull your hand back from a hot stove.

Why might this be? The next exercise will help you experience part of the answer.

EXERCISE: THOUGHTS AND EMOTIONS HAVE NO "ON/OFF" SWITCH

This exercise will help you get a sense of how futile it can be to try controlling your emotional reactions. Start by getting in a comfortable position. When you're ready, we'd like you to do the following: make yourself feel happy. Go ahead and try it now. Really work at it. Can you do it?

If you were successful, then you likely brought on the feeling of happiness in response to something else. For instance, you may have conjured up a memory of a pleasant experience from your past, visualized something you like, or thought of an event you are looking forward to. Yet this isn't what we were asking of you. We want you to feel exuberant for the sake of it, not as a response to something that may help make you feel that way.

Now, try to do the same by making yourself feel really anxious or afraid. Do it without thinking of something really scary or painful. We want you to try really hard. Just turn on the switch. Can you do it?

We hope that this exercise helped you learn that emotions have no on/off switch. It's next to impossible for anyone to feel one way or another just because they want to. Emotions just happen as we engage the world. They're not something we deliberately do apart from that world.

Emotions aren't something you can choose to have more or less of either. When you think and behave otherwise, you'll activate every aspect of your nervous system that keeps you feeling anxious and afraid. And you'll do things that end up keeping you stuck and miserable. You'll get more of the very thing you don't want to feel and think.

This happens because your body is a system with built-in feedback loops—your brain and nervous system. When you act against parts of this system—avoiding, suppressing, or escaping—it sends out reverberations to all other parts of the system. This mind-body connection is like a sensitive spiderweb in this respect. Everything is connected. Trying to run away from unpleasant experiences—be they feelings, thoughts, memories, anxiety, or bodily sensations—amplifies your pain. And your life will seem to be passing by too.

The next exercise (Hayes et al., 1999) will help you experience why struggling with unpleasant feelings and thoughts can make them worse. To begin, find a quiet place where you can sit and get comfortable.

EXERCISE: YOU'RE WIRED TO A PERFECT POLYGRAPH AND . . . ZAP!

Imagine that you're connected to the best and most sensitive polygraph machine that's ever been built. This polygraph is super effective at detecting anxiety. So there's no way you can be aroused or anxious without the machine noticing it.

Now here's your task, which sounds quite simple: all you have to do is stay relaxed—just stay calm—while thinking about a recent episode where you felt anxious. Just think about an episode where you were anxious . . . without getting anxious now. If you get the least bit anxious, however, this machine will detect it.

We know how important it is to you to be successful here, so we're going to give you a special incentive. If you can stay completely relaxed while you imagine the WAF scene, then we'll give you $100,000! (imaginary money, of course, but pretend that you'd get that cash payout).

The catch is that the polygraph is designed to give you a deadly shock if you show the slightest bit of anxiety or arousal. As long as you stay relaxed, you won't die. But if you get the least bit anxious or aroused—and remember this perfect polygraph will notice that immediately—the machine will deliver the shock and kill you. So just relax!

Take a moment to jot down what you think would happen in this situation.

_____

_____

Did you stay perfectly calm and get the payout? Or did you end up dead? We think we know the outcome and so do you—dead as a doornail. The tiniest bit of anxiety would be terrifying for you, and for *any* other person in this situation.

This isn't just another imaginary exercise either. Every day you wake up with your life at stake. You need to be calm, not panic, and avoid the thoughts and worries because your life seems to depend on it. And of course, there it comes: "I need to be calm at this social event. . . . Oh, no! I'm getting tense and anxious—zap . . . zap . . . zap." And there's another vital aspect of your life, missed or ruined.

There's no way to stay calm when you're connected to the perfect polygraph: your nervous system. This system is better than any lie detector at detecting anxiety. When the WAFs show up, you struggle to keep them at bay because everything you want in life seems to hang in the balance. As you do that, your nervous system kicks in. The web reverberates. And guess what you get: more anxious and panicky. And you get zapped too!

Take Joan, who was diagnosed with obsessive-compulsive disorder.

■ *Joan's Story*

Joan feared that she'd shout out profanities in public. She was truly horrified about the possibility of shouting out profanities during a church service. So she spent lots of time trying to figure out how to prevent that from happening. She tried really hard not to think about shouting profanities during church. And here's what ended up happening—she ended up consumed with thoughts about profanities, was extremely anxious, and eventually stopped going to church.

Here the very act of trying to suppress the thought brought about the unwanted thought and emotional experience. And it led Joan to act in ways to control the problem that ended up getting in the way of something that she greatly enjoyed doing. This is how it works with your brain and body too. It's all one big interconnected web that grows and grows as you age and develop new experiences. The more you act on your WAF web, the more it'll reverberate and spread into all areas of your life.

The way to stop the vibrations is to go after the source, the fuel, driving the WAF struggle-and-control machine. That source is unwillingness—your unwillingness to make space for *every* aspect of your experience and identity. The fuel for unwillingness is your judgmental mind talking to you, baiting you, and feeding you messages like "You can't have WAFs and be happy and live life fully. To have the 'good life' means that you must be free of WAFs."

So long as you buy this message, you'll be unwilling to allow your WAFs into your life. This unwillingness will add fuel to the fire driving more struggle and control. At this point in the workbook, you should have a good sense of what your time spent struggling has bought you. And we're almost certain that very little of it is vital and life expanding.

The good news is that living well doesn't require that you first start feeling and thinking well. Many people live with enormous pain and hardship and with every reason to cave in and give up on life. And yet, they continue to move forward in life with meaning, dignity, and a sense of purpose. You may wonder what secret they know that enables them to do that.

Their secret is this: they don't take the bait. They don't spend their valuable time on this earth struggling and fighting with their physical, emotional, and psychological pain. These individuals experience pain just like every other human being on this planet, and they've learned how not to get stuck in that pain. We'll start showing you how to do more of that too in the next chapter.

The simple lesson here is this: control works against you when applied to unwanted and painful aspects of your private world. To get out of this cycle, you'll need to first come to terms with the fact that deliberate control isn't a solution. It's the *problem*.

YOU CAN RUN, BUT YOU CAN'T HIDE FROM YOURSELF

There's another reason why you can't avoid and run away from feelings of anxiety and fear in the same way that you might run from or avoid dangerous objects or situations. That reason has to do with the source of the WAF emotional pain. That source is you.

Imagine a vicious dog or car is coming toward you. You can take quick and decisive evasive action by literally running for your life to avoid potential harm and danger. Running away from the source of danger gets you to safety. Here you're in control with your hands and feet because the source of danger is outside you.

Now picture this scenario: you've experienced a trauma, like a violent sexual assault or a terrible car accident. Memories of the event can pop up in your mind at any time—no matter where you go or what you do. If you're prone to having recurrent obtrusive thoughts ("obsessions"), such as "I could have contaminated myself," your experience will tell you that these thoughts can occur no matter what you happen to be doing or where you happen to go.

Or if you've experienced panic attacks, you know that they can show up in many different situations. Sure, some types of situations seem to make panic more likely, but many people who experience panic attacks over and over again know that panic can happen at any time or any place, even while sleeping in bed.

The bottom line is that your thoughts and feelings—the good, the bad, and the ugly—always go with you wherever you go. You cannot escape or avoid your feelings of anxiety, apprehension, and insecurity by going somewhere else for one simple reason: they are part of you. You take them with you everywhere, along with everything else going on inside your mind and body.

If this is true of your experience, then trying to run and hide from your WAFs is akin to trying to run and hide from you. You can certainly try to do that, but there's really no way to do it. Your WAFs are part of a larger package that helps define what is uniquely human about you. You cannot escape or avoid them so long as you're alive. To act against them is to act against your very being. To act against them also means that you'll remain stuck or that things might even get worse.

You Can't Argue Away Your WAFs

Have you tried getting a handle on your feelings of anxiety by changing your thoughts about what you're afraid of? It's a common strategy. We suspect you've found that it doesn't work well. Why can't you just talk your emotions away?

One reason why words are not very effective for changing our feelings has to do with the way the brain has evolved over time. The oldest part of the brain controls emotions such as fear and panic. This part of the brain doesn't respond very well to words and reasons such as "No need to be frightened" or "Just calm down."

In fact, the oldest part of the brain is very similar to the brain structure of more primitive creatures, like snakes and crocodiles. Have you ever tried arguing with a snake or a crocodile? Probably not, because if you had, you wouldn't be sitting here reading this book. It wouldn't have worked. You'd be dead! You can't talk a snake or crocodile into doing anything. Likewise, you can't change your unpleasant emotions by arguing them away.

You Can't Control Anxiety by Talking Yourself Out of It

Here's a story from our experience that nicely illustrates the impossibility of trying to talk anxiety away. The story takes place in a small town in a tropical part of Australia. Every year at the beginning of the rainy season, the whole town becomes infested with frogs. The frogs are everywhere.

Sometimes when people get in the way, the frogs jump up at them. These unexpected "frog attacks" startle and scare some people so much that quite a few residents develop frog phobias. The fear is that intense. Many people don't want to leave their homes. The possibility of an encounter with one of these "disgusting" creatures can be crippling.

Some people try to talk their fear away. They tell themselves something like "These little green frogs are absolutely harmless and couldn't hurt me." What they are really doing though is this: using reassurance by replacing one type of thought in their heads ("Frogs are disgusting") with another type of thought ("Frogs aren't really dangerous and actually look quite cute"). These mental gymnastics don't make a bit of difference. The fear and the disgust are still there and so too are the frogs. They can't talk themselves out of their unpleasant feelings.

People can run away and stay away from frogs but at significant cost to their personal freedom. What the Australians can't do is run away from their "froggy" thoughts and feelings. Their thoughts, feelings, and apprehensions about frogs follow them everywhere.

In the end, these individuals are faced with a choice, and many end up choosing to go nowhere and stay in their homes with their fears and apprehensions. It is often at this point of sheer frustration and despair that people finally seek help.

EXPERIENCING IS THE ANSWER

The oldest part of your brain doesn't respond well to words and reason, but it can learn from direct experience. You can teach your old brain something new if you give it something new. This is how our brains work—what goes in stays in. This means you can alter the mix. Doing something new adds something new. This can happen if you're willing to give up rehearsing old strategies—like running away from the thoughts and feelings you don't like—and instead do something new, like experiencing your WAFs for what they are.

In the next chapters, we'll cover some skills to help you experience your unpleasant thoughts and feelings without picking up the rope and fighting to defeat them. This, by the way, is exactly what helped the residents of tropical Australia get on with living their lives, even without overcoming their fear of frogs. You can do this too.

Instead of arguing with your feelings and thoughts, you can learn how to observe and stay with them—simply watching them come and go while moving with them as you engage your life more fully. When you do that, you'll be adding something new to the mix, and things will start changing in your life. You'll have room to maneuver and be able to start living a richer and less restricted life. This is one of the most important steps to leading a life no longer ruled by your WAFs.

THE TAKE-HOME MESSAGE

You cannot control your anxiety by running away from, avoiding, or suppressing unwanted sensations, feelings, thoughts, worries, or images—as much as you may want to. This only buys you more anxiety, frustration, and a sense of helplessness. When your WAFs show up, acknowledge feeling stuck, drop the rope, and make room for something new. Focus on what you can control to keep moving forward in directions you care about. Be mindful of this important point when WAFs show up in your daily life.

Trying to Control the Uncontrollable Is the Problem

Point to Ponder: Trying to control my WAFs makes my life worse, not better.

Question to Consider: Am I willing to give up trying to control what I cannot control so I can move forward with my life?

CHAPTER 9

You Control Your Choices, Actions, and Destiny

There are two primary choices in life; to accept conditions as they exist, or accept the responsibility for changing them. —Denis Waitley

The 3 areas you do have control: your choices, your actions, your destiny.

Conscious, deliberate, purposeful control works well in the external world, outside your skin, where the following rule applies: *If you don't like what you are doing, figure out a way to change it or get rid of it using your hands and feet. Then go ahead and do it.*

Unfortunately, this rule doesn't work nearly as well, or at all, when applied to the things you don't like that are going on inside your mind and body. You'd be much better off refocusing your attention and expending your energy on the three areas where you *do have control*: your choices, your actions, and your destiny.

YOU HAVE CONTROL OVER THE CHOICES YOU MAKE

You have full responsibility for the choices you make. Coming to terms with this can feel both sobering and liberating. Deep down you know that you cannot choose whether or not to feel panic, anxiety, or worry. Yet you can decide what you do with those feelings and thoughts when they show up.

you can't decide whether or not to feel panic, anxiety or worry. But you can decide what to do w/ those thoughts + feelings.

As you learn to recognize that every moment in life is about choices, you free yourself from being enslaved by your WAFs and the impulses they generate. In short, you're free to choose how you respond and what you do with your emotional upset and pain when you feel it.

It's your choice whether you stay with them, acknowledge their presence, let them be, and observe them with a sense of curiosity and kind acceptance, or whether you do as they say, pick up the rope, and give in to the impulses to act by choosing avoidance, escape, suppression, or other ways to try to get rid of or control the WAFs.

Taking Stock of Where You Have Response Choices

Let's take a look at some specific situations where you have the power to choose what you do when your WAFs show up:

- Observing what my mind says without further action versus doing what my mind says

- Meeting my WAFs with compassion and allowing them to be there versus struggling with them or trying to make them go away

- Observing what my body does versus listening to and doing what my mind tells me about what my body does

- Doing nothing about the WAF feelings and thoughts versus distracting myself, taking pills, and running away from them

- Practicing patience with myself versus blaming and putting myself or others down for having WAFs

- Moving forward in my life with WAFs versus struggling with them and remaining stuck

YOU CAN CONTROL YOUR ACTIONS

Your actions are what *you* do with your hands, feet, and mouth when WAFs show up and when they don't. How you respond to the unpleasant thoughts, memories, physical sensations, and feelings dished out by your body and mind is very much within your control. Learning to respond differently than you've done in the past is the key to getting unstuck.

Let's say you're in the mall and feel a panic attack coming on. Then you act on it: perhaps you take one of the pills you carry with you at all times; then you head for the exit. These are both actions. Alternatively, you might do nothing about the panic attack and simply notice it for what it is, not for what your mind says it is. You stay in the mall and focus on doing what really matters to you, even if that means taking the panic along for the ride. If you're really shaky, you could sit down or lean against a wall, observe what's going on, and wait until you're not quite as shaky anymore. Then you get up and buy your daughter the shoes you promised her. In both scenarios, you're doing something. And your choice of actions, in a very real sense, helps define who you are and what your life is about.

Looking at your experience will tell you how difficult it is to get a handle on the feeling part of your WAFs—the bodily sensations, nervousness, or sense of dread. Your experience will also tell you how hard it is not to give in to the action part of your WAFs—the impulse to do something.

Recall that the purpose of anxiety is to make us act. So when WAFs show up, the impulse to act on them is very strong. We understand it's easy to feel overwhelmed by WAF-driven impulses.

Your choice of actions in a very real sense, helps define who you are and what your life is about

EXERCISE: FINDING FRESH ALTERNATIVES TO THE SAME OLD WAF IMPULSES

Even an impulse to act is a feeling. There's a split second between the impulse and the action where you can ✱ intervene to determine what you're going to do and how you're going to respond.

To help you get a sense of this, go ahead and pull some of your LIFE forms from this past week. Select one episode where the impulse to act on your WAFs was strong and where the action kept you away from, or pulled you out of, something that was important or potentially vital for you.

Below, list the WAF feeling, what you did in response to it, and the costs of your actions.

WAF feelings (my thoughts, feelings, sensations): _____

_____

WAF impulse (my WAF coping actions): _____

_____

Consequences of my WAF response (what I lost or missed out on): _____

_____

You can step back and ask yourself, "Is it really necessary to act on these feelings (or this thought)?" What else might you have done here instead? Brainstorm some life-affirming alternative actions and write them down below.

Other life-affirming WAF responses: _____

_____

NOTICE IT FOR WHAT IT IS - NOT WHAT YOUR MIND SAYS it is.

Potential consequences of these new responses (what I would have gained in my life):

_____

The point of this brief exercise is to show you that you do have control and choices in this moment, no matter how powerful the anxiety feelings and impulses to act are.

It would be helpful at this point for you to go back and review the material in chapter 6, and ask yourself again what has cost you more: your anxious thoughts and feelings or how you've responded to those thoughts and feelings.

The costs we discussed in chapter 6 result primarily from your actions. Acting on your WAFs got you into trouble. This is where you need to take charge and make changes.

YOU CAN CONTROL YOUR DESTINY

The cumulative effect of your choices and your actions will determine what your life will become—in other words, your destiny. This is the prize!

This doesn't mean that the outcome of your choices and actions will always be what you want. Many events in life, both good and bad, will happen outside of your control. What most people hope for is that the cumulative effect of their choices and actions will yield a sense that their life was lived well. Everything you do from here on out adds up to that. Choice is destiny.

The cumulative effect of your choices and your actions will determine your destiny.

EXERCISE: CHOICES AND ACTIONS—MY LIFE AND MY DESTINY

Imagine you're driving through life on a long road toward a mountain—your "Value Mountain." It stands for everything you care about in life, and what you want to be about as a person. This is the place you want to go. You'll see it in the distance in the illustration below.

You're driving happily along the road toward your Value Mountain, and suddenly anxiety jumps out and blocks the road. You slow down and try to avoid hitting the WAF. You quickly turn right and find yourself on the "emotional avoidance" detour. This detour has its own road. It simply goes round and round in circles. You stay there because the WAFs are still blocking the road. So you go round and round, waiting, hoping, but going nowhere. You feel bad about going in circles. You feel mad at the WAFs for blocking the road. Your life ticks by.

This is what happens when people engage in a struggle with their unpleasant thoughts and feelings. They feel stuck, going around in circles, to nowhere. Nobody wants their life to be about driving on the control-and-avoidance detour. And yet it's so easy to get stuck on this detour when WAFs show up.

You're not alone on this detour. The illustration doesn't show how congested it actually is. Many people just like you are traveling on this road to nowhere. But there's an alternative.

You can take the WAFs—all those unpleasant feelings, physical sensations, thoughts, images, and worries—with you on your ride through life, without acting on them. You can choose to drive forward with them because choosing the old alternative costs you.

The first and most important task here is to make a choice to do something different when your WAFs show up. The second part requires that you be willing to take what you're thinking and feeling with you as you move forward. Unless you do, you'll continue to feel stuck.

LETTING GO OF THE STRUGGLE FOR CONTROL

Letting go of the struggle for control isn't as hard as it may seem. It begins with you making a decision to do so. The hardest part is putting your decision into action.

One of the chief barriers to action is failing to spot places where you have control and places where you don't have much control. Falling back into the old control agenda, where control isn't possible, is a surefire way to stay stuck.

To get unstuck and keep yourself from getting stuck, you'll need to develop greater ease in the early detection of situations where control is possible in your life: those are the places where you need to expend your time and effort. The exercise below will help you do just that. You can think of it as a sort of review and preparation for the hard work to come.

EXERCISE: THE DIFFERENCE BETWEEN WHAT I CAN AND CANNOT CONTROL

Read each statement and then, without much thought, circle the number next to each situation you believe you can control. Don't circle numbers for situations that are outside your control.

1. What someone else is thinking

2. The choices I make

3. How nervous I get

4. How I respond to other people

5. What other people value and care about

6. What I say and do in a situation

7. Worries I have from time to time

8. The direction I want my life to take

9. How others respond to my choices, expressed thoughts, feelings, and actions

10. How I behave with respect to other people

11. The choices others make

12. What I do when I get anxious

13. How often the same thoughts or images come back into my mind

14. How I respond to my thoughts and feelings (positive or negative)

15. Other people following rules or standards

16. Whether I follow through with commitments

17. What other people do

18. Whether I follow certain rules or standards

19. Other people liking me

20. If I prepare for tasks and do my best

21. What I feel at any point

22. What I do with my precious time on this earth

23. The thoughts I have from time to time

24. My values and what I care about

Now go back and look at the numbers you circled. All the odd-numbered items represent situations where you have absolutely no control. You may imagine otherwise, but if you go back and think carefully, you'll see that you truly don't have control in any of these scenarios.

Part of the problem is that your mind tells you that you do or *should* have control when you don't. Remember, when you struggle to control what you cannot control, you'll only end up feeling more anxious and disappointed. WAFs need this struggle to stay powerful. When they show up, you need to recognize them for what they are, stop, and then look for places where you can exert control over your choices and actions with an eye on what you want your life to be about.

The even-numbered situations represent a sampling of life circumstances where you do have control. They share one thing in common: they represent your actions, what *you* say or do.

THE BIG QUESTION: ARE YOU READY FOR A CHANGE?

Perhaps your fear is that anxiety will finally win and all the catastrophic events you've been trying to avoid will finally come to pass. So you do what you can to stay safe—protected from those strong feelings, scary thoughts, and worries. You remain vigilant, on guard, and anxious.

Here's an idea, one that we've hammered on throughout this chapter and those that came before: What if all this protecting and avoiding and hiding were the problem? What if there's no need to run away from anything? What if letting the WAFs be what they are—physical sensations, feelings, thoughts, or images—without doing something about them were the beginning of an answer?

You've tried the old ways long enough. They haven't worked. What they've done is created many more problems. The struggle just keeps playing out in your life. Are you ready for a change? What if you stopped struggling and dropped the rope?

Dropping the Rope: The First Step in Becoming a Life Manager

You may wonder how you can drop the rope to end your tug-of-war with WAFs. The first thing you'd need to do is give up your job as anxiety manager at WAFs "R" Us. If you haven't done that yet, are you willing to do that now? If so, make it a commitment by signing your resignation statement below.

I _____ [print your name] have worked as anxiety manager at WAFs "R" Us for _____ [insert number of months/years]. This position has been enormously challenging in many ways. I am no longer willing to continue with it. I am at a point in my life where I am ready for something new—ready for a position that makes room for aspects of my life that have been diminished or put on hold because of my job with this company. Thus, I formally resign from my current position, effective immediately.

Sincerely, _____ [sign your name here]

Once you've committed to giving up the old path, you're positioned to take up a new job of "life manager." This workbook is a job-training manual of sorts for this position. Taking charge of your life is a skill that you can learn, beginning with learning how not to get hooked by your judgmental mind and by the urge to pick up the rope and fight the WAF war.

Still, you need to be prepared for what you're getting into. Being a life manager means that you'll experience life's ups and downs. And sometimes you'll slip back into old habits—your old training at WAFs "R" Us. In fact, we can almost guarantee that you will. Anxiety is a powerful emotion. It won't just play nice because you've decided not to play.

When you decide to drop the rope, your WAFs will yell at you, be right in your face, and dangle that rope right in front of your eyes. WAFs need the fuel that comes from a good fight with you. It's not simply that struggling with WAFs drains you, but that WAFs themselves actually feed off and grow stronger because of your struggle with them. This is why dropping the rope and becoming an observer, not a player, can be so powerful. ✗

Up until now, the only choice you may think you've had is to use your old methods or newer ones like them, and to do that with more effort. Here, we're emphasizing that your old methods and those like them are actively making the "same old" experience worse. So the choice you have now is really

worries, anxiety and fears need the fuel that comes from a good fight with you.

about dropping the old methods to make way for something new. This is how you'll make your life better.

Many people have successfully let go of the struggle by learning to watch their sensations, thoughts, and feelings as they are, and not as what their mind says they are. Simply noticing what you feel means beginning to acknowledge and allow those feelings to be present. It doesn't mean liking what you feel or agreeing with what somebody has done to you.

It only means being aware of what you feel, acknowledging it for what it is—a thought, a feeling, a sensation, a memory, an image—without taking sides or doing anything about it. And it means recognizing that you and you alone have choices in how you respond to it.

Dropping the rope is also easier said than done. It's probably radically different from what you've done in the past. So in the coming chapters, we'll provide you with simple and powerful exercises that will help you drop the rope and expend your time and energy more wisely.

You'll become an expert observer of anxiety—not a participant with a stake in the outcome. You'll also nurture a deeper capacity for kindness and compassion for yourself too. It's like building a new relationship with your anxiety. When you do more observing than fighting, you'll find that you're freer to exercise your capacity to choose, take action, and create your destiny.

You Are Response-Able!

Responsibility means that you are able to respond, or "response-able." As you choose to take control of areas in your life where you have control, we can almost guarantee that your judgmental mind will come up with thoughts like "You're too weak," "Nothing will ever change," or "You've never succeeded in the past; why should things be different now." Heaping negative energy on top of negative energy by blaming and beating up on yourself isn't helpful. Neither is arguing back. Blaming yourself and arguing with your mind only feed anxiety and create more worries.

These and other thoughts are simply more old rusty hooks that are trying to snag you and keep you from doing something radically different than you've done before. The way not to get hooked is to not feed them. You do that by simply thanking your mind for those old thoughts and ceasing to dignify them with a response, giving them more value and importance than they deserve. Then, and only then, are you on the way to dropping the rope. No need to argue back.

Instead, ask yourself this: who has response-ability for the WAFs showing up or not? It's not you! Now ask yourself this: Who can choose and is truly *able* to respond differently than in the past when WAFs throw you the rope? Who has the power to persist in making life changes when your judgmental mind is trying to steer you off course? Like it says in the Cole Porter song, "You, you, you!"

Watch your sensations, thoughts and feelings as they are, and not as what your mind says they are.

Your behavior is something you can control
— even when it's in the grip of powerful emotions.

Are You Willing?

Responsibility for what you do begins with you. It's time to face this stark truth squarely. Your behavior is something you can control—even when you're in the grip of powerful emotions like your WAFs. This is good news.

At times, it will feel as if you have no choice but to resort to your old patterns of avoidance and struggle. Your mind will tell you that "It's too hard," "There's too much anxiety," and "You must get out of there." When that happens, it's important to nurture willingness.

Up to this point, we expect that putting willingness together with your WAFs sounds nuts. In fact, it's likely you opened this book with a deep feeling of unwillingness toward your WAFs.

You can get a sense of this yourself, by going back to your LIFE forms for the past week. Look at what you put down for your willingness rating for each WAF episode and then take a visual average of your ratings and place a mark to show that average on the scale below. If you haven't had WAF episodes in the past week, then give a best estimate of your willingness level right now using the same scale.

For the past week or so, my willingness to have my WAFs without acting on them (e.g., to manage, get rid of, suppress, or run from them) was at about this level:

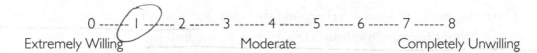

0 ------ 1 ------ 2 ------ 3 ------ 4 ------ 5 ------ 6 ------ 7 ------ 8
Extremely Willing   Moderate   Completely Unwilling

Many people think of willingness and unwillingness as feelings. And the rating you just made a moment ago may have been based on how you felt. As you'll see, willingness isn't a feeling. So when we encourage you to be willing, we aren't asking you to change how you feel. You can still think that your WAFs are unpleasant and you can dislike the discomfort.

With willingness, we're asking you to make a choice. That choice is to be with your WAFs when they show up and to stop trying to make them go away by acting in ways that hurt you and your life.

WILLINGNESS IS ABOUT DOING

Willingness means making a choice to experience anxiety for what it is—a bunch of sensations, feelings, thoughts, and images—and not the unacceptable stuff your mind tells you it is. Willingness is not about liking, wanting, putting up with, or tolerating. It's also not about enduring anxiety with brute force of will.

What if anxiety isn't the enemy?

In this sense, willingness is the opposite of control and avoidance. It means to show up and be open to experiencing anxiety as it is versus fighting anxiety with all you've got. We often find that people treat anxiety as their worst enemy. When you do that, it makes sense to fight it. But what if anxiety isn't the enemy? What if you could learn to develop some kindness and compassion for all your experience—including anxiety—and for yourself? Struggling would no longer be necessary. You'd cut the fuel line for your WAFs, and new options would become available to you. This is why developing willingness is so powerful.

Willingness is both a stance toward life and an activity. It is about doing, and doing in the direction of what you value and truly care about. So when we encourage you to be willing, we're asking you to be ready for action. And we're asking you to open up to every aspect of your experience, fully, and without defense.

Doing so allows you to put the serenity creed into action: When you're willing to experience what is, and to accept what cannot be changed, you're positioned to change what can be changed.

WILLINGNESS MAKES GROWTH POSSIBLE

You may think it would be much easier to be willing if you didn't have the pain you feel, if you weren't experiencing all those intense feelings and thoughts. Yet it is not the absence of trauma, pain, and intense, unpleasant feelings and thoughts that keeps people healthy.

Studies in many countries have found that the difference between health and suffering is whether people are willing to experience the totality of their psychological and emotional world and still do what matters most to them. Ultimately, willingness is about finding a way to live a meaningful and productive life with your pain. When you are willing to live such a life *and* take the totality of personal pains and joys along for the ride, you're on your way out of suffering.

We aren't saying this is easy. And yet this type of pain—having anxiety and doing what matters—is like a growing pain. Remember the story about the emperor moth in chapter 5. Being cut off from the experience of pain and struggle wasn't helpful to the moth. It never learned to fly.

At times, your old knee-jerk reaction of struggling with WAFs will occur so fast that it'll take a moment to recognize that you're caught up in the tug-of-war again. When that happens, notice what's going on and then let go of the rope. You've just been sucker punched into struggling. Give yourself three seconds to recover. Pull yourself up and then exert your response-ability for what you do next. It's just a passing phase before you can take off and fly.

Always remember that you can make a different choice by adopting the stance of willingness—by opening up and softening to the experience of anxiety. You can live a vital and meaningful life if you're willing to have and experience anxiety.

Willingness is both a stance towards life and an activity.

Willingness is about finding a way to live a meaningful and productive life with your pain.

EXERCISE: THE WILLINGNESS SWITCH

Imagine you had two switches in front of you. They look like light switches and both have an on/off setting. One switch is called "anxiety" and the other is called "willingness." It seems like both switches can be turned on or off. When you started reading this book, you were probably hoping to find a way to turn the anxiety switch off. Based on your experience, this turned out to be a false hope. The on/off toggle of the anxiety switch isn't working. This may even make you feel like you're a victim of anxiety, that you're helpless. And your mind says, "That sucks." You're disappointed over and over again.

So we'd like to share a secret with you. The willingness switch is really the more important of the two because it's the one that will make a difference in your life. Unlike the anxiety switch, you do control the willingness switch. When it comes to willingness, you're not a helpless victim because that switch is controlled by your actions. Remember, this is *the* place where you are *response-able*. It's your choice to flip the willingness switch on or off.

We're not sure what would happen with your anxiety if you switched the willingness on. We only know one thing: you really can switch it on if you make a choice to do so. And then things might start to happen in your life. You could start doing what you really want to do and start moving in the direction of your Valued Life Epitaph inscription.

In this metaphor, we're not talking about ignoring anxiety. We're simply encouraging you to turn your attention from what you cannot control to what you can control. You probably don't know what will happen to your anxiety if you don't attempt to control it. You may have a prediction. Yet, based on your experience, do you actually know? Have you ever approached anxiety with willingness to have it? What happens over time might surprise you.

WILLINGNESS IS DOING, NOT TRYING TO DO

"I'll try" is often the first response we hear when we talk to people about willingness: "Next time I'm anxious, I'll really try to be willing and not do what I usually do." And when things haven't worked out, we hear, "I've tried to go to work and face my fear of failure. I've tried *really* hard, but I just couldn't do it. My anxiety was just too high. So I stayed home."

The following brief exercise is a powerful way for you to connect with the fact that willingness is an all-or-nothing action: you do or you don't; it's not about trying to do something.

you can live a vital & meaningful life if you're willing to have and experience anxiety.

Willingness is an all or nothing action.

EXERCISE: THE TRYING PEN

To get a sense of what we mean, go ahead and have a seat at a table and place a pen in front of you. Now, we'd like you to *try* to pick up the pen. Try as hard as you can. Go ahead and *try* it. If you find yourself picking up the pen, stop! That isn't what we asked you to do. We want you to *try* to pick it up. After some effort, you're probably thinking, "Well, I can't do that. Either I pick it up or I don't." You're right. There's no way to try to pick up the pen and at the same time actually pick it up.

Trying is really a form of "not doing." This is why we never want you to try anything. You must first make a choice about whether you're willing to do something. If you are *completely* willing rather than just a bit willing, then go ahead and do it. And if you aren't willing, then don't do it. Remember willingness only has an on/off switch, not some type of dial you can move up or down a little. Just like a woman can't be a bit pregnant—either she is or she isn't—you can't be a bit willing.

Doing is not about getting it right or meeting failure. For instance, you could decide to pick up the pen and then find that it slips from your fingers and drops to the floor. Your mind might say, "You tried, but it didn't work." Yet your experience tells you that you could still bend over and repeat the act of picking up the pen, if that's what you're committed to doing. Some activities in life simply require persistence: you may need to do them over and over again before you've accomplished your goal. Failure is one of many subjective evaluations of what we like to call your *mind machine*, which comes up with a seemingly never-ending stream of judgmental thoughts. Such evaluations need not stop you from doing what is important.

So are you willing to go out with your hands and feet and take your anxiety with you? Remember, willingness is neither a feeling nor a thought. Willingness is simply a choice and a commitment to have what you already have. This frees you up to go where you want to go.

> *Your commitment is to do your best, it's not a commitment to success.*

If you're willing to make this commitment, then pick up a pen and sign your name on the line on the next page. If you cannot sign the commitment, then it's best to stop, go back, and dig into where you are in life with your anxiety before reading on. Look at the costs and the two epitaphs you worked on. See if you can connect with the life you truly want to lead. What's really holding you back now? You've already taken a bold step by opening this book and getting this far. You have everything you need to go on.

Willingness is simply a choice and commitment to have what you already have.

132

The Willingness Commitment

I am willing to take my WAFs with me
as I use my hands and feet
to move myself in the directions I want my life to take.

_____   _____

Signature   Date

THE TAKE-HOME MESSAGE

Instead of choosing to struggle with your WAFs, you can choose to drop the rope and be response-able. The idea of response-ability is a very positive and liberating one. You control your choices and actions, what you say, and what you do, including how you respond to your WAFs. All the remaining chapters are about fostering your ability to choose, take action, and move forward in your life. They are about maximizing control where you have it. This is how you create your destiny.

Response-Ability Is Control Over My Choices, Actions, and Destiny

Points to Ponder: I can choose how I respond to my WAFs. Making different choices than I've made in the past could improve my life. I am response-able. There's no try, only do.

Question to Consider: Am I willing to go out with my hands and feet and take my anxiety with me to move in the direction I want my life to take?

CHAPTER 10

Getting into Your Life with Mindful Acceptance

Water is fluid, soft, and yielding. But water will wear away rock, which is rigid and cannot yield. As a rule, whatever is fluid, soft, and yielding will overcome whatever is rigid and hard. —Lao-tzu (600 BC)

Take a moment and allow yourself to sit with the opening quote you just read. Then, when you're ready, insert the first noun that comes to mind as you consider each of the following statements.

My WAFs are like _____ (noun).

My responses to my WAFs are like _____ (noun).

Now stop. Look at what your mind came up with to characterize your WAFs and your response to them. Did you select nouns describing things that are soft, gentle, fluid, or yielding? We'd guess not. It's more likely that your mind came up with nouns describing things that are solid as rock and unyielding. When you put both statements together, what you are left with is something like this—rock against rock.

Your judgmental mind can readily turn anything that is normally fluid and flexible—like thoughts, feelings, sensations, memories—into something hard and heavy that's pushing you around and seemingly

— thoughts, feelings, sensations and memories are normally fluid + flexible?

ruining your life. Once your mind does that, it is natural to ramp up your efforts to alleviate the burden—the weight of the WAFs. The rub though is that resistance and struggle have a hard and weighty quality too. So there you are, carrying the burden of your WAFs and your unsuccessful struggles with them. Hardness begets hardness. This needs to stop.

Lao-tzu teaches us this simple truth: whatever is soft is strong. Take a second to let this powerful message sink in, for everything you are about to learn rests on this understanding. Packed in this pearl of wisdom is one of the most powerful antidotes to human suffering: nurturing your capacity for gentleness, kindness, and compassion in relation to your mind, body, and world. These softer, more fluid, more flexible, and, dare we say, more vital qualities are wrapped up in two words—mindful acceptance.

Mindful acceptance is a stance toward life: watching the struggle without judging it, feeling the pain without drowning in it, and honoring the hurt without becoming it. It's not a feeling or an attitude. It doesn't come from crystals or insight. Mindful acceptance is a skill—something that takes work to learn. We'll start showing you how in this chapter.

Before we do that, though, we'd like you to go back to the two fill-in statements you completed at the beginning of this chapter. And, with your most vexing WAF concerns in mind, we'd like you to do that exercise again, but with a slight twist.

Mindful acceptance is a skill.

EXERCISE: VISUALIZING THE SOFT-ROCK WAF SHUFFLE

This exercise is intended to help you connect with what a softer response can buy you in relation to your WAFs. Start by finding a quiet and comfortable place. And when you're ready, simply list words in the space below that come to mind as you think about your WAFs. Reveal the hardness.

Here's how Matt, a long-time panic sufferer, described his WAFs.

My WAFs are *nasty, crippling, intense, overwhelming, gripping, painful, a burden, a wall, a knife; screwed up, exhausting, shameful.*

Now it's your turn.

My WAFs are _____

_____.

Once you've got it all down, we'd like you to connect with the negative energy, the hardness in the words you used to describe your WAFs. Give yourself a minute to get into it.

Next, gently switch to the first statement from the list on the next page. Read it slowly and then close your eyes and sit with it. Imagine yourself doing what the statement says when your WAFs show up. Connect with the quality of each word in the list that follows. Let the quality of the word touch you. Try to become it. This is the softer response we're after.

We'd like you to repeat this exercise by shuttling back and forth between the *hard* words you came up with about your WAFs and each *softer* response option below. Continue this back and forth until you reach number 10. Imagine yourself meeting your *hard* WAFs with each *softer* response. Give yourself at least one minute with each new response option.

I will meet my hard WAFs with these qualities: worries, anxieties & fears

1. Softness

2. Gentleness

3. Kindness

4. Openness

5. Compassion

6. Love

7. Patience

8. Humor

9. Caring

10. Curiosity

As you did this brief exercise, did you notice anything? Did the quality of your thoughts about your WAFs change, even just a little bit, as you cycled back and forth through each softer response option? This may be hard for you to detect. If so, ask yourself this: after doing the exercise, would you write about your WAFs using the same words that you used before? Or, even if you choose to use the same words, do you really need to buy into them and do what they say?

Don't worry if you didn't notice anything dramatic here. The intent of this exercise is to reveal, even if only in a small way, what the softness of mindful acceptance can offer you. It can wear away your WAF rocks and the very need to do anything about them. But to truly get that, you'll need to practice developing the skill of mindful acceptance. Remember, softness will wear away rock—the hardness that underlies your tendency to struggle, to fight, and to pick up the rope.

You have the capacity to choose this softer, skillful alternative. And as you'll see with time and practice, mindful acceptance can be used in many areas of your life, not solely in places where anxious pain and hurt tends to get you sidetracked from where you want to go. You'll be learning skills that go beyond your anxieties and fears. These skills will improve your life in many ways.

mindful acceptance.

WHAT ACCEPTANCE IS AND CAN DO FOR YOU

Acceptance means "to take what is offered." This taking doesn't mean "taking it." Unfortunately, many people think of acceptance in this way. You know the message—to accept means succumbing to your pain, giving up, giving in, losing, being weak, or behaving like a loser or a patsy. This is what we mean by passive forms of acceptance.

These less vital forms of acceptance are not what we're going on about. They're unhelpful mainly because they keep you stuck—resigned to letting your WAFs (something you cannot control) guide your actions (something you can control). Giving up and bowing to your WAFs will lead you down the path of self-denigration and ultimately to more struggle and suffering.

With acceptance, you'll be doing something new. And as you do that, you can expect that your mind may not play nice. Your mind has fed you the message that your anxious pain is your enemy, and it has linked that pain to just about everything you want to be about as a person and with your life. And your mind tells you that your emotional pain stands between you and your life.

So it may seem that you are left with only two choices: sit and wallow with the emotional pain and do nothing, or struggle to get the pain out of the way while important aspects of your life slip away. The first is passive acceptance and the second is flat-out nonacceptance. Neither is good for you, and you know that from experience. Mindful acceptance is a third option that we want to explore further because it might just be good for you.

Mindful Acceptance Is Active, Soft, and Vital

Mindful acceptance is an active, fully conscious, softer stance toward your mind and body and your life experiences. It simply involves noticing what you think and feel and allowing those thoughts and feelings to be there—it doesn't mean liking or agreeing with them.

Acceptance is about acknowledging and experiencing what happened in the past and what's happening in the present moment without judging and getting all tangled up in that experience. This will help you wake up to reality as it is, not as your judgmental mind and past history say it is.

EXERCISE: "OH, WHAT A _____ ROSE"

To get a sense of that, do this: close your eyes and imagine a long-stemmed rose, freshly cut after a gentle rain, hovering in front of you. Look it over carefully. Notice all the details—the textures, smell, shapes, and colors. See the light and shadows, the dewdrops, and stem. In your mind, simply notice the qualities of the rose and your experience of it.

As you did this exercise, did your mind throw in evaluations of the rose? You might have thought, "How beautiful" or "It smells really nice." Your mind could have readily come up with more negative evaluations too, like, "That's an ugly rose," "It sucks," or even "What a stupid rose." It might have even brought to mind a memory of a loving moment, or a relationship that went sour.

Notice though that your evaluations don't change the rose one bit—the rose is a rose regardless of what your mind calls it. Notice also that your evaluations of the rose aren't the rose. The rose won't change because your mind calls it this or that. Mindful acceptance is a powerful way to notice when you're caught up in evaluations of your experience more than in the raw experience itself.

> *Acceptance means noticing and acknowledging what you experience—not liking what you experience.*

Mindful acceptance is *compassion in action.* With that, you cultivate your capacity to meet the hardness of your judgmental mind and emotional hurts with softness and gentleness. When you do that, you also weaken the tug and power of your judgmental mind to get you hooked by your anxieties, fears, hurts, shame, anger, or remorse—all the sticky negative energy that can pull you out of your life and keep you stuck.

Consider when you've been asked to go somewhere to do something where you know your WAFs are likely to show up. One of the first things you'll notice is this: you'll feel yourself hardening. Some people experience hardening as a tightening, tensing, or a sense of closing down. It can happen in an instant. You want to run, withdraw, and be somewhere other than where you are. Your judgmental mind pulls you out of the present. And with that, the old habitual comfort-seeking actions kick in, and wham—there you are, stuck, holding the rope, and struggling with yourself.

Mindful Acceptance Can Get You Unstuck

Mindful acceptance is a powerful way to get unstuck, unhooked, and moving forward. It starts with cultivating your willingness to stay with the urge to act on your own discomfort—without doing what your mind and history say ought to be done for the quick fix of temporary relief. It starts by recognizing and then softening to the urge to run from or avoid your worries, anxieties, and fears. And as you recognize and soften, you'll be free to make more vital choices.

There's no magic to this process. You decide to do it. And you do it by choosing to let go of the struggle with your inner painful and hurtful experiences, be they worries, anxieties, fears, or anger, hostility, or sadness. You let go by bringing kindness and gentle attention to unwanted WAF thoughts and feelings, by simply allowing them to be. Our colleague Jeffrey Brantley (2003) describes this process as one of becoming a friend to yourself and to your WAFs.

snared by what your mind is feeding you

It's very easy for all of us to run through life mindlessly, on autopilot. Our heads are in the past or the future or elsewhere. Yet you know that your life is only lived in the present because that's where you are. The present is the only place where you can make a difference in your life.

And there are many times when you've gotten hooked, snared by what your critical judgmental mind is feeding you. Our minds are constantly adding unnecessary baggage to our experiences, creating an illusion of a reality that simply isn't so. Recall that a duckling is a duck, regardless of what your mind says about it—an ugly duckling is as much a duck as a cute duckling.

This is where mindful acceptance can make a real difference. It'll help you learn to recognize the mind game for what it is—a substitute reality, not reality itself. Mindful acceptance will position you to break your identification with the thoughts that fuel your struggle. You'll start to see your urges to act on your WAFs as urges. You'll learn to sit with them without needing to change them or do what they say. And as you start cultivating a softer response to your mind, body, and world, things will change. Suddenly there will be space to move. You'll see how this works when you get to the Chinese Finger Trap exercise in a moment.

Mindful Acceptance Is a Skill and a Valuable Choice

People often associate mindfulness with religious meditative traditions such as Buddhism. Though there's a resemblance, you need not ascribe to a religion or be a saint to practice being mindful. Mindfulness is a skill of kind observing of your experiences, day in and day out—what's happening on the inside and outside—as it is.

The problem is that we live a good portion of our lives in our heads—interpreting, evaluating, and judging ourselves, the past and future, others, and our world. As we're doing that, we're not focused on what is really going on right now. Mindful acceptance will put you in fuller and more honest and open contact with everything you experience. You'll see things more clearly, gain perspective, and start to notice that what's happening is just what's happening.

This can be difficult, for we all have a natural reaction to run away as we open up and begin to face squarely things that we don't like very much. Yet acceptance isn't about liking unpleasant feelings. It just means acknowledging them and no longer fighting them or denying them. When you do more of that, you free up energy to create the life you want to live.

What we're after here is playfulness and transparency of the kind that would allow you to notice more fully the process of not liking, unease, discomfort, hurt, and even joy, goodness, and beauty. And we're after melding that with softer qualities of caring, compassion, and love. So as you develop the skills of acceptance, keep in mind that this isn't another clever fix to dull your WAF pain. If you find yourself using it this way, you're missing the boat. And you'll likely be disappointed with the results.

As you get into this, you'll see that your WAFs are just a collection of thoughts as thoughts, images as images, feelings as feelings, and sensations as sensations. That's it. You'll also be able to recognize judgments, negative evaluations, and pesky urges while bringing to those experiences a quality of gentle curiosity, kindness, compassion, caring, and wholeness. This isn't easy to do. And it's next to impossible to do without learning how to be a compassionate observer of your experiences. This is why mindfulness practice is an important part of active acceptance.

Mindful acceptance is best practiced at home as you begin, in a comfortable, safe environment. As you get more skilled at it, you can gradually expand to include more stressful, emotion-triggering situations, including those that involve your WAFs. A substantial body of research shows that this skill set can be enormously helpful in keeping you from getting hooked by your judgmental mind.

acceptance is the antidote to struggle.

Mindful Acceptance Makes Space for New Solutions

We focus so much on acceptance because struggling with your WAFs hasn't worked and acceptance makes room for new beginnings, new ways of responding. It's the antidote to struggle. It's vital. It gives you space to control what you do. Acceptance is doing something new!

You might be thinking that we're saying that your mind is the enemy. We're not saying that at all. Your mind isn't the problem—not even a critical judgmental mind that feeds you a stream of recycled scary thoughts and images.

Problems happen when you get hooked on thoughts and images, believing in them so strongly that you identify with them and allow them to pull you out of your life. At that point, you're completely caught up in your head. Mindful acceptance will help you to let go of the story line and just observe what's going on. It'll also help you see when your mind serves you well and when it doesn't. This understanding is key. *mindful acceptance will help you let go of the story line*

You cannot think yourself into a life. You cannot feel your way into a life. You need to get moving with your hands, feet, and mouth. Whenever your mind serves you well on this road—and sometimes it does—listen to it and do what it says. However, if listening keeps you stuck, then it's time to take stock: allow some gentle space between what your mind says works and matters and what your experience says works and matters. Then recommit to go forward with action because this is the only thing that matters. Mindful acceptance will help you gain the needed space to do just that.

EXERCISE: CHINESE FINGER TRAP

To get a sense of what we mean by creating space, imagine playing with one of those Chinese finger traps that you may have played with as a child. A finger trap is a tube of woven straw, about five inches long and half an inch wide. Perhaps you can find one in a novelty or party store and do the exercise for real. If not, just imagine doing it.

During this exercise (Hayes et al., 1999), you pick up the finger trap and slide one index finger into each end of the tube. After you fully insert your fingers, try pulling them out. If you were to do that, you'd notice that the tube catches and tightens. You'd experience some discomfort as the tube squeezes your fingers and reduces circulation.

You may feel a little confused. Pulling out of the tube seems like an obvious and natural solution. Yet it doesn't work. The harder you try to pull out of the trap, the more stuck you are. That's exactly how the WAF trap works too.

The finger trap shows that our instinctive solutions to our emotional and psychological hurts and pain often turn out to be no solutions at all. In fact, these so-called solutions create even bigger problems. Pulling away from anxiety and fear may seem like a natural and logical way to free yourself from the WAF trap. But your experience with anxiety tells you that this struggle has only brought you more discomfort and life problems. You're *trapped*!!

The good news is that there's an alternative that works and is supported by our research. To get there, you have to do something that goes against the grain. Instead of pulling out, you push in. This move will give you more space, more wiggle room. This is what acceptance offers.

Acceptance is doing something counterintuitive. As you practice leaning into pain and anxiety rather than pulling away, you'll be learning to stay with your experience. You acknowledge the discomfort and make room for it, allowing it to be, without doing anything about it and without trying to make it go away. This will give you enough room to move around and live your life.

THE FOUR QUALITIES OF MINDFUL ACCEPTANCE

Mindfulness and acceptance are difficult concepts to pin down for many people, including us. That said, there's a general consensus about four qualities that go into mindful acceptance. Jon Kabat-Zinn (1994, p. 4), a noted mindfulness scholar and therapist, packs the essential qualities of mindfulness into the following definition: "paying attention in a particular way: on purpose, in the present moment, and non-judgmentally." Let's unpack each part before we go forward with the practice.

Paying Attention

Paying attention in the here and now is enormously challenging because we all live with two sources of distractions: those from the world around us and those emanating from within our heads. Both

You lean into your experience.

sources can pull you out of the present in a flash. If you've suffered a past trauma or reexperienced painful memories, then you know this pull and spin quite well.

On top of that, your critical judgmental mind will often pull you out of the present too. So, you may spend your time thinking about your life, remembering the past, and contemplating futures that have yet to be. And you'll tend to react to people and situations based on old habitual patterns of thinking, feeling, relating, and behaving. These actions may have hurt you and others in your life. All of this activity pulls you out of the present moment—the place where your life is lived out—and can lead you in directions you don't want to go.

Learning to pay attention, fully and without defense, can liberate you from these traps and put you in fuller contact with yourself and your world as it is, right where you are. Paying attention means more contact with yourself and the circumstances of your life. More contact means more potential vitality. More vitality means that you'll likely feel better and grow. There's no way to learn and grow if you don't pay attention.

On Purpose

To pay attention, you must consciously choose to do it, and do it again and again, over and over throughout your day and your life. This alone can be difficult to do. Yet when you do it, you are doing something different than you've done before. You're taking the reins and noticing, with a gentle curiosity, what's happening as it's happening. As you do more of that, you'll interrupt the mind machine that's feeding you the same old unworkable strategies that have kept you stuck. Instead of pulling out of your experiences, you'll be deliberately moving into them.

Sometimes you'll get pulled back into the same old automatic patterns that have kept you stuck. The skill is to recognize when this is happening, recommit to acting with purpose, and get back to noticing what's really happening. And when those old habits rear their ugly heads from time to time, just notice them. Don't put yourself down for having "failed." Instead, be glad and grateful that you've recognized the old dead ends. You might just say, "There's my old history again." Then, after thanking your mind and body for that reminder, you can gently and purposefully return to what you'd really like to notice and do in the moment.

In the Present Moment

We all live in the here and now, but our minds can quickly take us elsewhere. You've had this experience too. If you pay attention you'll be amazed how often this happens on any given day. In fact, it happens more times than not. Taking a shower while thinking about what you're going to wear or the things you need to get done is a good example. Your body is in the shower, yet your head is elsewhere.

Or you may be driving while thinking about this or that, only to realize that you've gone five miles and can't remember a darn thing you've passed along the way. And you might have missed your exit too.

The point here is that we all can be readily pulled out of the present. And when that happens, you can and often will miss the here-and-now experience—the only place that is real.

Nonjudgmentally

Of all the qualities of mindful acceptance, this one is the most challenging to learn. And it will definitely be a gradual learning process. You'll remember from earlier chapters that we all have a tendency to evaluate and judge just about everything we do: good–bad, right–wrong, sour–sweet, should–shouldn't, and so on.

You may often judge situations, other people, and your own thoughts, feelings, and behaviors in a chain reaction of increasing judgment and distress: "This is horrible!" "What an idiot!" "How could I do that?!" "I can't take this anymore!" or "Here I go again." This is the fuel for the False Evidence Appearing Real, or F-E-A-Rful, struggle with your WAFs. And, if you look closely, you'll see that none of it is helpful to you.

Positive judgment can be every bit as problematic: "I need . . . ," "I want . . . ," "I should have . . . ," or "I deserve. . . ." All such judgments flow from thinking that you're missing out on something or that you must have something. When you hold on to these thoughts, particularly when they are automatic and intense, you can quickly lose focus, forget what's important, get caught in cycles of struggle and self-blame, or even become addicted to shopping, the Internet, drugs and alcohol, sex, relationships, or possessions.

All judgment creates an illusion of a reality that isn't so. When you fuse with False Evidence Appearing Real, you'll pull out of your experience and end up struggling to remove the unpleasantness or to get something you don't have. Perhaps that something is peace of mind, being relaxed, or even happiness. Your mind makes it seem like these qualities are something that you can have, hold, and keep. The evaluations seem real.

Stop here and check your experience to see if this is really the way it is: Can you get happiness and hold on to it like you can get a can of soda and keep it with you as long as you wish? Or does happiness tend to ebb and flow over time just like most thoughts and emotions? Are feelings something you can grab on to and hold like objects in the physical world? When you act as if you can hold on to them—and try to do what your judgmental mind says—you'll end up miserable.

Putting the qualities of acceptance—willingness, openness, compassion, kindness, and playfulness—into action is the single most powerful way to dilute the fuel that drives your WAF suffering. These softer qualities, when mixed with paying attention on purpose, nonjudgmentally, and in the present moment, will undercut the very need to struggle and will give you the freedom to do what matters to you.

You may have a hard time imagining bringing these nonjudgmental qualities to your experiences, particularly when unpleasant thoughts, memories, or feelings show up. And we can almost guarantee that your mind will continue to judge your experiences. Your task is not to stop your mind from coming up with judgments—that's virtually impossible. Yet you can learn to recognize judgments as products of your mind, and whenever they arise you can just label them "thinking." There is nothing mysterious about learning to become less judgmental over time. You have a choice here.

You can choose to continue to react to your unpleasant experiences with hardness and negative energy. Or you can decide to be kinder and gentler with yourself, to create space between you and what your mind (based on old history) is telling you. The choice here is entirely up to you. If you are willing to choose the softer path, then you'll be doing something new. It'll be a slow and gradual process with lots of setbacks on the path. The important thing is to keep going in a new direction.

LIFE ENHANCEMENT EXERCISE

Mindful breathing is a wonderful way to cultivate your observer mind. And it's relatively simple to do. Focusing on the breath is a skill that will be used in exercises in the chapters to come. You can do it anytime and anywhere.

You'll find an audio version of this exercise on the CD. We encourage you to use it during your home practice. This week, allow yourself to practice the Mindful Breathing exercise at least once each day at home, and then, as you get it, apply the skill anywhere you find yourself.

EXERCISE: MINDFUL BREATHING

Start by getting yourself comfortable in a place where you'll be undisturbed for five to ten minutes or so. You may sit on the floor or in a chair. Sit upright with your palms up or down on your lap.

Close your eyes and gently guide your attention to the natural rhythm of your breath in your chest and belly. Simply notice the breath as you breathe in . . . and out . . . in . . . and out. There's no need to make the breath faster or slower, deeper or shallower. Just allow your breathing to do its thing. Sense the air passing from the chest through your nose and mouth as you breathe in . . . and out.

Continue to notice your breathing with a sense of kindness and gentle allowing. There's nothing to do except notice your breath. Sink into its natural rhythm: the rising and gentle falling of your chest and belly as you breathe in and out . . . in and out.

If you find your mind wandering or you feel distracted, just kindly notice that, and return your attention to the rhythm of your breath and the rising and falling of your chest and belly. Continue this practice of kind observation for as long as you wish—just noticing your breath doing its thing.

Then, when you're ready, gradually widen your attention, and gently open your eyes with the intention of bringing this skill of kind observing to your experiences throughout the day.

THE TAKE-HOME MESSAGE

Everything we do happens now. This is where our lives are lived. By approaching WAF thoughts and feelings with mindful acceptance wrapped in compassion, you deprive them of the fuel they need to burn. You are no longer fighting. This will ultimately cool the flames feeding your WAFs and will free you to move in new and more vital life directions. You have control here.

Mindful Acceptance Can Pull Me Out of My WAFs and Into My Life

Points to Ponder: Acceptance is a vital and courageous activity. I can choose to acknowledge my WAFs without getting all tangled up in a struggle with them so that I can focus on what I really want to do with my life.

Question to Consider: Am I willing to approach my WAFs with more kindness and compassion?

CHAPTER 11

Learning Mindful Acceptance

In essence, the practice is always the same: instead of falling prey to a chain reaction of self-hatred, we gradually learn to catch the emotional reaction and drop the story lines. —Pema Chödrön

Developing any new skill takes practice and commitment. Mindful acceptance is no different. You must intend to be mindful. And you must be willing. And you have to do it over and over again to become skillful. Even then, it's best to think of learning mindful acceptance as a journey, not a destination. The more you do it, the better you'll become at it over time.

There isn't a cap on how mindful you can become. And there's no way to be mindful if your purpose is to make room for peace and calm only or to use it to quell the storm of your WAFs. You have to be open to everything that might show up—everything.

So ask yourself if there's enough room inside you to let all of you in—just as you are. If not, then what's standing in the way of you experiencing yourself? And if there's something that shows up, see whether you can make space for *that*—not liking or condoning it, just acknowledging that it's there with as much kindness as you can muster and without trying to fix it.

You have to be open to everything that might show up— everything.

BECOMING AN IMPARTIAL OBSERVER

If you want to really watch something, you have to plant yourself firmly in the present moment. The past and the future, where our thoughts so often dwell, must be abandoned in favor of the here and now. Remember: this is the place where your life is lived out.

You do this, first of all, by deciding to do it. You decide you want to understand the heart of the struggle, to fully experience everything that happens when you get anxious, afraid, in a panic, caught up in a bout of worry, or sucked into reliving a painful past memory. You can make this choice any time, even right now, and commit to it.

The second way you stay in the present is by listening to your body. You do that by noticing your breathing, your beating heart, your posture, and your areas of tension or hardness. You observe any significant sensations in your body—areas that hurt or that feel hot or heavy or shaky. This isn't an easy skill to learn, which is why we have exercises for you to practice every day. If you want to apply these skills in the heat of a WAF moment, it's best to practice them at other times first. The exercises help you do that.

The third way you stay in the present is to notice and track your conscious mind—your thoughts, emotions, and drives. During any WAF episode, you need to keep asking yourself some key questions. Here are a few:

- What am I feeling besides anxiety, panic, fear, or tension?

- What am I saying to myself? What "good" or "bad" or "right" or "wrong" thoughts am I experiencing?

- What am I driven to do now? Where's the urge to avoid discomfort trying to take me?

- What do I want to be about right now? What do I want my life to be about right now?

A useful strategy for staying in the present is to use a simple mantra as a reminder of your role as observer. We like the one that children are taught when learning about school-bus safety. That mantra goes like this: *Watch, look, and listen, or you won't see what you're missing.* When you see negative evaluation and judgment, don't feed it. And if you find yourself judging, then simply observe that—without judging the judging. Ultimately a judgment is just another thought. Don't allow it to hook you and suck you in. For the observer, there is no right or wrong—there's just noticing, experiencing, and learning.

The Advantage of Being an Observer

You may wonder why it's so important to be an observer and what it's actually like to be an observer. The advantage of being an observer is that you can watch what's going on (your experience) without having to take sides. It allows you to end the struggle and drop the rope.

Until now you've probably felt as if anxious thoughts and feelings rule you because they're so strong and powerful. In the heat of the moment, it may seem like they're taking charge of you—so much so that you get lost in those thoughts and feelings. At moments like that, it's difficult for all of us to see that our thoughts, worries, or feelings are just a part of us. They come and go. We don't own them. We can't make them go away. We can't hold on to them either.

In a sense we're like a house. Just as a house provides the space (e.g., rooms with walls, floors, and ceilings) in which people live, we provide the space for our experiences. The house remains the same regardless of what goes on inside it. And for all we know, the house doesn't care about who lives in it, what people do in it, what they think or feel, or what furniture gets put inside. The house just provides a place for all that living to occur.

EXERCISE: WHAT CHESS CAN TEACH YOU ABOUT BECOMING A SKILLFUL OBSERVER

Another way of learning to be an observer is to think about the game of chess (Hayes et al., 1999). That game takes two players, each with a team of pieces. The players engage in all sorts of moves to win the game. When one player makes a move, the other player takes a piece and makes a counter strike. Both players are working to outsmart each other.

Now imagine you're a part of this game. The black pieces are the team made up of your WAFs and everything that might trigger them. The other team represents your typical counter-strike responses. So, when the dark knight attacks (for example, you have the thought "I'm about to lose it"), you get on the back of the white knight, ride into battle, and do something to knock the dark knight out: breathe . . . think of something else . . . reassure yourself that you can make it. Looking back at your experience and the work you've done in the previous chapters, you can once again ask yourself if this approach has worked. Or does the WAF team always manage to come back and make another move to get you?

There's a tricky problem in this chess game. Unlike a real chess game, it's not a game with different teams and players. In this special game, the two opposing teams are really one team: *you.* The thoughts, feelings, and actions on both sides of the board are your thoughts, feelings, and actions. They all belong to you—you are *both* teams.

So the game is rigged. Both sides know the others' moves. No matter which side wins, one part of you will always be a loser. How can you win when your own thoughts and feelings compete against each other? It's a war against yourself. This is why it's a war you cannot win. So the battle goes on, every day, for years. You feel hopeless. You sense that you can't win and yet can't stop fighting.

Let's step back for a moment and look at this situation from a different angle. What if we said that those chess pieces aren't you anyway? Can you see who else you might be?

How about this: let's suppose you're the board. This is an important role. Without the board, there's no game. As the board, you see all the pieces and you can just watch the action without taking sides. If you're a player, the outcome of the game is very important; you've got to beat those worries, anxieties, and fears as if your life depends on it.

But the board doesn't care about winners or losers. The board just provides a space for the game and lets it happen. Being the board is a great relief because you don't need to be a player with a stake in the outcome. You simply provide a place for the game to play out. As the board, you can choose to be an impartial observer of your experiences.

If imagining being a chessboard is a bit hard for you, you may be able to relate more easily to a different sports-game metaphor—volleyball. In volleyball, two teams strive to keep the ball in play, back and forth from one side of the court to the other, without letting the ball fall on their side of the net. Each time a team sends the ball across the net to the other side, an opposing team player in the front row jumps up to block it with her bare hands. Behind the blocker are five other players strategically positioned to keep the ball in motion. If the ball isn't blocked, a player in the back row dives to the ground with her arms stretched out to pop the ball into the air as another teammate is set up to deliver a mighty spike to send the ball back to the other side. All the while, each player stands alert and ready, trying to read the opponents in anticipation of their next move.

EXERCISE: PLAYING VOLLEYBALL WITH TEAM ANXIETY AND TEAM STRUGGLE

Imagine that a volleyball match is going on inside your mind. Instead of volleying a ball back and forth, the teams inside your head volley thoughts about your WAFs. Much like competitive volleyball, your anxiety-related thoughts seem intense and forceful. And just when you thought they might be taking a rest, they're right back in your face, challenging you to take them on.

On one side of the court is Team A (Anxiety). Team A serves up the following thought: "If you go to the mall tomorrow, you're going to have a horrific panic attack. This could be the big one you've always been afraid of!"

Team S (Struggle) is ready for action, diving to the ground to prevent that thought from touching down: "Wait a minute. You've gone before and can do it again."

At this point, Team A keeps the ball in motion: "That's what you think now, but if and when you go to the mall, I'm going to be so big that you'll have to run away and then leave as quickly as you can. I'm going to yell right into your face and tell you to get out of that place. You might not even get out in time and could just end up lying on the floor with people staring at you."

Across the net the thought goes. Now, Team S fires back with this: "I'm going to ask my friend to come with me. She can help me if things get out of control."

Before that thought crosses the net, Team A blocks it with this: "But she can't really help you. When I attack you, you have no chance of beating me—no matter who is with you. I'm in control here, in case you hadn't noticed before."

Then Team S powers back with this: "Well, at least I can try to beat you."

And so the game goes, on and on. As soon as Team Anxiety serves up an unsettling thought, Team Struggle responds to that thought by somehow arguing with it. Notice how this mental volleyball marathon of worries, intrusive thoughts, and feelings has replayed itself over and over in your head and without resolution.

For the longest time, you've been a player in this game of endless struggle, and yet there's another option. Instead of choosing to be a member of Team A or Team S, you can choose to take the perspective of the volleyball court. As the court, you're an impartial observer, not a player with a stake in the outcome. Just like the chessboard, the court doesn't need to do anything. The court is merely there and watches and holds all of the players, the net, and the ball. In fact, the court doesn't care who wins or loses. The court doesn't worry about the outcome. The court will be around long after the game is over and as new players come and go.

You Are Not Your Worries, Anxieties, or Fears

Recall that your thoughts and feelings—all of them—are a part of you. This is important to understand. Anxiety and fear are emotions you experience periodically. They may explode into your awareness, and after a while, they recede. You—the person who experiences and observes your life—are separate from feelings of anxiety, panic, or dread. Like every other thought or emotion, your anxiety struts its moment on the stage, then slips into the wings. The only permanent, immutable thing is you—the audience, the watcher and doer of your life.

This perspective might help you take your WAFs a little less seriously. After all, they're just a moment in time—a wave on the sea of existence. You don't have to fight them. And you don't have to join them either. Your task, the work of mindful acceptance, is to disentangle from your WAFs. Just let the WAF waves come and go. Watch them from the safety of the shore.

Here's another way to look at it: all your feelings and thoughts are projections. You are the movie screen on which they play. While the screen never changes, the images change constantly. Millions of scenes can play out in a lifetime. When unpleasant thoughts or feelings show up on the screen, wait. They will morph into something else soon enough. The screen doesn't fight or resist the projections. It merely provides the space for the movie to play out and waits for that movie to end.

We talked earlier about the metaphor of the chessboard. You are the board upon which the pieces of your experience come and go. Each game has its own character and strategy, but the board never changes. One board might host a thousand struggles; one board might hold the moving pieces (thoughts and feelings) of a lifetime's challenges. Still, the board is not the game. You are not your thoughts or your feelings.

You might be thinking that we're asking you to become an automaton, a distant emotionless character like Spock from the popular TV series *Star Trek*. Mindful acceptance isn't about becoming numb or detached from your experience. In fact, it'll help you more fully engage your life, emotionally and mentally, as opposed to simply reacting to it with the same old habitual patterns of escape and avoidance. Being an observer gives you space to choose what to engage, what to let go, and what to do with your time and energy.

This fusion of feelings, thoughts, actions, and self is an illusion that our mind creates. It's time now to pull each element apart so your observing self can watch—with mindful acceptance—your WAF experience as it really is.

EXERCISE: USING YOUR WISE MIND TO UNHOOK FROM PARTS OF YOUR EXPERIENCE

To get a clearer idea of how to separate the pieces of your experience, let's look at Ellen's story. She's an office manager for a local ad agency. About six months ago, she was in a severe car accident. Ellen was fortunate to have walked away with minor physical injuries. Yet that event scarred her deeply.

Since then, she's been unable to drive or be in a car, suffers from painful memories of the accident, has nightmares, and has struggled with panic attacks that seem to come out of nowhere. She's on temporary leave from her job and fears that she'll lose her position.

When first asked to explain the fears, Ellen saw no separation between herself and any of her thoughts, feelings, or actions. They were all crushed together in one upsetting experience. Here's how it looked in a diagram. Notice all the circles are overlapping.

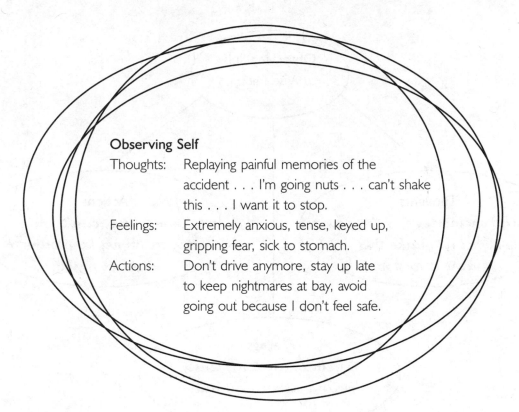

Observing Self

Thoughts: Replaying painful memories of the accident . . . I'm going nuts . . . can't shake this . . . I want it to stop.

Feelings: Extremely anxious, tense, keyed up, gripping fear, sick to stomach.

Actions: Don't drive anymore, stay up late to keep nightmares at bay, avoid going out because I don't feel safe.

Ellen's therapist asked her to do an exercise called Wise Mind. She was encouraged to take slow, deep breaths while focusing her attention on her diaphragm. Then the therapist drew a circle and wrote "Observing Self" inside it. Below it he drew a row of three more circles. In the first he wrote, "Thoughts," in the second, "Feelings," and in the third, "Actions."

"Keep your attention," he told Ellen, "just below your breath. This is the place we call Wise Mind. It's where you can see yourself; watch what's really going on. Now, with your wise, observing mind, fill in the other circles."

On the following page is what the exercise looked like when Ellen completed it. As you can see, the four circles aren't overlapping anymore. Thoughts, feelings, and actions are now separate and yet connected to and in touch with the observer self.

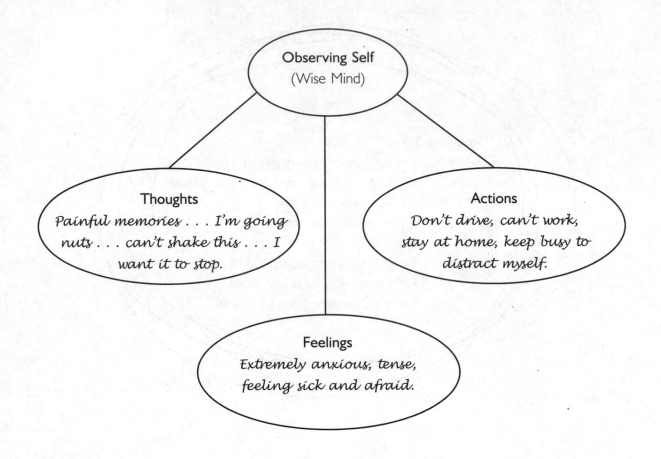

Right now, we'd like you to do the Wise Mind exercise with a recent WAF experience you've had. Pull out your LIFE forms and pick a form from the past week that captures a situation that was difficult for you. Briefly review what you wrote down.

Then, when you're ready, bring your attention to the gentle rising and falling of your breath in your chest and belly. Just notice it. Like an ocean wave coming in and out, your breath is always there.

Wait a few moments until you feel centered. Now visualize that WAF episode from the LIFE Form. Using your Wise Mind, observe each part of the experience. Separate your thoughts, feelings, and actions. Next, as Ellen did, write in the diagram below what you've observed.

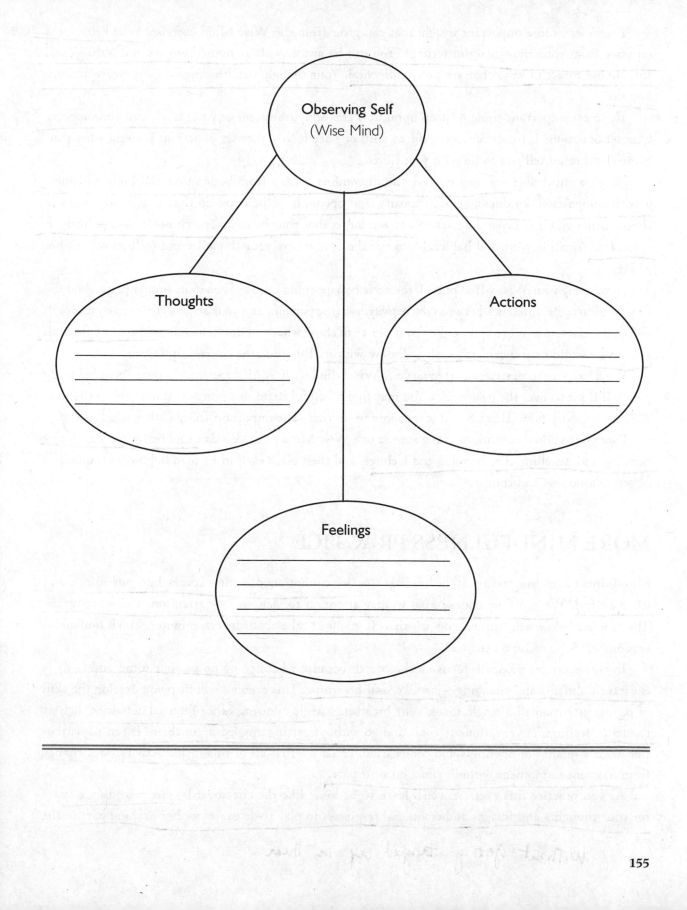

There's one more important insight that can grow from the Wise Mind exercise. Your behavior is separate from your thoughts and feelings. You can be awash with anxious thoughts and feelings and still choose to act in ways that are potentially vital. Your thoughts and feelings do not create actions. You do!

The most important thing to keep in mind is this simple awareness: you can choose your actions. One set of actions is to act on your pain, to stuff or bury it. Another set of actions is to do what your history and mind tell you to do with your hurts.

Here's a third one: you can observe the discomfort arising from your mind and body and meet it with compassion, kindness, gentle curiosity, and openness. When you do that, you'll have room to choose other vital life-expanding actions. If you forget that your behavior is a choice, you're unlikely to exercise it. You'll let your old habitual history take over, where your thoughts and feelings drive what you do.

Developing your Wise Mind puts all the activity happening inside of you in its proper place. And it'll help you learn the difference between *this activity*, *you* (the person), and your *actions*. This softer approach will give you space to move and awaken your power to chose what you do. Remember: You can fight with your inner world or you can stay with and move with it. This choice is entirely up to you.

We'd like you to practice developing your Wise Mind with WAF experiences you've recorded using your LIFE forms over the past weeks. You may find it helpful to do this practice, starting with the least difficult episodes first. That's fine if you choose to do that. The important thing is that you practice.

Pace yourself and commit to doing at least one Wise Mind practice a day. Get really good at simply noticing and watching the thoughts and feelings, and then place each in its own bubble with qualities of gentle kindness and compassion.

MORE MINDFULNESS PRACTICE

Mindfulness exercises are a way of learning that we cannot choose what comes into our minds and what we feel. We can only choose *what* we pay attention to, *how* we pay attention, and what we *do*. The exercise below will help you do just that. It ought to take about fifteen minutes. You'll find audio versions of the exercise on the CD.

In this exercise, we again focus on the breath because what's going on in your mind and body is constantly shifting and changing—just like your breathing. This exercise will help you develop the skill of paying attention to a single focus, your breathing, while allowing other internal activities such as thoughts, feelings, or sensations to come and go without getting tangled up in them. If you pay attention with a quality of openness and compassion, you'll see that all of this inside activity does change from moment to moment without effort on your part.

As you practice this exercise, you'll learn to be more like the chessboard—just providing a space for your thoughts and images and emotional responses to play their games without taking part in the

without getting tangled up in them

games. With time, you'll discover that no matter how bad an internal experience seems, it neither lasts forever nor can it do any harm.

Keep in mind that this exercise is not about making you feel different, better, relaxed, or calm. This may happen or it may not. The idea is to bring compassion and a kind awareness to *any* sensations that show up, including any thoughts or worries that come into your mind. It's about learning to stay with your WAFs with loving-kindness toward yourself, bringing as much warmth and compassion into the situation as you can. This is a concrete way of learning that anxiety isn't the enemy.

Remember that mindful acceptance is a skill that comes with practice. The goal is to develop the skill so that you can then apply it in your life, anytime or anyplace. There's no right or wrong way to practice. The important thing is that you commit to doing these exercises on the path of becoming a better observer and full participant in your life.

We suggest you simply select a quiet place where you feel comfortable and distraction is limited. Let's call this your peaceful place. The easiest way to do this exercise is by listening to and following the instructions on the CD that comes with this book. If you read the exercise and decide to commit it to memory, just do it slowly.

After practicing with the CD for a week or two, you may prefer to practice at your own pace without the CD. At any time, you can go back and do the exercise while listening to the recording.

EXERCISE: ACCEPTANCE OF THOUGHTS AND FEELINGS

Get in a comfortable position in your chair. Sit upright with your feet flat on the floor, your arms and legs uncrossed, and your hands resting in your lap (palms up or down, whichever is more comfortable). Allow your eyes to close gently.

Take a few moments to get in touch with the movement of your breath and the sensations in your body. Bring your awareness to the physical sensations in your body, especially to the sensations of touch or pressure, where your body makes contact with the chair or floor.

Now, slowly bring your attention to the gentle rising and falling of your breath in your chest and belly. Like ocean waves coming in and out, your breath is always there. Notice its rhythm in your body. Focus on each inhale . . . and exhale. Notice the changing patterns of sensations in your belly as you breathe in and as you breathe out. Take a few moments to feel the physical sensations as you breathe in and out.

There's no need to control your breathing in any way—simply let the breath breathe itself. As best you can, bring an attitude of generous allowing and gentle acceptance to the rest of your experience. There's nothing to be fixed, no particular state to be achieved. Simply allow your experience to be your experience, without needing it to be other than what it is.

Sooner or later your mind will wander away from the breath to other concerns, thoughts, worries, images, bodily sensations, planning, or daydreams, or it may just drift along. This is what minds do much of the time. When you notice that your mind has wandered, gently congratulate yourself—you have come back and are once more aware of your experience!

You may want to acknowledge briefly where your mind has been ("Ah, there's thinking" or "There's feeling"). Then, gently escort your attention back to the breath coming in and going out. As best you can, bring a quality of kindness and compassion to your awareness. See the wanderings of your mind as opportunities to bring patience and gentle curiosity to your experience.

When you become aware of bodily sensations and feelings, tension, or other intense sensations in parts of your body, just notice them, acknowledge their presence, and see if you can make space for them. Don't try to hold on to them or make them go away. Open your heart. Make some room for the discomfort, for the tension, for the anxiety, just allowing them to be there. Is there enough space in you to welcome in all of your experiences?

Watch the sensations change from moment to moment. Sometimes they grow stronger, sometimes they stay the same, and sometimes they grow weaker—it doesn't really matter what they do. Breathe calmly in *to* and out *from* the sensations of discomfort, imagining the breath moving in *to* and out *from* that region of the body. Remember, the purpose is not to feel *better* but to get better at *feeling and being with all that is you, as it is.*

If you notice that you're unable to focus on your breathing because of intense physical sensations of discomfort, let go of your focus on the breath and shift your focus to the place of discomfort. Gently direct your attention *on* and *into* the discomfort and stay with it, no matter how bad it seems. Take a look at it. What does it *really* feel like? Again, see if you can make room for the discomfort and allow it to be there. Are you willing to be with whatever you have?

Along with physical sensations in your body, you may also notice thoughts about the sensations and thoughts about the thoughts. You may notice your mind coming up with evaluations such as "dangerous" or "getting worse." If that happens, simply label those evaluations as "thinking" and return to the present experience as it is, not as your mind says it is, noticing thoughts as thoughts, physical sensations as physical sensations, feelings as feelings—nothing more, nothing less.

To help you experience the difference between yourself and your thoughts and feelings, you can name thoughts and feelings as you notice them. For instance, if you notice you're worrying, silently say to yourself, "Worry . . . there is worry," just observing worry and not judging yourself for having these thoughts and feelings. If you find yourself judging, just notice that and call it "Judging . . . there is judging" and observe that with a quality of kindness and compassion.

You can do the same with other thoughts and feelings and just name them as "planning," "reminiscing," "longing," or whatever you experience. Label the thought or emotion and move on. Thoughts and feelings come and go in your mind and body. You are not what those thoughts and feelings say, no matter how persistent or intense they may be. You are the place and the space for your experience. Make that space a kind space, a gentle space, a loving space, a welcome home.

As this time for formal practice comes to an end, gradually widen your attention to take in the sounds around you . . . notice your surroundings and slowly open your eyes with the intention to bring this awareness to the present moment and into the upcoming moments of the day.

experience

Return to the present ~~moment~~ as it is—not as your mind says it is.

Sometimes doing this exercise can be challenging. Don't let that challenge (a judgment) stand in the way of you doing the practice again and again over this week and the weeks to come. These judgments will usually show up when your practice is driven by achieving a particular result—like calm, peace, or anxiety reduction. If that result doesn't show up, it's easy to slip into thinking that the practice was a failure. This isn't so.

There's no right or wrong way to be mindful. Remember that mindful acceptance is a skill that needs to be cultivated in order to grow. It has many possible results, not one result. So, be kind with yourself as you do the practice.

It'll be helpful to track your experiences with this exercise over the next several weeks using the form at the end of this chapter. This will give your practice some structure and give you a place to chart your progress over time. We've included an example of how to complete the form. You'll also find the form on the CD so you can print out as many extra clean copies as you need.

LIFE ENHANCEMENT EXERCISES

Below is a list of activities that we think will be helpful to you. Put them on a to-do list of ways to take care of yourself each day. You alone can decide to do them. Once you've made a decision, commit 100 percent to doing them. Be realistic and commit only to what you know you can reasonably achieve. For instance, if you know in advance that doing the Acceptance of Thoughts and Feelings exercise once a day will be too much, then commit only to doing it every other day, or every other workday of the week and both days on the weekend. It's better to commit to less and follow through than to commit to too much and then break your commitments regularly. If you cannot commit to any of these exercises, then stop. Go back to the earlier material and ask yourself what is standing in the way. Perhaps you're taking things too fast. In that case, sticking with the earlier exercises a while longer might be helpful before going on.

Change can be scary, we know. Yet the prospect of doing the same old stuff that hasn't worked is even more frightening. If you want a different outcome in your life, you'll need to do something new, fresh, and different. Be patient. Do the work. It'll make a difference. Your experience will begin to tell you that.

- Practice the Acceptance of Thoughts and Feelings exercise once a day.

- Practice developing your Wise Mind.

- Practice being a mindful observer (the chessboard) during everyday activities at home and elsewhere—this can actually be very funny.

- Take stock of what you may still be giving up for anxiety this week.

THE TAKE-HOME MESSAGE

You can learn to stay with and bring patience to your WAFs and other forms of discomfort. This will free you to focus on the life you want to live. Learning to be more accepting and compassionate will make you more flexible—softer, kinder, and gentler with yourself, others, and the world in which you live. With that, you undermine and weaken everything your WAFs need in order to keep you stuck. You'll undermine the same old programming you've grown accustomed to.

Learning the Skill of Mindful Acceptance

Points to Ponder: Acceptance is a vital and courageous activity. I can learn to accept myself and be kinder with my WAFs on the road to living better.

Questions to Consider: Am I willing to accept myself with all my flaws, weaknesses, and vulnerabilities? Am I willing to be kind to myself so that I can move on and reclaim my life?

ACCEPTANCE OF THOUGHTS AND FEELINGS: Life Enhancement Exercise Practice Form

In the first (leftmost) column, record whether you made a commitment to practice the Acceptance of Thoughts and Feelings exercise that day and include the date. In the second column, record whether you actually practiced, when you practiced, and for how long. In the third column, note if you did or didn't use the audio version of the exercise that's on the CD. In the fourth column, write down anything that comes up during your practice.

Acceptance of Thoughts and Feelings Life Enhancement Exercise Practice Form			
Commitment: yes/no Day: Date:	Practiced: yes/no When practiced? A.M./P.M. How long (minutes)?	CD Audio: yes/no	Comments
Commitment: (yes)/no Day: *Saturday* Date:	Practiced: (yes)/no Time: (A.M.)/P.M. Minutes: *20 minutes*	*yes*	*Was a bit difficult to keep my focus; easily distracted by negative thoughts; felt a bit scary to open up; am I doing this right? I will keep at it.*
Commitment: yes/no Day: Date:	Practiced: yes/no Time: A.M./P.M. Minutes:		
Commitment: yes/no Day: Date:	Practiced: yes/no Time: A.M./P.M. Minutes:		
Commitment: yes/no Day: Date:	Practiced: yes/no Time: A.M./P.M. Minutes:		
Commitment: yes/no Day: Date:	Practiced: yes/no Time: A.M./P.M. Minutes:		
Commitment: yes/no Day: Date:	Practiced: yes/no Time: A.M./P.M. Minutes:		

PART 3

RECLAIMING YOUR LIFE
AND LIVING IT

CHAPTER 12

Taking Control of Your Life

Life is a choice. Anxiety is not a choice. Either way you go, you will have problems and pain. So your choice here is not about whether or not to have anxiety. Your choice is whether or not to live a meaningful life. —Steven C. Hayes (2005)

Early on in this book we talked a lot about what you cannot control. And we asked you to wade through this for yourself, by looking squarely at what WAF management and control has cost you in terms of energy, missed opportunities, and regret. These exercises were not intended to make you feel miserable. The intent was to position you to do something radically different than what you've done before—to give you space to exercise control in areas where you truly do have a choice.

The previous chapter on mindful acceptance was a step in that direction—taking control by learning to approach your WAFs differently, more softly, less judgmentally, and with kindness. You can keep nurturing these skills from here on out. They're what will get you out from under your WAFs and free you to move with them as you do more of what matters to you. Keep this in mind as you read on and do the work: *by letting go, I will grow.*

This chapter is about one more important area where you have control—acting to take charge and reclaim your life. As you do that, you'll discover, or perhaps rediscover, what's important to you.

This is a new moment to take stock. Look around the edges. Look deeply for places where your mind may be feeding you the same old false hope. Perhaps in the

By letting go, I will grow.

back of your mind you're still holding on to the idea that you can make the WAF monsters go away by attending to and appeasing them.

You may also think that if you trade in a little more flexibility in your life, eventually the anxiety monster will leave you alone. Does your experience tell you that this has ever really happened or that it's ever going to happen? If you find yourself still stuck in this place, this waiting place, then spend some time with the following story before moving on.

Stop Feeding the Anxiety Tiger

Think of your WAFs as a hungry, baby pet tiger. This baby tiger lives with you in your home. Although the tiger is just a baby, he's scary enough, and you think he might bite you. So you go to the fridge to get some meat for him, all the while hoping he won't eat you. And sure enough, throwing him some meat shuts him up while he's eating, and then he leaves you alone for a bit. But he also grows. So the next time he's hungry, he's just a little bigger and scarier, so you go to the fridge to get more meat to throw to him. Back and forth, over and over, the same drama plays itself out. The problem is that the more you feed him, the bigger he gets, and, with that, the more frightened you feel. Now eventually that little tiger has turned into a big tiger, and he scares you more than ever. So you keep on going back to the fridge to get more meat, feeding and feeding him, in the hope that one day he'll leave you alone, and for good. Yet the tiger doesn't leave—he just gets louder and scarier and hungrier. And then one day you walk to the fridge, you open the door, and the fridge is empty. At this point, there's nothing left to feed to the tiger . . . nothing . . . except *you!*

Each time you actively struggle with your worries, anxieties, fears, panic, or just about any form of emotional hurt and pain, you feed the WAF tiger and it gets just a little bit bigger. Remember: hardness begets hardness. In the short term, it may not feel this way. But in the long run, that's what acting on your WAFs does—it feeds your anxiety and cripples your life.

Take another look at some of the LIFE forms you've completed as well as your earlier epitaphs, and ask yourself this (say it out loud or as a whisper): "Am I making choices based on what I deeply value and care about for my life? And am I doing things that really matter to me and make my life worthwhile? Or have my choices and actions been driven more by avoiding or minimizing my pain—my painful WAFs?" Pause for a moment before going on.

Now is the time to face some critical questions: Who's running your life? Who's in control here? Is it you or is it the WAF tiger? You don't have to devote your life to feeding this tiger. You can stop feeding it by using mindful acceptance and growing compassion for what you experience. This will keep the tiger from crowding out your life space. Then and only then will you be able to see that you do have the power to choose a different direction.

EXERCISE: LIFE WITHOUT ACTING ON MY WAFs

Have you ever wondered what your life would be like if you weren't always struggling with your WAFs? Think about the kinds of things you'd do with your time and energy if you weren't consumed with handling the people, places, and situations that hurt. How would you spend your day differently? And how might your relationships be different?

Go ahead, sit back, close your eyes, and imagine your new life for a minute or so. Think—"This is my life as I'd like to live it." In the space below, jot down what you were thinking about.

_____

_____

_____

We have a hunch that some of the images that came up in your mind had to do with important aspects of your life that you're missing out on, or may have given up on, because of your WAFs. We'd like you to reconnect with some of these important parts of your life—because we know that you can have them back. And you can have them without winning the WAF war!

WHAT ARE MY VALUES?

Answering this question can be difficult. We're not asking you about your morals, beliefs, or philosophy —what you believe is right or wrong, just, or true. Values refer to actions—what you do. Believing that you should be a good parent is a question of morality; your actions in your role as a parent with your children are a question of values. Likewise, if you're someone who believes in helping others, you need to act in ways that are helpful. If you don't act out your values, they're just empty beliefs. Beliefs or morality without action are dead ends.

So, to answer the question above, you need to allow yourself time to think about areas of your life that are deeply important to you. These are the things that make your life worth living, that you cherish and nurture, and that you'd act to defend when necessary. By completing the exercises in this chapter and the next, you'll get a very clear sense of what *you* value.

Values Are Like a Beacon in the WAF Storm

You can think of values as the shining lighthouse in the sea of life, orienting you in a direction. Values serve as a map of sorts—showing you the way toward what's important in your life in the midst of life's ups and downs. Without values, you'll end up like the person in the image on page 168.

That person is stuck, being tossed about in the relentless churning seas, wind, and dense fog of the WAF storm. They are focused on the storm, not the shining light in the distance. You may feel that way too—directionless, pulled and pushed around in a sea of worry, anxiety, and doom and gloom. There seems to be no hope, no way out, and no place to go. That is, unless you bring your attention to the light coming from the lighthouse.

That light, that wondrous and wonderful light, is waiting for you—calling out to you, "This is the way toward the things that matter in your life!" You need to look for it to see it. You need to focus on ways that you might move toward that light instead of bobbing in place, wallowing, and waiting for the storm to pass.

This much we know: if you stay in that boat where you are, you may feel safe. We also know that if you do that, you'll be trading in important aspects of your life for that fleeting sense of comfort. You'll be stuck.

Values are the lighthouse that can help guide you out of the storm and into your life. You don't need to wait for the storm to pass. You can move yourself, storm or not, in directions that are important to you. You know that your WAFs come and go just like the weather—sometimes strong, sometimes weak, sometimes surprising, and at other times entirely predictable. Your other thoughts and feelings do this too. Yet your values tend not to change the way your mental and emotional weather does. The trick is to start looking for those values and nurturing them.

When you do that, you'll probably want more of it, WAF storm or not. Once those value-guided directions are clearer to you, you can begin to focus your efforts on moving in those directions. This is how you create a life.

Values Help You Stay Focused

Focusing on living well instead of thinking and feeling less anxious is a radical and vital step. And keeping your sights set on your values and life will help motivate you to keep up with the exercises in this book. We know that this isn't easy and requires commitment. We also know that few things worthwhile in life are easy. In fact, living well is hard work—period.

The investment you make in reading and working with this book will pay off. As you start spending more of your time living consciously and consistently with what you value, and do so mindfully and with compassion, your life and everything you want to be about will come into focus. Valued living plus mindful acceptance is *compassion in action*!

Life is energy—and this energy is a precious gift. Right now, you're beginning to nurture that energy by developing mindful acceptance skills. These skills, and there will be more of them as you read on, will help shift your attention and energy from WAF struggles and utter exhaustion to a place where you have energy to focus on and engage other more meaningful life activities. Remember this: you can choose how you expend your energy.

In fact, you can think of your energy as being like a hammer. You can use a hammer to build or destroy. You can also spend your energy constructively or destructively. It's up to you. You can choose to waste your energy struggling against WAFs or you can decide to focus that energy on being a loving partner, a good friend, an athlete, or whatever else is important to you. As you explore your values, keep this question in mind: "How can I use my time and energy wisely?"

Values Are a Wise and Vital Alternative to WAF Struggle

Values serve as a benchmark for deciding which actions are useful and which aren't. This is especially important when you feel anxious, worried, or panicky and wonder what to do. At those times, you know from your experience and work with the material in the earlier chapters that your mind will put you in overdrive, feeding you all kinds of "solutions" that haven't really worked. Even now, you may still feel the pull of your old history: "Listen to us. . . . Give us one more go. . . . Maybe it'll work this time." In those moments, it's critical to focus on your values because they'll guide you toward the actions that you want your life to be about.

When you're in the grip of your WAFs, you will know what to do and what not to do by answering one important question: "Does this action I want to take move me closer to or farther away from my values?" Our experience tells us that in most instances, it won't be difficult for you to come up with the right answer. Thinking about this question and answering it will help you move forward rather than resorting to old strategies that haven't worked. To help you remember the value question, we put it in a special box on the right.

> *Does this action move me closer to or farther away from my values?* *

Values don't act as a distraction from WAFs. Instead, they help you decide what matters: winning the battle with WAFs (or at least keeping them at bay) or living well. As you become aware of your values, situations will arise that require a choice from you. There are really only two options here. One choice is to continue spending your life managing anxiety. Another choice is to move with your anxiety in the directions you want your life to take.

PROBLEMS WITH FINDING VALUES

We've found that some people struggling with anxiety have problems identifying their values. At times, they also get bogged down by confusing goals with values and have a hard time separating values from feelings. If left unchecked, these and other concerns can keep you stuck. To help you avoid that, we'll briefly discuss them.

I Don't Have Any Values!

Sometimes we hear people say they don't really have any values. When we ask more questions, it turns out that most people do have values but feel too helpless and afraid to move in valued directions. They're overwhelmed by their WAF barriers.

Take the example of Doug who suffered from obsessive-compulsive disorder and excessive worrying. He told us, "I don't really care anymore about friends and intimate relationships. Every time I try to get closer to people I like, they just seem to push me away. And after going on a date with a new potential partner, I find they're usually not interested in seeing me again—probably because they noticed some of my peculiar habits."

On the surface, it sounds like Doug doesn't care about his social life and intimate relationships. Yet if you look more closely, you'll see that he mentioned reaching out to people in his life and that he, in fact, does care! To help Doug out of this apparent dilemma, we asked him to reframe the way he identified his values. Instead of asking "Can I *achieve* this?" we recommended he ask himself "Do I *care about* this?"

Doug was thinking about his values in terms of goals and achievements. He was disappointed that he hadn't reached his goal of having a number of close friends and an intimate relationship with a woman he cared about. However, he certainly cared about having meaningful personal relationships. So we brainstormed things he might do to support his social values. And we acknowledged that forming loving and deep social bonds takes time.

Doug also got stuck thinking that values are about achieving outcomes or results. This is a trap. Value-focused living, like life in general, is a journey, not a destination. Destinations are the steps along the way of creating a life, but the outcomes—good, bad, and sometimes ugly—of reaching certain destinations don't diminish the value that led you to go forward in directions you care about. The point of valuing is that you do your part and you do what's most important to you in life. And you do it in the here and now. You do it because doing matters. It's not about outcomes.

Consider parenting as a value. Most parents wish the best for their children and do what they can to help make that outcome more likely. Yet engaging the value of parenting is no guarantee that your children will be healthy, safe, and grow up to be good citizens or functional adults. Yet not knowing the outcome for their children doesn't stand in the way of parents, who value parenting, doing what they can as parents. The same is true of other values that involve actions that might be risky or outcomes that are largely uncertain—for example, with career and financial stability, health, love and friendship, or recreation.

The point here is that values focus your attention on the here and now—the process. If you choose values solely on the basis of results and outcomes, you'll be waiting a very long time to see them. And you'll likely be disappointed if things don't turn out a given way.

When you persist, you'll progress. Each day you're given 86,400 seconds to use wisely or to squander. Time is a nonrenewable resource. It can't be saved and stored for tomorrow. If you don't use it, you'll lose it. So spend your time wisely each day. Use all of it. When you do that, you'll position yourself to be able to say at the end of the day, "There were 86,400 seconds lived well." And you may find that the results and outcomes will likely be more or less what you are looking for.

Choose Your Values

When thinking about values and goals, listen to your heart and don't just blindly follow your mind. When we ask people about what's important to them, we sometimes hear them say, "It's important for me to contribute to my community" (a value) or "I want to be a good parent" (a value) or "I want to spend at least two nights a week reading to my children" (a goal). And yet they don't sound very enthusiastic when talking about any of their values and goals. As you come up with values and goals, always ask yourself, "Is this really important to me, or am I doing it because I'm supposed to?"

We find that some people don't freely choose values that they hold dear. They choose a value because it sounds socially appropriate, makes them look good, or because of what their loved ones expect of them. What's important here is that you listen to your heart, not outside pressures to conform to valuing this or that. Be sure that your values are *your* values, not values that society, friends, or family impose on you. Ask yourself: "Why am I doing this? Am I doing this for me or for someone else, or to avoid someone else being hurt or disappointed by my choices?" Remember that the pursuit of values is about discovering or rediscovering what's truly important in your own life—what *you* want your life to stand for, not what other people want from you or for you.

Goals can help you physically move in your valued directions, but in order to regain your quality of life, you need to judge the quality and vitality of each activity against your values. This sound advice was shared with us by two of our colleagues—Joanne Dahl and Tobias Lundgren. We think their advice is right on the mark.

Vitality is your benchmark. Moving toward important values makes you feel energized and alive. Sometimes you'll experience that vitality as you take a step, but other times you won't. Some steps might not come with a "good feeling." Here, just think of something you care about in life and important things you've done in the service of that important value. You've probably had many "not feeling great at the time" steps along the way.

In fact, reading this book and doing the hard work of changing your life for the better (a value of health and wellness) isn't all roses. Yet you persist, because when you look back at your steps against the backdrop of your values, you can say, "Yes, my actions are part of something bigger. . . . They leave me feeling more vital and alive at the end of the day." When you can say that, you've found a value and a goal that really strikes a chord in you.

If you find that what seemed like a worthy goal doesn't advance your sense of vitality, then reexamine that goal and adjust course. This is a smart thing to do. Adjustments are normal steps on your valued path, and if you keep your values in sight, they'll steer you in the right direction.

Without identifying the direction you want to move in, and without a plan on how to move in that direction, you're unlikely to go anywhere. This is why goals are so important. Setting goals allows you to establish a game plan for the way you want to express your values in your life. In chapter 18, we'll help you set goals based on your values. For now, it's enough that you understand the difference between goals and values, and that you choose values that are truly your own.

Is It a Goal or a Value?

It's easy to confuse goals with values. Here's how to think about the difference. Goals are stepping-stones that lead you down the path of a valued life. Goals involve actions you can put on a list, complete, and then tick off. Once you reach a goal, the work is done, and you're finished.

Taking out the garbage is a good example. If you set that as a goal, you could put it on a list and tick it off when you're done. Other goals might include losing ten pounds, taking a vacation, getting a degree, or mowing the lawn. Even the act of getting married fits our definition of a goal. Once that ring is on your finger, your goal is achieved. So you can tell if something is a goal by whether you can do it and then tick it off your list.

Unlike goals, values are lifelong journeys. You can't answer the question "Am I done yet?" about values. Values have no end point. Instead, they direct us throughout life. If values are the map or compass that shows you the direction you want to move in, then goals are the waypoints on the map, places you plan to visit as you move in the direction of your values.

For example, reaching a particular goal (getting married) is just one of many steps in a valued direction (being a loving partner). The value of being a loving, devoted partner isn't complete the moment you say, "I do." Being a loving, devoted partner is something you must keep working toward—as you'll learn more about in a bit when we share Danny's experience—and there's always room for growth.

The same can be said of parenting as a value. Reaching your goal of spending two hours of quality time with your child every weekend doesn't complete the value of being a good parent. Values such as being a loving person or a good parent are ongoing commitments that are reflected in moment-to-moment actions. You cannot ever "finish" a value.

Although values and goals aren't the same, they're related. Just think of one or two goals you have set for yourself. Be open to the seemingly mundane here too—things like taking out the garbage. To determine the value that underlies the goal, you can simply ask yourself, "Why am I doing this?" "What am I trying to accomplish in my life with this goal?" and "Where am I heading with this?"

Answers to these questions will point you in the direction of your values. And they'll change the way you look at things too. You may find that the simple act of taking out the garbage reflects a value of helping, being part of a family, and/or being a supportive spouse. It's no longer a stinky "I have to do it" task. Taking out the garbage with an eye on your values changes the act of taking out the garbage. See if you notice the difference the next time you take out your trash.

Values are ongoing commitments that are reflected in moment to moment actions.

Valuing Involves Action, Not Feeling

Many people assume that valuing is about how they *feel* about a particular area in their lives. This is a potential trap. Here's why. You do lots of things in life regardless of how you may feel at the time. Breathing is one of them. If you waited to feel good or happy before taking your next breath, you'd be in serious trouble. Many other actions are like this too. We do many things despite how we think or feel at the time.

You probably go to work in the morning regardless of whether you feel anxious, sad, irritated, worried, or happy. Or you may have paid a visit to Aunt Edith even if you don't like her very much. Let's take this a step further.

Suppose you value social interactions and feel anxious about talking to a group of strangers. Not waiting to feel less anxious in this situation means that you can still talk to them regardless of how you may feel inside. Or if you're feeling panicky while attending a ball game with your son, you can stay in the stadium even though you feel like heading for the closest exit.

Put simply, values are the cumulative effect of what you spend your time doing, not what you think and feel about what you're doing. Many research studies have shown that if you focus on your actions, your feelings will eventually follow suit and take care of themselves.

This is why we stress that valuing is all about doing things. You actually value with your hands, feet, and mouth (that is, by what you say). So valuing your career means that you're acting on that: working to build your career. If you don't work to build your career, then you don't value it, regardless of how you *feel* about it. Values are expressed in action—period.

Emotional Outcomes Are Not Values

When we ask people what's important to them, they often make statements such as these:

- "I want to be calmer, more at peace."

- "It's important for me to be happy."

- "I want to feel more confident."

- "I want to be less anxious and more easygoing."

- "I want people to like me."

- "I want people to accept me so I can accept myself."

All these statements sound like values, but they're really goals masquerading as values. In fact, they're emotional goals—different types of feelings. Being calmer and happier are emotional outcomes too. You could even tick them off when they show up. They are states that may or may not happen *after* you start moving toward your values. Remember that you can't really control what you feel or think or how others think or feel about you. You can only control what you do.

You set yourself up for disappointments if you make feeling better, happier, more confident, or more accepted the reasons for your actions. Chances are that you'll *sometimes* feel better about yourself once you start moving in the direction of your values. But when you do things just to feel better, you're walking on thin ice, because no matter what you do, you won't always feel good, calm, confident, and accepted. Feelings are fickle. They come and go. That's why they cannot serve as a solid foundation for your actions.

If you look deeply inside yourself, you can connect with aspects of your life that are precious—for whatever reason. Those precious things are that way just because they are. You don't need to justify them. They're present despite your emotional weather, much like the stars are forever present even on an overcast cloudy evening. You know the stars are there even when you sometimes can't see them. And you know they'll be back in view. Even the clouds don't stick around forever, but the stars sure will. Your values are like the stars in a way. They don't change overnight, nor do they go away. This is why values provide a more solid foundation for your actions than fleeting feelings ever could.

YOU'RE AT A CROSSROADS

Right now, you're at a critical crossroads in your life. You can choose to live your life in a way that upholds your deepest and most cherished desires, or you can choose to live the same old way, constantly avoiding or struggling against WAFs. It's up to you.

Take a look at how Danny handled this important choice in his life.

■ *Danny's Story*

Danny came to us suffering from panic disorder. His panic was taking a huge toll on his life, snuffing out just about everything that mattered to him. One of Danny's values was being a loving husband. Danny was faced with a tough choice—his panic or his relationship.

Danny and his wife enjoyed classical music. Yet they hadn't been to a live performance in years because to do that meant that Danny would need to sit in a concert hall for two hours amidst hundreds of people. Then, the unexpected happened.

Danny's wife approached him with some exciting news. Her friend had offered her two tickets to the symphony at a bargain price. That news sent Danny's mind into a tailspin and headed straight into a pit filled with the usual worries and scenarios: "What if you have a panic attack? It'll be difficult to leave. Everyone will stare at you as you try to make it to the exit in the middle of the show."

[handwritten margin note:] Feelings are fickle – They come and go.

In the past, Danny's default response was a flat-out "no!" And he knew that opting out made him feel safe and then sad. His wife would feel unhappy too. That's how it went when his choices were about panic management. This time, though, things were a bit different.

He asked his wife for a bit of time to think about it. He knew how much his wife would love to go with him, all dressed up by his side. And he was well aware of his deep love for her (and for the music). So he took time to think about it and make a choice. This wasn't easy. He wanted to go and tell her, "Yes, let's go." Yet his mind was feeding him doom and gloom—cycling through an endless stream of frightening scenarios of what might happen at the concert. His old history was at work here, and it was pointing him to the same tiresome conclusion: don't go—stay home.

He was torn and didn't know what to do. It was at this point that Danny remembered the value question we had talked about. And focusing on this question helped him resolve his dilemma. He saw that listening to his mind and staying at home wouldn't move him any closer to his value of being a loving husband. And with that, he made a courageous choice to go to the concert with his wife.

Like Danny, you have an important choice to make: Are you going to start living the life you want to live or are you going to keep on trying to avoid or struggling with your WAFs?

You can think of these choices in this way. Imagine life as a walk down a long corridor with many doors on either side. You have the power to choose which doors to open and enter. One of those doors is labeled "no more anxiety." You've chosen the no-more-anxiety door for so long that you may have lost sight of other doors available to you. Now's the time to venture out and open up other doors. You can do this!

What choice do you want to make? Going back to the no-more-anxiety door sure sounds tempting. Now consult your experience: has this action moved you closer to your values or further away from them? By now, you know the answer. If not, just go back to the Costs of Anxiety Management exercise in chapter 6.

Now is the time to muster the courage to explore other doors in your life corridor. Think about your life. Besides the no-more-anxiety door, what other doors would you like to open? Maybe there's a door labeled "love" and another sporting a sign that says "physical fitness." There's a door to professional satisfaction and another that leads to political activism. Yet another is marked "inner peace." It's a long corridor with many, many doors.

LIFE ENHANCEMENT EXERCISES

In chapter 11, you created a to-do list of ways to take care of yourself each day. Continue to practice the following exercises from that chapter. Remember that you're learning new skills, and be patient with yourself. Make your practice an important part of your daily routine.

- Practice the Acceptance of Thoughts and Feelings exercise once a day.

- Practice developing your Wise Mind with the Wise Mind exercise.

- Practice being a mindful observer (the chessboard) during everyday activities at home and elsewhere—and have fun with it.

- Take stock of what you may still be giving up for anxiety this week.

THE TAKE-HOME MESSAGE

You can take charge of your life by focusing on what you can control: what you do with your hands, feet, and mouth. Instead of struggling with WAFs, you can identify what truly matters in your life and then focus your energy on pursuing goals that will move you in those directions.

Your values will help you choose a course of action that moves you closer to your dreams.

Focusing on My Values

Points to Ponder: My values are the beacon guiding my actions. My actions are what others see about me. My actions create my life.

Questions to Consider: Am I willing to let my actions be guided by my values rather than my WAFs? Am I willing to make valued living a priority?

Finding Your Values

When you have a sense of your own identity and a vision of where you want to go in your life, you then have the basis for reaching out to the world and going after your dreams for a better life. —Stedman Graham

Identifying your own values is one of the most important steps on the road to living the life you want to lead. It may also seem like quite a daunting task. And you may even think that you have no values. Asking yourself a few simple questions will always point you in the right direction: "What do I want my life to be about?" "What really matters to me?" The epitaphs you completed in chapter 7 have already primed you to get to a place where you're able to consider such questions.

WHAT ARE MY IMPORTANT VALUES?

Now, we'd like you to explore these questions more deeply by completing the exercise below using the Valued Directions Worksheet. This worksheet will help you identify areas of your life that are most important to you. And it will help you make fuller contact with how you would like to conduct your life vis-à-vis the things that matter most.

The worksheet explores ten areas of life that people value to varying degrees: family relationships, intimate relationships, social relationships, parenting, work/career, learning/education, leisure, health, spirituality, and community life. What *you* value and consider important may not be exactly what others value and consider important. This is exactly how it should be.

We're concerned with your quality of life in the areas that are most important to you. What people do in these areas adds up to a life lived well. Failure to act in these areas because your WAFs show up will naturally diminish the quality of your life.

Be forewarned—this exercise will take a while to complete, and it should. It's also one of the most important exercises in this book and your life. We'll guide you along. You'll see it's time well spent. Here's how you do it.

EXERCISE: THE VALUED DIRECTIONS WORKSHEET

Step 1: Make Your Importance Ratings

Start by rating the importance of each area by circling a number on the Importance Scale (0, 1, or 2). It's okay if you don't value all areas, or you don't rate them as being equally important. Simply rate each area according to *your own personal sense of its importance*. It's also fine if you end up rating only one or two areas as very important or if you rate most areas as important to you. What matters here is that you look inside yourself and make an honest rating of what's important to you personally.

If you rated an area as unimportant (0), then move on and rate the next area. Continue until you've rated the importance of all value domains.

Step 2: Rate Your Satisfaction

Go back and focus on areas that you rated as moderately (1) or very important (2). Pause and reflect on those areas. Then, using the Satisfaction Scale, rate how satisfied you are (0, 1, or 2) with the quality and depth of your life in each important area.

Step 3: Write Your Intentions

After completing your ratings, go back to each value you rated as either moderately important (1) or very important (2) and write down your intentions. An intention is a statement that reflects the direction you want to move in for the foreseeable future. It's simply a statement of how you'd like to live your life. It should capture what's most important to you in that area. These statements should be real in the sense that they genuinely reflect your wishes. So listen to and follow your heart. Really make an effort to come up with statements rooted in your experience. This will give your values greater pull over your actions when your WAFs are in danger of pulling you away from where you want to go.

Value intentions are not goals. They have no end point at which you can say, "Now I've accomplished that." You shouldn't be able to tick them off a list. Instead, they should speak to how you want to live every day of your life. If you're having difficulty coming up with an intention statement because you're unsure what a particular domain is about, ask yourself the questions we list in each area.

Now go ahead and write your value intentions directly on the lines provided. Do this for all areas you rated 1 or 2 in terms of importance:

The Valued Directions Worksheet

1. Work/career

Importance: 0 = not at all important   (1) = moderately important   2 = very important

Satisfaction: 0 = not at all satisfied   1 = moderately satisfied   (2) = very satisfied

Intention: What do I want my work or career to be about or stand for? What is important to me about my work (for example, financial security, intellectual challenge, independence, prestige, interacting with or helping people, and so on)?

_____

_____

2. Intimate relationships (e.g., marriage, couples)

Importance: 0 = not at all important   (1) = moderately important   2 = very important

Satisfaction: (0) = not at all satisfied   1 = moderately satisfied   2 = very satisfied

Intention: What kind of partner would I most like to be within an intimate relationship? What type of marital or couple relationship would I like to have? How do I want to treat my partner?

_____

_____

3. Parenting

Importance: 0 = not at all important   1 = moderately important   (2) = very important

Satisfaction: 0 = not at all satisfied   (1) = moderately satisfied   2 = very satisfied

Intention: What type of parent do I want to be? How do I want to interact with my children?

_____

_____

4. Education/learning (personal growth)

Importance: 0 = not at all important   1 = moderately important   (2) = very important

Satisfaction: 0 = not at all satisfied   (1) = moderately satisfied   2 = very satisfied

Intention: Why is learning important to me? What skills, training, or areas of competence would I like to acquire? What would I really like to learn more about?

_____

_____

5. Friends/social life

Importance: 0 = not at all important   1 = moderately important   (2) = very important

Satisfaction: 0 = not at all satisfied   (1) = moderately satisfied   2 = very satisfied

Intention: What kind of friend do I want to be? What does it mean to be a good friend? How do I behave toward my best friend? Why is friendship important to me?

_____

_____

6. Health/physical self-care

Importance: 0 = not at all important   1 = moderately important   (2) = very important

Satisfaction: 0 = not at all satisfied   (1) = moderately satisfied   2 = very satisfied

Intention: How and why do I take care of myself? Why do I want to take care of my body and my health through what I eat, by exercising, or by being physically fit?

_____

_____

7. Family of origin (family relationships other than marriage or parenting)

Importance: 0 = not at all important   (1) = moderately important   2 = very important

Satisfaction: 0 = not at all satisfied   1 = moderately satisfied   (2) = very satisfied

Intention: How do I want to interact with my family members? What type of sister or brother do I want to be? What type of son or daughter do I want to be?

_____

_____

8. Spirituality

Importance: 0 = not at all important   1 = moderately important   (2) = very important

Satisfaction: 0 = not at all satisfied   (1) = moderately satisfied   2 = very satisfied

Intention: What are the mysteries of life before which I stand in awe? What are the things larger than my own life that inspire me? In what (if anything) do I have faith?

_____

_____

9. Community life/environment/nature

Importance: 0 = not at all important 1 = moderately important **②** = very important

Satisfaction: 0 = not at all satisfied **①** = moderately satisfied   2 = very satisfied

Intention: What can I do to make the world a better place? Why are community activities (such as volunteering, voting, recycling) important to me? What do I care about in the environment or nature (e.g., being outdoors, gardening, hiking, camping, communing with nature)?

_____

_____

10. Recreation/leisure

Importance: 0 = not at all important **①** = moderately important   2 = very important

Satisfaction: 0 = not at all satisfied **①** = moderately satisfied   2 = very satisfied

Intention: How do I feed myself through hobbies, sports, or play? Why do I enjoy these things?

_____

_____

CREATING YOUR LIFE COMPASS

The Valued Directions Worksheet is the foundation for creating a "life compass" (adapted from Dahl & Lundgren, 2006). We call it the Life Compass because it gives your life direction—with it, you'll know where to go from here. The next exercise will help you create it.

EXERCISE: BUILDING YOUR LIFE COMPASS

We've broken this exercise up into four easy steps. Referring back to your Valued Directions Worksheet will make building your Life Compass easy. The Life Compass appears at the end of the exercise.

Step 1: Focus on Life Domains You Find Important

You'll notice that there are two small, blank boxes attached to each value in the Life Compass below. These boxes are for rating each value in two different ways: how important the value is to you ("i" is for "importance") and how often you have actually moved in that direction over the past two weeks ("a" is for "action").

Let's start with the importance rating. Go back to the Valued Directions Worksheet and copy your importance ratings into the "i" box connected to each value.

Step 2: What Are Your Intentions?

Write a brief intention statement in those value boxes you rated as either moderately important (1) or very important (2). You can start by going to the intention statements on the Valued Directions Worksheet. We've found that these statements tend to be one or two sentences long. We suggest that you boil these down to a shorter statement that will fit into the box of the Life Compass so that you'll be able to remember the intentions more easily when you're in the grip of WAFs. Do this for all areas you rated 1 or 2. If you have three or more areas that you rated as very important (2), you might want to focus on those and write in an intention for only those areas. Remember, intentions are statements about how you would like to live your life in that area—what is most important to you. Now go ahead and write your intentions in each box.

Step 3: Are You Doing What Matters to You?

After you've finished writing down your intentions, please think about your activities in the past two weeks. Are your actions consistent with your intentions in each area? We call these activities "your feet." So, were you doing things consistent with the intentions you just wrote down? For each intention, rate how often you've done something to move you toward your important values during the past two weeks. Use the following scale for your ratings: no action (0), one or two actions (1), three or four actions (2), and five or more actions (3). Write your ratings in the "a" (actions) box next to the "i" box that's connected to each value. We're not asking about your ideal in each area or about what others may think of you. Just rate how actively you've been living out your intentions over the past two weeks.

Now go back and look at your intentions and actions. How well do they match up for each value domain you rated as important to you? Take stock here. Look for areas where the "i" number is larger than the "a" number. This mismatch means that you're not living your life as you want to live it. For instance, if you consider family very important (say, "i" is rated a 2) and your action rating is low ("a" is rated a 0 or 1), you're living a life that is quite different from the one you want. If you're like most people with anxiety problems, you might find discrepancies between your importance and action ratings.

Step 4: What Stands in Your Way?

Discrepancies between your intentions and actions in valued areas are often related to barriers. Barriers are anything that stands in the way of you living out your values. Go back to each value area that's important to you and examine what exactly stands in the way. Perhaps it is a fear of a panic attack or other intense feelings; thoughts about being overwhelmed, embarrassed, or exposed; intrusive unwanted thoughts that seem to show up out of thin air and invade your mind; painful images or memories; specific worries about what will happen if you move in that direction; thoughts about failure, incompetence, or inadequacy; or other worries and doubts. Whatever the barriers may be, just write them down (in a word or two) in the signs on your Life Compass. These signs are the barriers between you and your values.

Recreation/leisure   i =   a =

Work/career   i =   a =

Intimate relationships   i =   a =

Parenting   i =   a =

Community life/ environment/ nature   i =   a =

Education/learning   i =   a =

Spirituality   i =   a =

Family of origin   i =   a =

Health/ physical self-care   i =   a =

Friends/social life   i =   a =

Now stop and review your Life Compass. If you look carefully, you'll see that many of your barriers have to do with your WAFs—thoughts, negative evaluations, judgments, feelings, and bodily sensations you don't like. The barriers are happening inside you.

Worries about anxiety and what might go wrong can definitely sidetrack you from seeing your valued intentions and following through with them. This isn't something to beat yourself up over—many people with anxiety problems are in the same boat that you're in.

Here's what you can do: you can choose to take what you've learned during this exploration of your values and use it as inspiration to stick with this workbook and to learn how to bring your life into alignment with your values. If you find that WAFs have steered you away from the life you value, the next chapters will show you a way out of the avoidance detour and back on the road toward your Value Mountains. This is the opportunity that this book offers you: learning to live the life you want without being held back by your struggles with WAF barriers.

LIFE ENHANCEMENT EXERCISES

Below is a list of activities that we think will be helpful to you. We've added a new activity about your values. Add it to your daily to-do list and commit to doing all the activities as best as you can.

- Practice the Acceptance of Thoughts and Feelings exercise from chapter 11 once a day.

- Practice being a mindful observer (the chessboard and the Wise Mind exercises from chapter 11) anytime, anywhere.

- Do something in line with your most important value(s) at least every other day.

Doing the exercises won't always go smoothly. And you won't always get the result you may be hoping for. That's okay. Be patient and trust that doing the work will make a difference. We've seen the exercises make a difference with many people who have worked with this program.

THE TAKE-HOME MESSAGE

The values you choose are the road map for getting the most out of your life. They help you stay focused on what's important. When WAFs are demanding your attention, you can stop, observe your thoughts and feelings, and then listen to your values and do as your values say. A life lived well is a product of many small, valued actions. You write your own eulogy and epitaph through the choices you make and the actions you take every day. Each day provides you with opportunities to move in valued directions *and* to take your anxious thoughts and feelings with you.

a life lived well is a product of many small, valued actions.

Identifying and Thinking About My Values

Points to Ponder: Life is short. My values are lived out by my actions and make my life worthwhile. Anxiety management is not a vital value!

Questions to Consider: What do I want to be about in this life? How consistently am I living out my values? Am I letting my WAFs get in the way of my values? Am I willing to make valued living a priority? Am I willing to do what I care about with or without my WAFs?

CHAPTER 14

Getting Ready to Face Anxiety with Mindful Acceptance

When we are motivated by goals that have deep meaning, by dreams that need completion, by pure love that needs expressing—then we truly live life.
—Greg Anderson

The epitaph and other values exercises in previous chapters have shown you that you don't want your life to be about an endless struggle with WAFs. The exercises also provided you with an opportunity to find out what you care about. Now it's time to start taking the first steps in directions that you really want to be headed.

You may ask, "But what about my anxiety? If I start doing all those things I want to do, my WAFs are going to stand right in the way and keep me from going forward."

You may feel that your situation is like the one depicted in the drawing you see to the right. Notice that

the anxiety monster is blocking the way to Value Mountain—where you want to go with your life. The anxiety barriers are still there, hurting you. Your experience has shown you that listening to and doing what your WAFs ask you to do has only made the space they occupy larger while your life space has become smaller and smaller.

YOU'RE IN CHARGE

In this and the following chapters, we'll teach you skills and strategies to help you move with your WAF barriers rather than waiting for them to go away or trying to push them out of the way. Many of these skills build upon those you've started practicing already—a more gentle and friendlier approach to your anxiety, panic, thoughts, and bodily sensations. By continuing to practice and apply mindfulness and acceptance skills, you'll gradually come to see your anxiety for what it is rather than what your mind screams that it is. We'll also teach you new skills to make more space for what your judgmental mind comes up with and to handle all the hooks and snares that pull you out of your life.

The foundation for all this work is your values. You've already created a compass to guide you. Now it's time to take some steps. Living out those values is a rewarding alternative to staying stuck in the anxiety management and control trap. It makes the hard work ahead worthwhile.

We hope that having learned about your values will inspire you to take steps in a more vital, meaningful direction—one where you and not the WAFs are in charge. Are you willing to face your WAFs and make living a valued life a reality for you?

WHAT TO DO WHEN YOU'RE ANXIOUS OR AFRAID

As you're getting ready to face your WAFs, one nagging question may be on your mind: "What do I do when I'm getting anxious or afraid?" The answer is both simple and challenging: do something radically different than you have done before! The exercises below will help you do that. They build upon the skills you've been learning about and practicing. Give yourself time with them.

Choose What You Do and Attend To

This is probably the most important choice you will make when you notice your WAFs coming on: You can choose to attend to and listen to what your WAFs are telling you and do as they say. Or you can choose to move with your hands and feet, guided by your values.

MOVING WITH BARRIERS

As you embark on your journey of acceptance and as you put your values into action, you'll find the road to be full of barriers. Some barriers are external, such as lack of money, time, opportunity, physical space, geographical constraints, or even foul weather. You can work through some of these barriers by brainstorming alternatives or by talking with a good friend to get some perspective and fresh ideas. Yet by far the most frequent and tricky barriers that you'll face are those nagging, pesky WAF-related thoughts, feelings, bodily sensations, or impulses that have slowed you down in the past.

In this chapter, we want to help you get ready for the moments when WAF barriers show up. These are the moments to employ some of the observer, mindfulness, and acceptance strategies you've been learning in this book. These are also the moments of choice where you can determine the direction that you're headed by controlling what you do with your hands and feet.

Remember that we're brought up and socialized to believe that when a barrier comes up, we should just get rid of it—overcome it. The problem with this strategy is that getting rid of and overcoming a barrier awakens our natural inclination to struggle. You know by now that struggling with your WAFs doesn't work well. So when a barrier comes up, you need to listen to and trust your experience, not your mind!

You don't need to get rid of WAF barriers on your road to living your values. The key is to accept and move *with* the barriers—take them along for the ride! You can deal with any WAF-like obstacle in the same way that you deal with other thoughts and feelings: You don't push them aside. Instead, you make room for all the unwanted stuff that has been stopping you from doing what's best for you. You acknowledge that stuff, watch it with your Wise Mind observer perspective, let it be without getting involved with it, *and* keep on moving in the direction you want to go—all at the same time, just like the person in the cartoon to the right.

EXERCISE: DRIVING YOUR LIFE BUS

You can think of yourself as the driver of a bus called "My Life." You're headed north toward your Value Mountain _____ [insert one of your important values here].

Along the way, you pick up some unruly passengers, like frightening thoughts and images that your mind comes up with. Other passengers on the bus traveling with you are feelings of panic, apprehension, and tension. These passengers are loud and persistent. They frighten and try to bully you as you drive along your chosen route: "Don't go there! It's too dangerous. You'll make a fool of yourself. STOPPPPP!"

After a while, you realize that while you were busy trying to come up with arguments and strategies to quiet them, you missed a road sign and took a wrong turn. Now you're an hour out of your way, headed south. You are, in a sense, lost. So you stop the bus and focus on getting your passengers in line. This time you turn around, face them, and let them have it: "Why can't you leave me alone? I'm sick of you. Just give me a few moments to relax."

Look at what happened here: You've stopped the bus, let go of the steering wheel, turned yourself around, and your eyes are looking at the back of the bus instead of staying focused on the road ahead and your real destination. You're not moving. Instead, you're paying attention to the stuff that has nothing to do with your values.

Now you have a choice again: you can stay tangled up in arguments and strategies to calm the passengers down or you can let them be, get back in the driver's seat, turn on the engine, and find your way back onto the road toward your Value Mountain.

If getting to the mountain is important to you, then what you need to do is stay in the driver's seat of the bus and drive north toward the mountain no matter how much noise those other passengers are making. Thoughts and feelings cannot prevent you from turning your bus around and heading north again toward the mountain—unless you give them that power.

The unpleasant passengers are still on the bus with you. You can't kick them off. While you're driving your Life Bus on the road to your Value Mountain, every now and then they creep forward and scream, "Pay attention to us! Turn around! Go back! Take this detour—it's safer, easier—and it'll make you feel better."

Here life is asking you to make a choice again: what will you do? Stopping won't get you to the mountain and neither will the detour. Only you can take yourself to where you want to go—and you have no choice but to take the whole crowd with you.

Remember, your WAF passengers will grab every opportunity to steer you off course. They'll try to convince you that you don't feel like doing this anymore, that it's all too much, too difficult, not worth it . . . *and* you can still choose to keep on moving north. You can't control what kinds of feelings, thoughts, or fears will ride along with you. What you can control is where your Life Bus is going—you control the steering wheel with your hands and the accelerator with your feet.

TUNING IN TO JUST SO RADIO INSTEAD OF ANXIETY NEWS RADIO

Several of the earlier exercises have shown you that you need not fight and struggle with your WAFs—you can choose to observe and accept them instead. The bottom line is that you can choose what you pay attention to.

This choice is humorously illustrated in the Anxiety News Radio metaphor from our colleague Peter Thorne, a clinical psychologist working in England. Peter shared an interesting comment with us from one of his clients. We'll call her Amy.

Long before Amy came into therapy, she'd been an avid radio listener. The station she tuned in to most often was WANR—Anxiety News Radio—and she was sick of it. This wasn't the kind of radio most of us think of, nor was it something that Amy wanted to listen to. This radio was broadcasting from her head, and she couldn't tune it out or turn it off. This brought Amy to Peter. And, over time, she learned something that she hadn't thought of before: she didn't have to stay tuned in to WANR around the clock, slavishly believing all the broadcasts inside her mind. The idea that she could tune in to more helpful sources of information out there in her world of actual real-life experience was a new direction for her. Perhaps it will be for you too. Read the next exercise to find out.

EXERCISE: CHANGING RADIO STATIONS

Anxiety News Radio (WANR)

Here's the message you've been getting:

Welcome to Anxiety News Radio, WANR, broadcasting inside your head twenty-four hours a day, seven days a week. It's the news station you've grown up with, and now it comes to you automatically, 24/7. Anxiety News Radio is compelling listening, and guess why! When you wake in the early hours, we'll be there to make you aware of all the unhappy aspects of your life, even before you get out of bed. We'll bring you all the things that you find most disturbing and distressing—anytime, anywhere. So don't forget that, and if you should forget us and act without seeking permission, then we'll broadcast all the louder. Our mission is to drown out your values. Our goal is to take over and control your life. Pay attention! Anxiety News Radio knows what's best for you. We guarantee that our products will pull you out of your life in a flash. Remember: what you think and feel inside your skin can be really awful. So stay tuned. We know how to keep people stuck.

Just So Radio (WJSR)

Here's an alternative station, with a very different message. If you chose to tune in, you'd hear something like this:

Wake Up! Anxiety News Radio is just a station—you can tune in or you can tune out! One thing is guaranteed, though: whatever the time of day, you'll hear the same old stuff on WANR. If that's been really helpful to you, then go ahead, tune in and stay tuned. If not, then tune in more often to Just So Radio. We bring you the news of actual experience, in the moment—all live, as it is, all the time. Living well is our business! We'll give it to you straight—real experience as it is, not as what your mind says it is. We'll bring you into fuller contact with the world outside and inside your skin. We'll help you wake up to your life and to your experiences as a human being—and it's entirely free! Our listeners tell us that tuning in to WJSR is vital and can even bring you joy. Just So Radio brings you information about how things are, not how you fear they might be. Just So Radio invites you to step forward and touch the world, just as it is, and to touch your life, just as it is. We get louder the more you listen to us. So stay tuned. Give us a fair trial and if not convinced by your own experience (please don't take our word for it), then WANR—Anxiety News Radio—is still there on the dial.

The text files of both radio broadcasts are also on the CD. We suggest that you print the two parts of this metaphor on the back and front of a piece of paper and take it with you in your pocket, purse, or briefcase—whatever is most convenient. This way you have them handy when you're sick of WANR and are ready to tune in to WJSR. You can also listen to the messages of the two radio stations on the CD. Notice the different style and tone of voice of the two messages.

Freeing Yourself from Your Mind Traps

Your mind and the simple language conventions you've learned over the years can play tricks on you that keep you stuck where you are. Recognizing them and making some simple and subtle changes in what you tell yourself can make a big difference in your life. Let's have a look at two insidious mind traps: yes-butting and buying into your thoughts.

Getting Off Your But(t)s

At some point you've probably said something like "I'd like to go out BUT I'm afraid of having a panic attack." Snap—you just got caught in the "yes-but" trap.

Anytime you put "but" after the first part of a statement, you undo what you said; you make the first part of the statement go away by denying it. This is the literal meaning of the word "but."

So when you say, "I'd like to go out BUT I'm afraid of having a panic attack," you "undo" your interest in going out—and then you won't go out. You'll stay home because that "but" takes the "like to go out" away. "But" makes going out impossible. You're quite literally stuck on your butt. If you pay close attention, you may find that you use the word "but" many times every day as a reason for not acting on your values. This unnecessarily restricts your life and reduces your options.

Now imagine what would happen if you replaced the word "but" with "and." "I'd like to go out AND I'm afraid of having a panic attack." This little change can have a dramatic impact on what might happen next. If you put it that way, you could actually go out *and* be anxious *and* be worried all at the same time. Most importantly, it would actually allow you to go out and do something vital even though you might feel anxious. It would also be a more correct and honest statement.

Imagine how much more space you'd have in your life, if starting today, you were to say "and" instead of "but" every time a "but" is about to keep you stuck on your butt. How many more opportunities would you gain to do things? Getting off your but(t)s could be one of the most empowering things you've ever done.

Don't Buy Into Your Thoughts

let go of your story

You may have come across a saying that goes something like "Sticks and stones may break my bones, but words will never hurt me." But thoughts, evaluations, memories, and the like can hurt when you take them literally—when you treat them as if they were the same as sticks and stones in the real world. This is why it can be dangerous if you buy into your thoughts.

You can learn to not buy into what your mind tells you if you start to recognize your thoughts and images for what they really are. For example, when you say, "I'll have a panic attack if I go out," you can say out loud or think, "*I am having the thought that* I'll have a panic attack if I go out." Or if you find yourself thinking, "If I don't learn to control my anxiety and worries, then things are going to go downhill for me," you can say out loud, "*I am having the evaluation that. . . .*"

You can apply the same strategy to scary images or feelings. With images you can say, "*I'm having the image that* I'm being attacked." With feelings, you can say, "*I'm having the feeling that* I'm about to die" or "*I'm having the feeling that* [insert whatever you typically feel]."

If you find this too cumbersome or difficult, there's an even simpler way of labeling. Whenever a thought comes up, whatever it may be, just label it "thinking" or "Oh, there's thinking." Whenever an image comes up, just label it "picture" or "There's a picture." And when sensations come up, just label them "sensations" or "There are sensations."

Developing these new labeling and language habits will help you see thoughts as just thoughts, images as images, and feelings as feelings. Even when the most scary and intense thoughts, images, or feelings are highly believable, they're still only thoughts, images, or feelings.

It takes a while before you develop these new habits. Every time you catch yourself yes-butting or buying into thoughts, you can apply these techniques. And the more you do so, the more they'll help you create more space between you, your evaluations of yourself, your experience, and your old history. You'll become a more skilled and wise observer.

Riding Out Your Emotions

Imagine for a moment an ocean wave as it approaches the shore. It's steep and tall and hasn't crested yet into a breaker. Now imagine the wave nearing a group of gulls floating on the water. The birds don't fly away. They simply ride up the facing slope, round the top, and drift down the long back of the wave.

That's what you can learn to do with your WAFs too. All emotions are wave-like and time limited. They ebb and flow. Like a wave, emotions build up, eventually reach a peak, and drift away. WAFs come and go in a similar way. They don't last forever, even if it feels like they will.

We encourage you to ride the wave of your WAFs. You must initially face the steep leading edge. At this point, the wave is tall and scary. You may feel that it will go on forever; that you may drown. Finally the emotion reaches its zenith; instead of getting stronger it starts to recede. You may feel yourself slipping down the back of the wave, the WAFs quieting.

That's how anxiety works if you don't try to control or block it, just allowing the wave to run its course. If you refuse to ride out the wave and try to fight it, then you'll never get over the top. You'll stay stuck on the wave's leading edge. Eventually—sometimes after hours or days—the anxiety wave crests and crashes. Then you're caught churning helplessly beneath the surface of the water, at the mercy of the full force of the crush and undertow.

All emotions are wave like and limited. Like a wave, emotions build up, eventually reach a peak, and drift away.

EXERCISE: WAF SURFING

Right now you have a chance to learn to ride the wave of your WAFs. If you are willing, then think of a recent situation where you felt afraid, panicky, nervous, worried, or upset. Visualize the scene and remember how you felt.

Notice the worrying and disconcerting thoughts. Perhaps you'll notice images of disaster too. Keep focusing on the upsetting scene as well as on the judgments you made about it and what was happening inside you. Let your anxiety rise till it's at least a 4 or 5 on a scale of 10.

Good—now go back to the white room like you did in chapter 5. Observe what your body might be doing. Notice the sensations and how your mind evaluates them. Simply label them all—"I am noticing. . . ." Notice the sensations of warmth and of tightness. There's the thought that it's dangerous, that you're losing control. Just let your body and mind do their thing.

Do the same with worries, other thoughts, and images that show up—the old story line. None of them are right or wrong, true or false. Acknowledge their presence without trying to control or change them; without trying to push them away. Simply label them and keep watching your mind and body.

As you do that, notice the emotional wave in the room with you. Be aware of the point where your WAF stops climbing. Feel it leveling off and starting to diminish. Experience the slow ride down the back of the wave. Accept wherever you are on the wave. Don't hasten to get past it. It moves at its own speed—all you can do is let go and let it carry you.

So you can watch your thoughts and bodily sensations entering and leaving the white room. And you notice the progress of the wave, nothing more. Keep watching until the WAF has completely passed.

Emotions proliferate through our internal dialogue

Using the Energy of Anxiety Wisely

Pema Chödrön (2001) describes an intriguing way you can use the energy of anxiety wisely. Emotions proliferate through our internal dialogue—what your mind is telling you about your anxiety. If you label those thoughts as "thinking" when you notice them and just observe what's going on, you may be able to sense the vital, pulsating energy beneath them. This energy underlies all of your emotional experience; and there's nothing wrong or harmful about it.

The challenge is to stay with this underlying energy: to experience it, leave it as it is, and, when possible, put it to good use. When anxiety arises uninvited, let go of your old story line about it and connect directly with the energy just below. What remains is a *felt* experience, not the story line your mind is feeding you about what's happening.

If you feel, and can stay with, the energy in your body—neither acting on it nor suppressing it—you can harness it in the service of actions that move you forward toward achieving your valued goals. The raw energy of anxiety is fuel. You get to choose to use that fuel for you or against you.

LEARNING TO ACCEPT YOUR ANXIETY

Mindfulness exercises are a way of learning that you cannot choose what comes into your mind and what you feel. You can only choose what you pay attention to, *how* you pay attention, and what you *do*. The exercise below will help you do just that.

In our previous exercises, we have used the breath as the focus of attention. When your mind wandered off and started focusing on thoughts, worries, images, or feelings, you were asked to notice these thoughts and feelings and then gently redirect attention back to your breath.

In this exercise, we're simply building on the skills you've been learning. What's new is the expanded focus of the practice. Here, you'll be actively and openly inviting into your awareness bodily sensations and unwanted thoughts, worries, and images so that you may learn to approach them in a more accepting and compassionate way. Just like the finger trap and tug-of-war exercises, this exercise encourages you to lean into anxiety rather than fight it. This will create space for you to feel your emotions and think your thoughts as they are, not as your mind tells you they are.

You'll practice opening up to uncomfortable feelings and thoughts rather than rushing to fix or change them. As you do that, you're dropping the rope and willingly making space for WAFs when they're present—because they're present anyway. And with that, you'll get more space to do the things with your life that you may have put on hold for a long time. Are you willing to do an exercise to help you do that?

If you are willing, we suggest you select a quiet place where you feel comfortable and distraction is limited. Let's call this your kind space, your peaceful place. Go through the exercise slowly and pause after each section. It will take about fifteen minutes.

The easiest way to do this exercise is by listening to the recording (the male- or female-voice version) on the CD that comes with this book. After practicing with the CD for a week or two, you may prefer to practice at your own pace without the CD. If you'd like, you can occasionally go back and do the exercise while listening to the recording again.

EXERCISE: ACCEPTANCE OF ANXIETY

Go ahead and get in a comfortable position in your chair. Sit upright with your feet flat on the floor, your arms and legs uncrossed, and your hands resting in your lap (palms up or down). Allow your eyes to close gently.

Take a few moments to get in touch with the physical sensations in your body, especially the sensations of touch or pressure where your body makes contact with the chair or floor. Notice the gentle rising and falling of your breath in your chest and belly. There's no need to control your breathing in any way—simply let the breath breathe itself. As best you can, also bring this attitude of kind allowing and gentleness to the rest of your experience. There's nothing to be fixed. Simply allow your experience to be your experience, without needing it to be other than what it is.

It's natural for your mind to wander away to thoughts, worries, images, bodily sensations, or feelings. Notice these thoughts and feelings, acknowledge their presence, and stay with them. There's no need to think of something else, make them go away, or resolve anything. As best you can, allow them to be . . . giving yourself space to have whatever you have . . . bringing a quality of kindness and compassion to your experience.

Allow yourself to be present to what you are afraid of. Notice any doubts, reservations, fears, and worries. Just notice them and acknowledge their presence, and don't work on them. As you do that, allow yourself to be present with your values and commitments. Ask yourself, "Why am I here?" "Where do I want to go?" "What do I want to do?"

When you're ready, gently shift your attention to a thought or situation that has been difficult for you. It could be a troubling thought, worry, image, or intense bodily sensation. Gently, directly, and firmly shift your attention on and into the discomfort, no matter how bad it seems. Notice any strong feelings that may arise in your body, allowing them to be as they are rather than what your mind tells you they are. Simply hold them in awareness. Stay with your discomfort and breathe with it. See if you can gently open up to it and make space for it, accepting and allowing it to be while bringing compassionate and focused attention to the discomfort.

If you notice yourself tensing up and resisting, pushing away from the experience, just acknowledge that and see if you can make some space for whatever you're experiencing. Must this feeling or thought be your enemy? Or can you have it, notice it, own it, and let it be? Can you make room for the discomfort, for the tension, for the anxiety? What does it really feel like—moment to moment—to have it all? Is this something you *must* struggle with, or can you invite the discomfort in, saying to yourself, "Let me have it; let me feel what there is to be felt because it is my experience right now"?

If the sensations or discomfort grow stronger, acknowledge that, stay with them, breathing with them, and accepting them. Is this discomfort something you *must not* have, you *cannot* have? Can you open up a space for the discomfort in your heart? Is there room inside you to feel that, with compassion and kindness toward yourself and your experience?

As you open up and embrace your experience, you may notice thoughts coming along with the physical sensations, and you may see thoughts about your thoughts. When that happens, invite them in too . . . softening and opening to them as you become aware of them. You may also notice your mind coming up with judgmental labels such as "dangerous" or "getting worse." If that happens, you can simply thank your mind for the label and return to the present experience as it is, not as your mind says it is, noticing thoughts as thoughts, physical sensations as physical sensations, feelings as feelings—nothing more, nothing less.

Stay with your discomfort for as long as it pulls on your attention. If and when you sense that the anxiety and other discomfort are no longer pulling for your attention, let them go.

As this time for practice comes to a close, gradually widen your attention to take in the sounds around you. Take a moment to make the intention to bring this sense of gentle allowing and self-acceptance into the present moment and the rest of your day. Then, slowly open your eyes.

This exercise can be challenging. This is the first time you're deliberately welcoming in your WAF experiences and practicing a new response to them. Don't let that challenge (a judgment) stand in the way of you doing the exercise again this week and in the weeks to come. It'll get easier over time.

Remember that mindful acceptance is a skill. Like a seedling, it needs to be cultivated in order to grow. It has many possible results, not just one. You may feel relaxed during or after the exercise, or you may not. You may feel tense and keyed up at some point, or you may not. You may experience sadness or regret, or you may not. These and other responses are just fine.

The best possible outcome of this exercise is when you find yourself better able to stay with your anxiety-related thoughts and feelings rather than fight them or push them away. So be kind with yourself as you do the practice. Remember, the ultimate purpose of being more accepting of your experience is that you can move forward with your life. Acceptance empowers you to do what you really want to do *and* experience whatever you may experience along the way.

It will be helpful to track your experiences with this exercise over the next several weeks, using the form at the end of this chapter. This will give your practice some structure and give you a place to chart progress over time. We've included an example of how to complete the form. You'll also find the form on the CD. Print out as many extra clean copies as you like.

LIFE ENHANCEMENT EXERCISES

Use this week to practice the exercises in this chapter, adding them to the to-do list introduced in chapter 11. Allow yourself opportunities to practice the Acceptance of Anxiety exercise (described above) at least one time each day. You can continue to do any of the exercises from earlier chapters. In fact, we'd encourage you to do them as often as you can. Play with them. Get good at using them. Look for opportunities to practice using them too.

THE TAKE-HOME MESSAGE

Anxiety can be a monster crippling your life, or it can be a temporary experience that comes and goes pretty much all by itself. It's all a matter of how you respond to it. There's nothing in your head or heart that can keep you from doing what you want to do. You have choices. We hope that you're starting to experience that for yourself. Everything in this chapter builds on skills you've been cultivating throughout the book so far. Every WAF moment can be an opportunity for you to learn a new way of responding. So continue to nurture your capacity to act with kindness, gentle observation, patience, and wholeness, and all with an eye on your values. You can't control the passengers that ride along with you on your Life Bus. What you can control is how you respond to them and whether you keep on moving north toward your values.

Facing My Anxiety, Getting On with My Life

Points to Ponder: Pain is part of life. When I shut down to WAF pain, I shut down to my life. Softening to my pain is the way to get my life back.

Questions to Consider: Am I willing to face, openly and honestly, my WAF pain for what it is, and take it with me where I want to go? Am I ready to take a stand and accept WAF discomfort in order to get my life back?

ACCEPTANCE OF ANXIETY:
Life Enhancement Exercise Practice Form

In the first column, record whether you have made a commitment to practice the Acceptance of Anxiety exercise that day and include the date. The second column asks whether you practiced, when you practiced, and how long you practiced. In the third column, note whether you used the CD audio file or not. In the fourth column, write down anything that came up during your practice.

Acceptance of Anxiety			
Life Enhancement Exercise Practice Form			
Commitment: yes/no **Day:** **Date:**	**Practiced: yes/no** **When practiced?** A.M./P.M. **How long (minutes)?**	**CD Audio:** yes/no	**Comments**
Commitment: (yes)/no Day: *Saturday* Date: 8/4/2007	Practiced: (yes)/no Time: (A.M.)/P.M. Minutes: *20 minutes*	*yes*	*Was tough to be an observer; felt the pull of negative thoughts, physical tension; felt some scary sensations; had some space too. I'll work at being the board next time.*
Commitment: yes/no Day: Date:	Practiced: yes/no Time: A.M./P.M. Minutes:		
Commitment: yes/no Day: Date:	Practiced: yes/no Time: A.M./P.M. Minutes:		
Commitment: yes/no Day: Date:	Practiced: yes/no Time: A.M./P.M. Minutes:		
Commitment: yes/no Day: Date:	Practiced: yes/no Time: A.M./P.M. Minutes:		
Commitment: yes/no Day: Date:	Practiced: yes/no Time: A.M./P.M. Minutes:		

Bringing Compassion to Your Anxiety

Though we all have the seeds of fear within us, we must learn not to water those seeds and instead nourish our positive qualities—those of compassion, understanding, and loving-kindness. —Thich Nhat Hanh

We've talked a lot about anxiety monsters and bullies on the bus. That's what your WAFs appear to be most of the time: a frightening, overbearing enemy that's about to swallow you whole. The problem with terms like "monster" and "bully" is that they keep one toxic myth alive. That myth is this: WAFs are your enemy—an enemy that must be defeated. You know by now that this fight has cost you dearly. You also know that you can't win it because you can never win a fight with yourself.

So here's an important question: must anxiety be your enemy? What if you were willing to approach anxiety with some compassion and kindness instead of with a declaration of war in your hand? If you did that, you'd find out—over time—that your worries, anxieties, and fears would become better travel companions. And you'd see that you can move with them, not against them.

Compassion and kindness can literally take the sting out of anxiety, panic, fear, and worry. This will transform your WAF roadblocks into something you can live with and move with on your way toward your Value Mountains.

To develop compassion, you must cultivate your capacity for loving-kindness just like that of a mother toward her newborn child (Dalai Lama, 1999). The next exercise will help you do that.

EXERCISE: TRAVELING WITH MY ANXIETY CHILD

What if anxiety didn't look like the dark menacing monster from the cartoon in the previous chapter? What if it looked more innocent and childish like the cartoon figure below.

Perhaps you could treat this WAF child as you would your own child if he or she were acting out and being noisy. Think about how you might respond.

Some parents deal with the pulsating energy of their kids by lashing out, fighting, and screaming. The kids, in turn, bear the brunt of this unfettered negative energy as they take one punishment after the next.

Yet we know from countless research studies that these strategies are poor ways to encourage more appropriate behaviors. Parents end up feeling bad, tired, and frustrated, and the kids go on being kids, but now with frustrated, tired, and angry parents.

Other parents opt for a softer, yet firm, approach. They don't resort to fighting or punishing behavior simply because their child is behaving badly. They see through that first impulse (which would be to react with negative energy), and instead, they redirect, refocus, and reconnect. They see their child as part of them. They wish for that child to know kindness and love, and so they respond in a way that shows that. They also act as a pack leader of sorts and take the child in directions the parent wants to go and in directions that are best for the child too. Research shows that this kinder way of relating is highly effective as a parenting strategy.

So what's your parenting strategy with your anxiety "child"? Do you yell, scream, and struggle? If you do that, has it worked? Or do you end up feeling worse—frustrated and tired out by the constant nagging?

Perhaps it's time to refocus, reconnect, and redirect. After all, your WAF child is a part of you. What would it be like for you to treat your WAF child with kindness and love? You'd be firm too. You wouldn't let your WAF child sidetrack you or get you tangled up in wild antics.

You'd also take that child with you. You'd do what you set out to do when you left home. Are you willing to do the same with your anxiety child, taking that child with you as you drive into life?

PRACTICE ACTS OF KINDNESS AND TENDER LOVING CARE

We've found that people with anxiety disorders are very hard on themselves. They're often frustrated with how constricted their lives have become, and so they get caught in the self-blame game. "Why can't I snap out of it? I'm so silly. I know it's all in my head. I'm angry at myself and I'm angry at the world. I hate my panic attacks—I just hate them."

Many people with PTSD, in particular, struggle with anger and anxiety almost every day. They find themselves being hateful and angry at the perpetrator who abused them or the soldiers who committed war atrocities. They also blame themselves for not being able to "cope" better, or they wallow in shame, remorse, and regret for things they did or failed to do during the original traumatic event.

The answer to all this blaming and hating is loving-kindness and compassion. You've got to learn to be kinder to yourself first and then to others if you want to stop being at war with your WAFs and your life. Compassion and kindness make mindful acceptance vital and liberating.

Practicing acts of kindness toward yourself and others is a behavioral antidote to anxiety and anger. This practice will make it easier for you to stop fighting with your mind and body. It's a simple thing you can do to bring more peace and joy to your life.

How to Be Kind to Yourself

You'd like to be kinder to yourself, but maybe you don't know how to start. Here's something to do: make a commitment to practice at least one act of kindness toward yourself every day. Start each day with this commitment. Think about something you could do to be kind to yourself. These acts are particularly important when *TLC problems* arise—when you feel tired/stressed, lonely, and are craving things like nurturing, praise, stimulation, food, or drugs. These TLC problems can be undercut if you remind yourself to meet them with compassion and kindness wrapped in tender loving care.

Compassion and kindness are not feelings. They're actions. Acting with compassion toward yourself and others means acting in a caring and loving way. You stop being a whipping post. If you're ready to make such a commitment, write it down, or, better yet, share it with someone you care about.

You can attend to TLC problems by nurturing tender loving care toward yourself. This might involve taking time to practice meditation, reading a good book, going for a walk, listening to music, gardening, or preparing a good meal. You do this not because you deserve it. You do it "just because."

Valued living and being kind to yourself are related. Whenever you do something that moves you closer to one of your values, you're also being kind to yourself. Return to your Life Compass in chapter 13 and identify something you can do, however small, in the service of one of those values. Write it down in the space below. Then commit yourself to doing it. Give yourself tender loving care every day. Make it a priority.

_____

_____

Make Your Mind and Body a Kind Space

Remember the chessboard and volleyball exercises we talked about in chapter 11. In those exercises you learned that you can be a player with a stake in each battle or you can be the board that provides a space for the game. In the next exercise, we'd like to help you practice making that space a kind space. You can listen along using the audio version of the exercise on the CD.

EXERCISE: LOVING-KINDNESS PRACTICE

Loving-kindness is soft and gentle. It is how you might handle a newborn child or the way you might touch and hold something fragile. In those moments, you open up and handle what you're given with the greatest care. You can do the same with WAF thoughts, bodily discomfort, and painful memories too. The power of kindness cannot be underestimated.

Start by getting comfortable in your kind space. Sit upright, feet flat on the floor, arms and legs uncrossed, and palms, facing up or down, resting gently on your legs. Close your eyes and bring your attention to your breath as you've done with other exercises.

Continue to focus on each gentle inhale and exhale, simply noticing the rhythm of the rising and falling of your chest and belly. As you follow the soft flow of your breath, imagine a halo of kindness sweeping over you. It starts at your head and slowly moves, ebbing and flowing, past your face and then on to your chest and belly.

As it passes, silently say to yourself on each inhale, "May I meet my experience with kindness," "May I bring peace and gentleness to my experience," "I am complete," and "I am whole." Continue as the halo gradually sweeps down past your hips, over your knees, and flows over your toes. See if you can bring the intention of kind allowing to your experience as you imagine breathing in compassionate kindness.

As you do, bring to mind someone you know who is struggling and suffering. Perhaps it's a parent, a brother or sister, a friend, spouse, or coworker. It could be a child, an older person, or someone you've heard about in the news or on TV. See if you can imagine their suffering. Make them present with you now.

Now look into your heart and into your capacity for healing and kindness. Imagine that the person you are thinking about is in the room with you and that you could extend healing to them, that you could restore their mind, broken body, failings, hurts, struggles, and pain, and make them whole. Silently repeat, "I extend kindness and healing to you."

In your mind's eye, see yourself wiping away their tears and extending love. Open your arms and wrap that person in your kind embrace—extend your heart. Allow yourself to connect your kindness with that person. They are no longer alone. You are not alone. You are uniting with them in their suffering and in yours too. By your generous act, you are sharing your capacity for kindness and healing. Stay with them as long as you wish.

Continue to sit quietly with this moment in time. And when you are ready, gradually widen your attention to the sounds around you. Open your eyes with the intention to extend loving-kindness to yourself and others each moment of this day.

Kindness begets kindness. It's uplifting energy that will weaken the power of your judgmental WAF mind that's keeping you stuck. Kindness waters the seeds of compassion and acceptance in you. Many people find that their capacity for loving-kindness grows as they practice the loving-kindness meditation by bringing other people to mind, such as someone they may respect or like, someone they don't get along with particularly well, or someone they don't know all that well. You can do the same as you develop this important skill.

Practice Kindness with Your Wounds

Being kind also includes practicing acceptance and compassion toward your feelings, memories, and hurts. Many of us have old wounds from losses, unfair treatment by others, and sometimes even real abuse. When painful feelings, images, and memories come up, your first, instinctual response is to push them away. If you catch yourself doing that, please stop. This is a golden opportunity to embrace old hurts with compassion and acceptance.

Why should you do that? People who have been hurt continue to inflict pain on themselves and others because they haven't taken care of their wounds. They haven't allowed their wounds to heal. If you don't take care of your wounds, you may pass them on to your children, spouse, friends, colleagues at work, and other people in your life. Hurt can be recycled many times.

For a moment, think about what you would do if something was physically wrong with you, like a bleeding knee or a problem with your stomach, your back, or your teeth? We suspect that you'd stop what you were doing and attend to your bleeding wound or sick organ. You'd take really good care of them. That makes sense. We suggest you do the same with your open WAF wounds—all those feelings of fear, panic, worry, and shame, along with all the anger and blaming you inflict on yourself and dole out to others.

To break the cycle of anxiety avoidance and life constriction, you have to start by taking better care of yourself. You do that by practicing being kind to yourself and by embracing anxiety with compassion. You do this by no longer buying into all the thoughts your mind comes up with about you and your emotional pain. Just as with your physical organs, your anxiety and emotional pain are parts of you.

Even when you're in the throws of your WAFs, you can take good care of your anxiety. That's what embracing anxiety with compassion means.

You can take care of yourself, your anxieties, and your wounds by giving yourself loving-kindness. This is something you can learn to do. You don't need to rely on other people to do that for you. Thich Nhat Hanh (2001) developed a beautiful exercise to practice self-compassion. It is both powerful and simple. It shows you how you can take care of your WAFs as if they were your sick baby or child needing your love and attention.

EXERCISE: GIVING YOURSELF LOVING-KINDNESS

Remember when you were a little child and you had a fever? You felt bad. So a parent or caregiver came and gave you medicine. This may have helped, but it was nothing like having your mom there. Remember that you didn't feel better until your mother came and put her hand on your burning forehead? That felt so good! To you, her hand was like the hand of a goddess. When she touched you with her hand, freshness, love, and compassion penetrated into your body. The hand of your mother is alive in your own hand. Go ahead and touch your forehead with your hand and see that your mother's healing hand is still there. Allow the energy of your mother's loving and tender touch to radiate through your hand and into you. Bring that quality to your experience.

As with the finger-trap exercise, this is the time to take an unusual step and be open to what may happen. Here is what you can do: close your eyes, touch your forehead, and think of your mother's hand touching you when you were young and sick. The kindness of her hand is alive in yours. And you can give that kindness to yourself, right now and anytime, anywhere.

Practice Compassion with Anxiety

Another powerful way out of suffering and into happiness is to stop avoiding pain and chasing pleasure. This rat race is the root of much unhappiness. The path out of it is doing the opposite. You invite in what feels bad and give away what's good and joyful. You breathe in the discomfort and receive it and breathe out and away what you so desperately want and think will bring relief. You're doing this for every person out there, and in so doing, you're doing it for you.

If you let the words go—drop the story line—and just feel the discomfort and sit with it without all the holding and chasing, you share what we all share. That's what compassion really means. Experiencing this sense of shared humanity has tremendous healing power—as Pema Chödrön (2001) tells us, it's the path out of misery and into vitality.

Breathing in pain and breathing out relief is the basis of an ancient form of meditation known as Tonglen (meaning "giving and receiving"). Welcoming your pain and giving away good may strike you as odd. It goes against the grain. This is precisely why it can be so powerful. When you embrace what you don't like, you transform it. That transformation will release you from attachment to pleasure seeking, fear, and self-absorption, and it will nurture your capacity for love and compassion. The next exercise will help you develop this important skill.

EXERCISE: EMBRACING THE "BAD," GIVING AWAY THE "GOOD"

Start by getting yourself comfortable in a place where you'll be undisturbed for five to ten minutes or so. You may sit on the floor or in a chair. Sit upright with your palms up or down on your lap.

Now, close your eyes and gently guide your attention to the natural rhythm of your breath in your chest and belly. After a few moments, bring to mind something painful or hurtful, perhaps a recent event or a time in which you felt very anxious. Then, with your next inhale, visualize taking in that negativity and painful upset. Breathe in the discomfort with the thought in your mind that what you're feeling in this very moment is being felt by millions of people all over this world. You're not alone with this. This anxiety has been felt by countless numbers of people from the beginning of time.

Your intention here, for yourself and others, is for you and them to be free of the suffering, the struggle, blame, and shame that can happen with the pain that you and they experience. With that intention in mind, on each exhale, breathe out relief, joyfulness, and goodwill. Do it slowly with the natural rhythm of your breathing. Continue to connect with your pain as you breathe in, and with each out breath, expend goodwill and a wish that others may find relief from the suffering they get caught in when they experience hurt and discomfort.

If you find breathing in anxiety gets too heavy or tight, you can imagine breathing into a vast space, or that your heart is an infinite space. Imagine breathing into your heart, making it bigger and bigger with every out breath until there's enough space for all the worries, anxieties, and concerns. With each out breath, you're opening up your whole being so you no longer have to push the WAFs away—you're opening your heart to whatever arises.

If you find your mind wandering or you feel distracted, just kindly notice that and return your attention to the intention of welcoming in your pain and hurts, and releasing goodwill and kindness. Continue this practice of giving and receiving for as long as you wish.

Then, when you're ready, gradually widen your attention and gently open your eyes with the intention of bringing this skill of kind observing to your experiences throughout the day.

You can also practice Tonglen in everyday life. Whenever anxiety shows up, you can remind yourself, "Other people feel this too. I'm not alone with this." It will help ease the sense of isolation and burden of feeling that you're alone with your WAFs.

When you notice yourself getting anxious and not wanting to be anxious, you can practice on-the-spot Tonglen for all the people out there who, just like you, get caught in the struggle by pushing their discomfort away when they notice it. Right then, wherever you are, you can start breathing in—acknowledging the discomfort—and breathing out and giving away a sense of peace and calm. With every moment you're willing to stay with uncomfortable anxiety, you learn more and more not to fear it.

Practicing Forgiveness Is Kindness

Learning to forgive is the single most powerful way to soften the pull of your painful past. Studies report that the ability to forgive can be learned, and it improves health—physical, emotional, and spiritual. Those who learn this important skill report experiencing less hurt, stress, anger, depression, and illness, and more energy, hope, optimism, compassion, love, and a greater sense of well-being. These are the concrete benefits of forgiveness.

Many people think forgiving is a sign of weakness or that it means condoning or forgetting past wrongs, or ignoring hurt and pain. None of these are true. When Pope John Paul II met to forgive his assassin, he wasn't condoning the wrong that was done. Instead, he was extending mercy and compassion. He was letting go, and the assassin still sat in prison for his crime.

Forgiving is the most courageous and beneficial thing you can do for yourself. It's a gift to yourself. It's about letting go. It's not a feeling either. It means letting yourself off the hook. It's letting go of attachment to being a victim as well as the feelings of shame, anger, regret, and pain.

You and you alone can do this. And you do it for you because not doing it virtually guarantees that you will remain stuck, the victim, wanting and waiting for a resolution that may never come. Unforgivingness ultimately hurts you, not those who once wronged you.

Below we describe a brief exercise that outlines four steps on the path to learning forgiveness. We'll have another forgiveness exercise in chapter 17. The steps are as follows:

- **Step 1: Awareness**—waking up to hurt and pain as it is, without judgment or denial

- **Step 2: Separation**—softening using your Wise Mind while inviting healing and change

- **Step 3: Compassionate witness**—extending compassion to your experience and others

- **Step 4: Letting go and moving on**—releasing grudges and resentment that fan the flames of your suffering, and then moving forward in your life in directions you want to go

EXERCISE: LEARNING TO FORGIVE

Take a moment to reflect on some past event that you continue to recycle over and over again in your mind. Look for a situation or event that leaves you feeling angry, hurt, resentful, bitter, and demanding justice. Get a piece of paper and jot down the details of the past transgression. Make it as detailed as possible.

When you're ready, close your eyes and bring the event to mind. Really get into it as best you can. What happened? Who did the wrong—you or someone else? How were you or others hurt? What didn't you get then that you are longing for now? Allow yourself several minutes to really open up to this experience.

Become aware of the pain surrounding that past event. Allow yourself to experience the pain as it is. Where does it hurt now? See if you can face it squarely. What does it feel like? What does it look like?

Notice your mind linking your pain with judgment, blame, and negative evaluations. See if you can use your Wise Mind to separate the judgment from the pain you are having now. Notice judgment as judgment, blame as blame, and bitterness as bitterness, without engagement. Simply watch and separate the pain itself and the suffering from the evaluations of the pain.

See if you can step back even further as if you're watching this event play out on a giant movie screen. Imagine being in the audience, simply watching, as though you're someone seeing this drama unfold for the first time. See if you can open up your heart to be a compassionate witness to the actors in this scene. See who's doing the hurting. See who's receiving the hurt. See who's responsible for doing the hurting. See the person responsible for the felt pain, then and now.

Now kindly ask yourself this: who's responsible for letting go now? Who has control over that happening or not happening? Who's in control over the resentment you feel now? Who is getting hurt, right now, by holding on to the memory of the past wrong? Who has the power to let go and move on?

The answer is *you*. You can let go of holding on to the wish and hope for a resolution. You can take the energy and effort focused on resolving, fighting back, or getting even and put it to more vital use. You can bring kindness to your experience by facing your pain squarely for what it is. Own it because it is yours, and then choose to let it go.

If you're willing to let the resentment and rage go, then do that. If you're having trouble doing that, then think about who's getting hurt by holding on—is it you or the person that once wronged you? Imagine what you'd do with your mental time and energy if you were no longer consumed by resentment and recycled rage. What would you think about instead? What would you feel? What would you do?

Put Kindness Toward Others into Action

In addition to being kind to yourself, be mindful of any chance you get throughout your day to act in a kind and compassionate way toward others. These acts of kindness could take many forms. You might practice saying "Please," "Thank you," and "You're welcome" more often. You might open a door for someone, offer a helping hand, extend a smile to a stranger, or let a driver merge into traffic. Give a hug or a kiss to a loved one. Show understanding, compassion, and forgiveness when you feel hurt and the urge to strike back.

The point of these activities and other random acts of kindness is that you're doing something positive and personally uplifting for the sake of doing so—"just because." You're expressing the value of kindness and compassion. Doing so may feel contrived at first, but don't let this feeling get in the way of your commitment to act kindly. You don't need to wait to feel peaceful and loving before you decide to act in a kind and loving way. You can just do it regardless of what you feel.

Look for moments when you can share. Watch for times when you can show care and moments when you can offer gratitude or extend warmth. Look for times when you can offer hope, love, or a helping hand. Do this when you'd rather shut down, tune out, or explode. These are the moments when the benefits of practicing tender loving care with your hands, feet, and mouth are needed most and when they will benefit you and others most.

With practice, acts of kindness will become automatic and bring with them an increased sense of peace, love, and trust. You'll find that people will be more likely to gravitate in your direction when you practice acts of kindness. This outcome can only enrich your relationships. Be mindful, however, that you may not always get kindness in return. The point is that *you* are taking charge by being kind. This is something *you* can do.

Regardless of the target or the outcome, kindness is fundamentally about you! Nurture it. Develop it. Make it the core of your being and how you choose to live.

LIFE ENHANCEMENT EXERCISES

Expand the to-do list introduced in chapter 11. Practice nurturing tender loving care toward yourself and your WAFs:

- Starting today, and for the next seven days, do something kind for yourself every day—however small that something may be.

- In addition, be kind to your WAFs by practicing acceptance and compassion toward your feelings, thoughts, memories, and hurts. You can do this by practicing the Acceptance of Anxiety exercise (from chapter 14) and at least one of the Loving-Kindness exercises (from this chapter) at least once each day.

- Nurture your capacity for forgiveness too—let go of the resentment and regret associated with past wrongs committed by you or others.

- Integrate acceptance into your daily life by continuing to practice labeling of thoughts and feelings without getting tangled up in them. Whenever uncomfortable thoughts and feelings show up, notice them, label them, let them be, and move on with whatever you were doing. If the emotions are intense, take a moment to practice WAF surfing (described in chapter 14). Then move on.

THE TAKE-HOME MESSAGE

Although WAFs feel like monsters, they're more like kids. Like most kids, they respond better to tender loving care than to reprimands, rebukes, or harsh punishment. You can learn to bring more compassion to your worries, anxieties, and fears by practicing acceptance of your thoughts and feelings instead of trying to get rid of them. And you can practice kindness to yourself and others. Do this every day. Even small acts of kindness matter. Over time and with regular practice, compassion and kindness will become a habit. And they'll take the sting out of anxiety, panic, fear, and worry. This will make it easier for you to stay on the road to your Value Mountain without being steered off course.

Learning to Bring Compassion to My Anxiety

Points to Ponder: Anxiety need not be my enemy. I can learn to bring more compassion and kindness to myself and my experience. Kindness and compassion are shown by my actions. They will help me heal and move with my anxiety instead of remaining stuck, struggling with anxiety.

Questions to Consider: Am I willing to meet my WAF children with friendliness and compassion? Am I willing to give kindness and forgiveness to myself and others so that I can move on and reclaim my life?

CHAPTER 16

Developing Comfort in Your Own Skin

When we come to that compassionate awareness that is not afraid of the fear, that can embrace the fear, we are able to heal the wounds of the child and the adult and begin to live the lives we've always wanted to live. —Cheri Huber

Everything you've been learning in this book up until now has prepared you for this moment. To embrace, perhaps for the first time, the fears and anxieties that have kept you stuck for so long.

You might be thinking, "Oh, here it comes—they're going to ask me to face my fears." In a way, this is true, but this isn't about white knuckling your way into your discomfort for its own sake, or about proving something to yourself. This chapter is bigger than that. It's about facing your life—what you care about—while practicing staying with your discomfort just as it is. This is probably the kindest thing you can do for yourself.

And you won't be doing this naked, without any tools. You have the tools—skills to help you to make a choice to be kinder, more compassionate and mindful, and less prone to get caught up in struggle with your bodily discomfort. You've been practicing these skills up to this point in the book.

The exercises in this chapter are simply more opportunities to practice flexibility with and softness toward unpleasant bodily sensations that have tended to keep you stuck. In the next chapter, we'll help you approach mental barriers that feed the mind-body WAF connection. Take your time with the exercises in this chapter and the next.

Pain is part of living well. When you shut down to pain— you shut down to life.

FACING YOUR PAIN, LIVING YOUR LIFE

Pain is part of living well. When you shut down to pain, you shut down to life. When you open up to life, you must open up to pain in all its forms. This is how it works. To have it all, you must be willing to have it all—the good, unpleasant, and sometimes ugly.

We're pretty certain that your WAF bodily discomfort is linked with doing what you care about—living out your values. In fact, if you look closely, you'll see that as you take a step in a direction you want to go, you'll probably get something that you don't want to have—unpleasant bodily sensations. These sensations are the barriers we talked about in chapter 14.

The solution is simple—to move into your life, you need to let go of the urge to act on your WAF discomfort while moving into and with your feelings and bodily sensations, just as they are. This can be difficult to do, just like many other things in life that are potentially good for you. Think about that for a moment.

Recall some vital and important things that you do now and that were once difficult to do. Think simple and expand out. What was it like when you first learned how to eat with a fork and knife, or to use a toilet? How about when you first started learning your ABCs, writing letters of the alphabet and eventually your name? How about learning how to read or use money? Go further.

Consider the steps involved in first starting an exercise routine, playing an instrument, riding a bike, hitting a baseball, starting a career, driving a car, all the way up to navigating your daily routine and your varied roles as friend, teacher, partner, spouse, or parent, and more—learning to love, share, care, give, and forgive.

You should see that your life up until now has been a journey of small moments. The things that you do and want out of life often start out seeming difficult or impossible. And to do the things you want to do calls on you to move with and through difficult moments, often many times. Had you not done that, you might still be wearing a diaper, be illiterate, or need to be spoonfed by someone else. To get the life you want, you must open up to difficulty now and then.

When you witness and accept your WAF discomfort and hurt, you'll be moving with and through what may seem difficult too. As you do that, you'll be making room for compassion, kindness, and forgiveness. In the process, you'll continue to soften and learn several new things:

- You'll develop greater honesty about your experience. You'll learn to acknowledge bodily discomfort and other unpleasant sensations, without engagement, as you feel them.

- You'll nurture the courage to do nothing, to just sit with your WAF discomfort. This part is critical. You'll learn to stop running from yourself and you'll develop comfort in your own skin.

- You'll continue to develop your wise observer's perspective with your experience. Watching without judgment and engagement will allow you to disentangle yourself from what your mind and body are doing. This will give you control to act in ways that matter to you rather than reacting without control. This stance will free you to let go and move forward in your life.

So when your mind gives you "This is difficult" or "This is too much," kindly recognize those thoughts as a signal that you are on the path of something new and potentially vital. To help you along, we'll give you lots of opportunities for practice in this chapter and the next using FEEL—Feeling Experiences Enriches Living.

Watching without judgment & engagement will allow you to disentangle yourself from what your mind and body are doing.

FEEL EXERCISES

FEEL exercises have one purpose only—to help you engage your life to the fullest. They're a natural extension of the exercises you've been doing up to this point.

Here, you'll get a chance to practice being an observer of your WAF bodily sensations, just noticing and experiencing them as they are while meeting them with a quality of kindness and compassion. When you do that, you'll be defusing the urge to avoid, run, or fix what your body is doing. Instead, you'll have the room to focus on what you want to do, what you want to be about, and where you want to go. As you get better at feeling, your life will grow.

FEEL Steps, in a Nutshell

The steps are straightforward. The first step to start any of the exercises is to flip your willingness switch to on—fully. Remember, you can control this switch. And unless you choose to turn it on, you'll continue to get what you've always got.

The second step is to think about what you care deeply about—your values. Having your sights on your values—what you want to do and where you want to go—will allow you to practice a new response to the bodily discomfort that has stood between you and your life for so long. You'll want to have your Valued Directions Worksheet and Life Compass handy and look for places where bodily discomfort has stood between you and your valued intentions.

The third step involves playing with exercises in which you gently bring on bodily sensations that normally send you into a tailspin and keep you stuck. As you practice just noticing the bodily discomfort without acting on it, and bring to the experience a sense of kind allowing, you'll be letting yourself off the hook. This part calls on your Wise Mind and mindful acceptance skills.

To sum up, FEEL exercises involve you making a choice for willingness, experiencing your bodily discomfort with gentle kindness and allowing—always with an eye on the things you care about and want to do. You'll have opportunities to create and watch bodily discomfort show up and then to practice letting that discomfort be as it is. As you do that, you'll be learning new skills that will transform discomfort *difficulty* into discomfort *vitality*.

Importance of Practice and Pacing

All of the exercises require practice, practice, practice. You'll be walking into familiar territory—you know the discomfort. You know what's there. What's new is this: approaching your dark discomfort with the bright light of a kinder and more compassionate response. This more skillful way of relating needs to be nurtured—and it can happen over time.

Take it slow. Don't rush through the exercises. It's best to repeat them several times in one sitting and over several days. Practice at home first. Find a place in your home to do the practice and make it your kind space. As you develop the skills, you can put that practice into action in your daily life. Let willingness and compassion be your guide.

It's okay if your willingness switch seems to toggle on and off during the exercises, at least early on. The important thing is that you recognize that and are willing to keep going the next time. When you are able to keep your willingness switch in the on position with minimal or no disruption, then you're ready to move on to another exercise.

A Word of Caution

We're pretty certain that you'll experience some discomfort as you do the exercises. And we're pretty certain that your old history will be right in your face—urging you, begging you, to stop, pull out, or run. The results of many research studies show that if you stick with the exercises and allow your old history to do its thing without doing what it says, then you'll get some relief too.

That relief may take several forms. Some people experience it as peace. Others report feeling less anxious or fearful. Many more feel like a burden has been lifted. They tell us the discomfort is still there once in a while. And sometimes that discomfort is very intense. But underneath all of that, they notice a profound shift in the experience of WAF discomfort. They are no longer fighting with it. And they notice that letting go of the struggle with their bodily discomfort has given them relief in the form of newfound freedom.

Don't do the FEEL exercises for the purpose of chasing emotional goals—like feeling less anxious, keeping panic at bay, or stopping your mind from doing its thing. We talked about these familiar dead-end goals early on. They are more of the same stuff that hasn't worked. Don't fool yourself into thinking that freedom from fear will work now.

The goal of FEEL exercises is to help you develop comfort and kindness in your own skin—to take the stance of being the chessboard or volleyball court and not of being one of the struggling teams. This shift in perspective will free you up to live better with whatever your body and mind may be doing.

Anxiety will take a backseat because you'll be spending less time with your WAF discomfort *and* more time focused on and engaging your life *with* your discomfort. That's how it works. That's how you get your life back. And that's the path to thinking and feeling better too. You can't experience peace so long as you remain in a fight with your mind and body.

FEEL EXERCISES FOR YOUR BODILY DISCOMFORT

The exercises below will help you practice being with and moving with the barriers you listed on your Valued Directions Worksheet and the Life Compass in real-life situations. Before going on, take a moment to review these forms and look for places where avoidance or struggle with your bodily discomfort has stood between you and what you wanted to do—your values.

We've found that people benefit most when they do all of the exercises. The reason is that each exercise provides you with skills to undo potential barriers. And doing all of them gives you a chance to practice developing flexibility with different forms of bodily discomfort.

The form below is to help you track your progress with the exercises. You'll see that it is easy to fill out. And it gives you a nice opportunity to chart your progress each and every time you do one of the exercises. You'll find versions of the form on the CD. You'll want to print several copies and have them handy for your practice.

You can't experience peace as long as you remain in a fight with your mind + body.

FEEL* BODILY DISCOMFORT FORM

Date: _____ Time: _____ A.M./P.M

0	1	2	3	4	5	6	7	8	9	10
Low					Moderate					Extreme

Exercise	Sensation's Intensity (0–10)	Anxiety Level (0–10)	Willingness to Experience (0–10)	Struggle with Experience (0–10)	Avoidance of Experience (0–10)
Staring at a spot					
Spinning					
Head between legs					
Shaking head					
Breath holding					
Breathing through straw					
Breathing fast/deeply					
Fast walking					
Jogging in place					
Climbing steps					
Staring at self in mirror					
Other _____					

* Feeling Experience Enriches Living

How to Do the FEEL Exercises in Seven Simple Steps

All of the FEEL exercises follow the format below. You'll want to have a watch or clock close by as you do them. Remember to apply all of the skills you have been learning up to this point as you do each exercise. Here are the steps:

1. **Identify a valued domain.** Get an index card or small piece of paper and write down one of your important values. Before each practice, take a moment to connect with that value and keep it in mind as you do the exercises. Think of the things you want to do in one important valued area. Later, you can also switch to another valued domain and repeat each FEEL exercise with your intentions in mind for that area.

2. **Practice a FEEL exercise.** Start the exercise and continue it for thirty to sixty seconds after you first notice sensations of discomfort, and five minutes beyond the point at which you might experience disturbing thoughts or images.

3. **Apply your mindful acceptance skills.** Continue to simply observe, with kindness and gentleness, for one to two minutes after you stop each exercise. Simply observe and make space for what you're experiencing.

4. **Chart your progress.** Use the FEEL Bodily Discomfort Form to record your reactions and progress. Complete the form right after you do each exercise.

5. **Reflect on your practice.** Gently reflect on the exercise you just did. Look at your ratings. Did you experience high levels of unwillingness, struggle, or avoidance? If so, try repeating the exercise again more slowly. As you do, watch for sticky judgmental thoughts like "This isn't working" or "I can't stand this anxiety anymore." See if you can simply notice these thoughts from your Wise Mind perspective. The next time you do the exercise, approach it from an observer perspective, and when sticky thoughts show up, notice them, and gently say to yourself, "*I am having the thought* that this isn't working" or "*I am having the thought* that I can't stand this anxiety anymore" or "*I am having the thought* that this is too much." Or simply label them all as "thinking."

6. **Repeat FEEL exercises.** Practice is critical for skill development. So repeat the exercises during your home practice sessions. Shoot for at least two to three repetitions of an exercise per practice session when you start out. Allow yourself a mindful rest period between exercises where you can sit comfortably and just notice your thoughts and sensations as they are.

7. **Review your ratings on your FEEL Bodily Discomfort Form.** You'll be ready to move on to a new exercise when you notice that your willingness ratings hover at 7 or higher and your struggle and avoidance levels are at 3 or lower. These ratings are your benchmark for progress. This is why recording your reactions is so important.

Keep the seven FEEL steps handy as you first do the exercises. Commit them to memory.

PHYSICAL HEALTH CHECK

If you haven't done so already, do check in with your doctor to see that you are physically able to do the exercises. Most involve mild-to-moderate physical activity. If you suffer from any of the following health conditions, we strongly suggest that you *not* do the FEEL exercises until you've talked with your doctor.

- Asthma or lung problems
- A heart condition
- Pregnancy

- Epilepsy
- Physical injuries (neck, joint, back)
- History of fainting/low blood pressure

Should your doctor recommend against you doing one or more of these exercises, you can still practice the ones that have been approved for you. If your doctor recommends against all of these exercises, you can still practice your mindfulness skills and taking the observer perspective when you experience intense physical sensations as part of your regular daily activities. Remember that the goal is to practice staying with discomfort in all its forms without getting tangled up in it, whenever and in whatever form the discomfort may take.

EXERCISES: BEING WILLINGLY DIZZY

This set of exercises will help you practice mindful acceptance with sensations of dizziness, unsteadiness, or vertigo. The experience of dizziness will be different for everyone. It's an experience that occurs when you move your head and body through space at a rate too fast for your brain's balance system to keep up with.

Some people experience light-headedness, a sense of imbalance or floating, and nausea too. These are all expected reactions. And there are several ways that you can create them yourself. Here are some FEEL exercises to do just that:

- **Staring at a spot.** Position yourself about one to two feet from a nearby wall. Find a small spot on the wall and stare at it for about two minutes. Try to resist blinking as much as you can. Then, turn away quickly and focus on something else in the distance.

- **Spinning.** Using a swivel chair, spin yourself round and round as quickly as you can by pushing off of the floor as often as needed. Do this with your eyes open. You can then vary this by spinning while standing up with arms outstretched.

- **Head between legs.** Get in a sitting position. Place your head between your legs (at the knees) and hold that position for about thirty seconds. Then sit upright quickly. Do this gently if you have a history of back problems. You can play with this exercise by repeating it from a standing position.

- **Shaking head.** From a standing position, move your head back and forth and from side to side, slowly, with your eyes open. Do that for at least thirty seconds or until the sensations of dizziness are first noticed. Again, do this in a way that is steady and not too vigorous. Then stop and focus straight ahead.

To start, get set up in your kind space where you won't be disturbed and have a clock or watch nearby. Be sure to position yourself in a spot where you won't fall or hurt yourself during the practice. Select the first dizziness activity and then follow FEEL steps 1 to 7 as you practice. Stay with and repeat that exercise until you notice that you are able to be with any discomfort without needing to stop or resolve it (willingness ratings at 7 or higher, and struggle and avoidance levels at 3 or lower). Then, move on to the next dizziness exercise and so on.

It is best to keep your eyes open as you do the exercises. It's fine if you need to sit down between practice sessions. Just watch that you don't immediately go to sitting or lying flat on the floor as a default coping strategy. If you can remain in a standing or sitting position while dizzy, you'll notice that the sensations will pass without you having to do anything about them.

Being willingly dizzy may have been hard for you. The experience can readily make anyone feel like they are losing touch with reality. The experience is not harmful to you. The discomfort does pass. Congratulate yourself for practicing a new response to it.

EXERCISES: BEING WILLINGLY OUT OF BREATH

The exercises in this section allow you to practice making room for discomfort with the experience of feeling out of breath, short of breath, or with sensations coming from your heart and chest, such as heart flutters and chest tightness. Along with those sensations, some people experience light-headedness, dizziness, a sense of detachment from themselves, blurred vision, tingling, or numbness in areas of the body.

These experiences are normal. They happen as a consequence of what we do—many activities have the potential to bring them on. They are a natural by-product of our normal blood-gas balance getting out of sync, specifically the balance of oxygen and carbon dioxide. Your body is set up to restore this blood-gas balance without effort on your part.

You can willingly bring on these sensations with any of the FEEL exercises below:

- **Breath holding.** For this exercise, simply take a deep breath and hold it for as long as you can. Start by doing the exercise while sitting down with your eyes open. You can then vary it by doing it longer the next time, while sitting, and then standing with eyes open or closed. Play with it. Be willingly creative with your discomfort.

- **Breathing through a small straw.** For this FEEL exercise, you'll need to get a hold of some inexpensive small- or large-bore straws. During the practice, breathe through the straw while you pinch your nostrils closed with your free hand. See if you can do it for at least thirty seconds the first time, and work up from there. You can vary this exercise, as you may have done with breath holding, by doing it with eyes closed or open, while standing or sitting, or even while walking up and down stairs. The important thing is to take it slow. When you can be with the discomfort without pulling out from it, you are ready to gently up the ante in terms of length or new variations.

- **Overbreathing.** Just about everyone has had the experience of being out of breath. When you breathe too quickly or too fast and deeply, you take in too much oxygen relative to the carbon dioxide in your body. The technical label for this is *hyperventilation*. Though you may typically experience this response as beyond your control, you can bring it on by taking rapid inhales and exhales at a pace of about one breath every two seconds. When you first do this exercise, start in a sitting position. Take in a deep breath and then exhale fully, and repeat. Use a watch with a second hand and see if you can do it for at least sixty seconds at first and then work your way up to two or three minutes. This exercise is a powerful way to create a host of uncomfortable sensations that can keep you stuck and off track. And it is a great way to practice a new, more mindful response to them.

Before moving on, take a moment to review your practice and your progress on the FEEL Sensations Record Forms. Are you making a conscious choice to turn on your willingness switch? Are you meeting the discomfort that you are producing with a new, less engaged, and softer response? As you did the exercises, were you keeping your values, and living well, in focus? Take stock. There's no need to rush. And it's okay if this doesn't come easy. Be kind and patient with yourself. These small moments will add up to something new in your life.

EXERCISES: BEING WILLINGLY AEROBIC

Engaging your life requires action in the form of aerobic activity. If you've avoided activities, exercise, and the like because of the potential for WAF discomfort, then it's time to practice willingness by deliberately moving with physical arousal that must happen within your body as you get moving. You'll see that there are many ways you can do that, and most have the added benefit of being good for your health. Here are a few:

- **Fast walking.** Walking engages your entire body. And it's a great way to practice making space for bodily discomfort. You can do this exercise indoors or outside. Start slow and work up to a fast and comfortable pace. As we describe in FEEL steps 1 to 7, allow enough walking time so that you're able to notice and experience bodily WAF discomfort. It's best to do this exercise without other distractions (such as listening to music). When you can willingly be with your body while walking, you can then add the headphones.

- **Jogging in place.** This will get your heart and respiratory system going. And it can be practiced in your kind space at home. Let FEEL steps 1 to 7 be your guide.

- **Climbing steps.** Simply go up and down a few steps, over and over again, until you begin to notice bodily discomfort. You can then increase the number of steps and duration of practice (such as two steps, five steps, ten steps, a flight or several flights of stairs).

- **Other aerobic exercises.** The list of possible aerobic exercises is only limited by your imagination. For instance, you could do aerobic FEEL exercises while doing household chores like vacuuming, cleaning, mowing the lawn, or raking the yard—anything that gets your body going. You might apply them in the context of swimming, going for a hike, shopping, running errands, sexual activity, or taking a bike ride. Just follow FEEL steps 1 to 7 as you play with the possibilities.

All of the aerobic FEEL exercises get you out and moving. And all are good for you in more than one way. They'll buy you a renewed sense of freedom, increase your vitality, range of options, and more. Remember to keep your values in view as you move into your discomfort.

EXERCISE: BEING WILLINGLY PRESENT WITH YOURSELF

Most of us don't like what we see when we look at ourselves in the mirror. There's always something about our bodies that could be different, better, or that we'd like to keep just as it is. The same is true of our sense of who we are—the part of us that is more than our hands, eyes, breasts, hips, or feet. It can be uncomfortable to see yourself exposed, just as you are. Learning to be with yourself, just as you are, involves embracing your vulnerabilities and imperfections. This skill is particularly important in your interactions with other people.

This exercise involves looking at yourself in front of a full-length mirror for two to five minutes or so. It's a bit different than the earlier exercises because it'll bring up many things for you, some of them uncomfortable. The exercise is more powerful if you can do it undressed and fully exposed.

Start by standing fully naked in front of a mirror so that you can see your entire body. Take a moment to look at yourself, really look. What do you see? What's it like to stand with yourself, unmasked, just as you are? Just notice any sensations coming from your body. See yourself from a kind perspective—there's nothing to be fixed, no need to hide anything. You are you.

Then shift your attention to your head and face. Notice the top of your head—your hair and skin. What does it really look like? Study it, noticing the textures, shape, and colors. Then gradually move to your face—eyes, nose, mouth, and cheeks. See if you can look closely into the perfection of your eyes—the colors, depth, and textures. Are those eyes something to be disliked or hated? What do you want to do with your seeing eyes, hearing ears, or your lips and mouth? See if you can allow yourself to be with your experience and let your mind do its own thing.

Then gradually move your attention to the area just below your chin. Slowly scan the midsection of your body—inside and out. What do you see as you gently focus on your shoulders, chest, belly, and each arm and hand? What do these parts of your body look like? Notice colors, textures, shapes, contours, and sensations from this region of your body.

Each is a part of you. Each has its own story to tell. What is your mind telling you about them now? Perhaps there is regret, shame, embarrassment, humiliation, or thoughts such as "too big, too small," "ugly," "beautiful," "wrinkled," "smooth," "attractive," or "unattractive." What are you experiencing on the inside? Can you be with your body and mind just as they are—just as you are? Must you hide from yourself? Allow yourself time to just notice the labels your mind may be giving you and then see if you can focus back on the raw, unedited experience of you.

Continue your body scan slowly as you move your attention down to your feet and toes. Notice any inner discomfort that may show up. See if you can be with your discomfort as you spend this time with you. Is there anything about you that must be fixed?

Allow yourself to be with you just as you are—whole . . . complete . . . unique . . . perfectly imperfect . . . and vulnerable . . . like everyone else.

WHEN *FEELING* BODILY DISCOMFORT GETS TOUGH

This section is for times when you find yourself experiencing high levels of unwillingness, struggle, or the urge to avoid or stop your practice. This isn't a time to cave in to what your mind might be feeding you. What you need to do here is to take your practice more slowly and with greater simplicity of focus. So instead of being with the entire experience, bring your kind attention to two or three bodily sensations, one at a time.

EXERCISE: STAYING WITH INTENSE BODILY DISCOMFORT

Start with one bodily sensation that is particularly difficult for you. As you bring your attention to this sensation, simply acknowledge it—"There is tension," "There is fast breathing," "There is my heart beating," or "There is dizziness, light-headedness, or the sensation of heat or cold."

Acknowledge the presence of the discomfort, stay with it, breathe with it, bring kindness to it, and open up to it. As in the Chinese Finger Trap and Tonglen exercises, this is the perfect time to lean into the discomfort and invite it in rather than struggle with it.

If you need to, you can slow the process down even more. To do that, close your eyes for a moment, allowing _____ [insert the uncomfortable sensation] to be what it is—a feeling in your body, nothing more and nothing less. Ask yourself a few key questions:

■ Is this something I need to push away from, or can I acknowledge its presence and make room for it? Can I make space for it?

■ What does this sensation really feel like? Where does it start and where does it end?

- Must this particular feeling be my enemy, or can I just have it as a feeling, a sensation?

- Is this sensation something I must not or cannot have? Even if my mind tells me that I can't have it, am I willing to open up a space for it in my heart?

- Is this something I absolutely must struggle with, or is there room inside me to feel all that and stay with it? Can I make my inside space a kind space?

As you make space for each sensation, one by one, you may notice that your mind is feeding you all sorts of labels—old F-E-A-R (False Evidence Appearing Real) labels—like "dangerous," "getting worse," or "out of control." When that happens, simply thank your mind for such labels and then gently shift your attention back to watching and noticing with gentle curiosity, openness, and compassion.

This exercise is a good reminder that you can control where you put your attention and to choose to meet your discomfort with a quality of softness instead of hardness. You don't need to like what you are feeling in order to be willing to have it.

You may also reframe your "Don't do it" mind by using some of the mindfulness strategies you were learning in the previous chapters, and those metaphors and exercises that you learned to help you move with barriers. For instance, this is the time to practice getting off your but(t) by transforming "I want to get better BUT . . . this is too hard . . . too much . . . too difficult" into a more honest and correct statement, like "I want to get better AND I'm thinking this is too hard." Remember that you drive your Life Bus!

LIFE ENHANCEMENT EXERCISES

For the next two weeks, commit to making the following activities a priority on your to-do list:

- Practice the FEEL exercises in this chapter for your bodily discomfort. If possible, do some every day. Make sure you record your commitment and progress with them.

- Practice the Acceptance of Anxiety exercise (introduced in chapter 14) once a day with or without the CD.

- Practice mindfulness and observer skills when anxiety shows up during daily life activities, and don't leave out your practice of loving-kindness and acts of tender loving care.

THE TAKE-HOME MESSAGE

Facing your discomfort and letting it go are two necessary steps out of anxiety and into a more vital life. Developing comfort in your own skin is something you can choose to do—anytime, anywhere. You need to practice this important skill—it needs to be nurtured. When you choose to be with your WAF discomfort, just as it is, you are letting yourself off the hook. Situations or triggers that evoke discomfort—many of them associated with what you care about in life—will be less likely to get you sidetracked from what you want to do and where you want to go. This discomfort vitality is how you'll get your life back. Look for it instead of waiting for it to look for you. Practice and play with the exercises.

Facing My WAF Discomfort Is Vital and Liberating

Points to Ponder: It's easy to duck, run, and hide from bodily discomfort. The harder and more vital path is to face my discomfort openly and honestly for what it is—plain old physical, mental, and emotional pain. Approaching my discomfort with kindness and compassion will result in discomfort vitality and freedom from fear.

Questions to Consider: Am I willing to experience unpleasant bodily sensations and not let them stand between me and what I want to do? Am I willing to face my discomfort as it is, accepting myself with all my flaws, weaknesses, and vulnerabilities?

CHAPTER 17

Developing Comfort with Your Judgmental Mind

There are only two ways to handle tense situations: you can change them, or you can change the way you look at them. There is enlightenment to be had in changing the way you look at things. —Paul Wilson (1996)

Your mind can be your greatest friend and your worst enemy. It all depends on what you do with it. There's nothing packed between your ears that can do you harm. Thoughts are just thoughts, ethereal, without form or substance. Things that you might imagine or visualize in your mind are like that too. They can seem quite real, but when you look at them, you'll find that there really isn't much to them at all.

This chapter is an opportunity for more growth and change, a chance to expand your practice by stepping back and watching your critical mind for what it is—a machine whose job it is to produce thoughts, images, memories, judgments, and evaluations (more thoughts), and to connect them with you, your body, your experiences, and your actions. Often these body-action-mind (BAM) connections can serve you well: they help you do what you care about doing. At other times, they can keep you stuck—BAM!—not doing what you care about.

Using your Wise Mind skills will help you see that these barriers to your life are really not barriers at all. You have a choice to do something else when your mind baits you with fuel for your suffering. Practicing compassion with your catastrophic mind is a powerful way to defuse all this activity and give you clarity and freedom to make more vital choices and take more vital actions. This is what this chapter is about.

Practicing compassion w/ your catastrophic mind

YOUR MIND MACHINE

Your mind is constantly at work, producing a never-ending stream of thoughts. It creates. It evaluates. It solves problems. It helps you make sense of your experience. And it can create futures that haven't happened or pull you into a past that once was. It is the instrument of love and kindness and the fuel for anxiety, hatred, blame, and self-loathing. This is what a mind does. It's remarkable, really.

Your mind machine will always be doing its thing so long as you are alive. Yet you have choices in how you respond to it. You don't have to buy into everything that your mind does. You can step back and watch. You don't have to take the bait.

The exercise below, shared with us by ACT colleague Richard Whitney, will give you a better sense of what we mean.

EXERCISE: UNHOOKING YOUR JUDGMENTAL MIND

Our minds work like a good fly fisher whose job it is to catch weary trout by managing to trick them into taking the bait. Good fly fishers take time to match their artificial flies to the insects that trout are feeding on. And they carefully present those flies with each cast. When they get it right, the trout can't tell the difference between a real insect and the fake fly. The trout sees it floating by, buys that the fly is real, bites, and gets hooked. The trout then finds itself in a fight for its life.

Here, let's just imagine that one of those trout is you. Just like a skilled fly fisher, your mind creates thoughts, worries, and images that look like carefully crafted flies—just the ones you will bite on. Your mind casts them out onto the stream of life, again and again, here, there, and just about anywhere. They seem so real to you that you "buy" them.

So you bite and get hooked. Perhaps it's on the "Wingless Nutcase" or "Blue-Winged Panicker" or the "Soft-Hackled Worrier." You may even get snared by the "Hopeless Dun," "Out-of-Control Dragonfly," or the "Mad-and-Angry Streamer." Once you're hooked, there's nothing left to do but struggle. The struggle sets the hook deep. You're now in a fight for your life, being pulled in directions you don't want to go.

There's one important difference between a fly fisher and your mind: your mind can only tie flies on barb-less hooks. Your mind will *tell* you there is a barb on the hook and that you can't get off, and it also feels like you can't get off. But if you pause from the struggle and observe the hook more closely, you can see that the hook really has no barbs. You can let go of the hook.

As you swim in the stream of life, flies are floating by on the surface all the time. As you get better at recognizing them as barbless hooks—"Oh, that's just another WAF fly floating by; I don't have to bite"—you'll get hooked less often. At other times, your mind will trick you again, and you'll bite. Getting hooked once in a while is part of being human. The skill is in noticing that you've been hooked. Once you do that, you can then make a choice to let go and move on.

Thoughts Are Just Words Too

Our minds tend to take words literally, and before we know it, the thought has become the "real thing" in our mind—no longer just a thought or words. If we can step back a little and begin to notice the thought as just a bunch of words, we can open our minds to more than the automatic conclusion we draw from those words.

This next exercise, inspired by an activity developed by our colleagues Matthew McKay and Catharine Sutker (2007), will help you see for yourself that thoughts are just words.

EXERCISE: DEMOTING YOUR WAF MIND PLAYFULLY

Let's start with the word "spider." When you think "spider," what does it look like in your mind? Can you see it crawling? You may even feel a little anxious or disgusted if spiders scare you in real life. Now sit somewhere near a clock. Say that word "spider" out loud, over and over, as fast as you can: "Spider, spider, spider. . . ." Do it for forty seconds and no longer.

When you're done, reflect on what happened to the meaning of the word after forty seconds. Did it still make you feel creepy (if you did feel creepy) and did it continue to summon the image of the spider? Did the words start running together? For many people, the word just starts to sound like an odd sound—"ider, ider, ider . . ."—and the meaning dissolves during those forty seconds.

This is a useful exercise for helping you see that the products of your judgmental mind can create an illusion of WAF monsters that are really not monsters at all. The monsters are words, linked with images and sounds, and with meanings that we assign to them. When you understand that about language, you can alter your relationship with your unpleasant thoughts, feelings, and images.

Right now, go back to your Valued Directions Worksheet and Life Compass that you worked on in chapter 13. Look at one of your important values and the WAF barriers that seem to stand in the way. Select one barrier and give it a one-word name—like "worry," "panic," "anxiousness," "aloneness," "space," "airplane," "sadness," "death," "dirtiness," "sickness," "heights," "crashes," "crowdedness," or the like. You may also bring to mind a negative word that you think about yourself, like "unattractive," "stupid," or "boring." Or perhaps it's a painful image that seems seared in your mind's eye.

Now say that word out loud as fast as you can for about forty seconds. Does it still sound as believable? Can you see how it's also just a word, a sound with no meaning or truth?

You can create even more space by doing the following: Say the thought out loud and *slowly*, like "woooooorrrrrryyyy," "stuuuuupid," or "unreeeeeal." Say it in another voice—as a child or an old person, as Minnie Mouse or Donald Duck, as someone intoxicated, or as a grumpy person. Notice what happens as you add a playful quality to the thoughts.

To add another layer of play, you can put your thought to music. Take the thought and sing it to yourself. Put it to the melody of a favorite holiday tune, children's song, or whatever song you'd like. Start with something simple like "Jingle Bells" or "Row, Row, Row Your Boat." See what happens to the thought as you put it to music.

This is a powerful exercise. You can do it anytime or anywhere. As you practice it, you will develop your capacity to get unhooked and to see thoughts, evaluations, and the stories you may tell yourself as just more thoughts. Some of it might even make you laugh.

Your Mind Machine and Your Values

We said that your mind can be your worst enemy and your greatest friend. The way to tell the difference is by first noticing what your mind is telling you and then asking yourself this: "If I listen and do what my inner voice tells me right now, will I do more or less with my life in this moment? What

> You can choose to stay hooked or let go.

does my past experience tell me?" If the answer is "less" and you do what your mind says, you won't move forward. You'll remain hooked and struggling.

So what are you to do? The answer is to do something radically different than you have done before. This means watching, with mindful compassion, your mind's hooks and choosing to let them be just thoughts, a brief moment in time, not nets that keep you trapped. The exercises below will help you do more of that.

FEEL EXERCISES TO UNHOOK YOUR JUDGMENTAL MIND

The FEEL exercises below build on what you've been practicing in chapter 16. If you need to, go back and review the basic FEEL steps and guidelines. The only difference here is that you'll be practicing being with your judgmental mind—your WAF thoughts, images, memories.

You'll want to be mindful of the thoughts, images, or memories that you listed as barriers to your values. So take a moment to review your Valued Directions Worksheet and the Life Compass. Look for places where avoidance or struggle with your mind has stood between you and what you wanted to do—your values.

As you did in chapter 16, begin each FEEL practice by bringing an important value area to mind. Put that value in writing on an index card and list some of your behavioral intentions too—the things you'd like to do in that area. Connect with what the card says and keep it close by as a reminder of why you're doing the exercises. Let your willingness switch be your guide!

You'll expand your skill base most when you do all of the exercises. It's fine if just a few exercises seem to resonate with you. To get to that point, though, you'll need to allow yourself time with each of them. So we encourage you to work with all the exercises.

You can use the form below to chart your progress with the FEEL Thought and Imagery exercises. You'll see that it's similar to the FEEL Bodily Discomfort Form you used in chapter 16. You'll also find an electronic version of the form on the CD. Print several copies and have them handy.

FEEL* THOUGHT AND IMAGERY FORM

Date: _____   Time: _____ A.M./P.M

0	1	2	3	4	5	6	7	8	9	10
Low					Moderate					Extreme

Exercise	Sensation's Intensity (0–10)	Anxiety Level (0–10)	Willingness to Experience (0–10)	Struggle with Experience (0–10)	Avoidance of Experience (0–10)
Demoting mind play	_____	_____	_____	_____	_____
Bubble wand	_____	_____	_____	_____	_____
Kind allowing images	_____	_____	_____	_____	_____
Candle of forgiveness	_____	_____	_____	_____	_____
Leaves on stream	_____	_____	_____	_____	_____
Other _____	_____	_____	_____	_____	_____
Other _____	_____	_____	_____	_____	_____

* Feeling Experience Enriches Living

FEEL Exercise for Nagging Worries and Doubts

The exercises in this section are meant to help you get back behind the wheel, driving your Life Bus in directions you want to go. These exercises build on everything you've been learning up to this point in the book. They provide you with opportunities to stay with your judgmental mind and do something kinder with it.

The next exercise is quite long, and it's one of the most important ones in this book. Set aside ten to fifteen minutes for doing it. We recommend that you start by listening to the audio recording of the exercise on the CD. You can follow along, or you can read through the script a few times first and then close your eyes and do the exercise.

EXERCISE: BUBBLE WAND

Go ahead and get in a comfortable position in your chair. Sit upright with your feet flat on the floor, your arms and legs uncrossed, and your hands resting in your lap (palms up or down, whichever is more comfortable). Close your eyes and take a few deep breaths. Allow your body to rest without drifting off to sleep. Bring an intention of kindness to this practice.

Now bring into your awareness a recent situation where you found yourself in a bout of endless worry. Perhaps it's a situation you know all too well or one from your LIFE forms over the past weeks.

Really work to bring this experience into your full awareness and right into the room with you. Make it as real as possible. Continue to visualize the situation until you can really notice a wave of unpleasant changes sweeping over your body and mind. Allow yourself to connect with the experience. Relive every bit of it as best as you can. Keep doing so until you're at a point where you feel taken over by anxiety and tension and a strong desire to do something about it.

Now, we want you to go more deeply into this experience. Imagine that you have a large bubble wand like the kind that kids sometimes play with at the beach or in the park. Go ahead and fill the wand with bubble soap. Then look within you and notice all the elements of the unsettling experience. Start by locating one of the most obvious judgments or worrisome thoughts.

For each one, take your bubble wand and sweep it through each worry thought. Trap each thought in a giant bubble. Then, one by one, notice each thought in its bubble and label it as you watch each drift upward in the gentle breeze—"There goes worrying . . . what if-ing . . . second-guessing . . . judging . . . blaming . . . shaming . . . criticizing." Keep watching the bubbles go higher and higher until they're out of sight. Then take a few slow, deep breaths.

Allow yourself to go more deeply into this experience. See if you can find the next thought underneath the first worry. For example, if you worry about not having enough money to make ends meet, then you might gently ask, "And if that were true, then what?" Watch what your mind comes up with. Perhaps it's the thought "I won't be able to pay my bills." Notice that thought and place it in a giant bubble and watch it float upward. Follow this with "And then what?" Keep going with an attitude of gentle curiosity and kind allowing.

As you go more deeply into your worry, you'll likely notice more physical bodily sensations of anxiety: heart pounding in the chest, feeling shaky, trembling hands, shortness of breath, feeling hot, or the sensation of an upset stomach. There's tension everywhere. You may feel like you're about to pop. As that unfolds, notice your impulses to respond and label these sensations one at a time: "There is my impulse to shout . . . run away . . . shut down . . . struggle . . . make a fist . . . lash out . . . point my finger . . . or stop this exercise."

Your task now is both simple and difficult: Do nothing! Sit with these thoughts, sensations, and impulses. Feel the restless energy in this situation. Sitting still and doing nothing is the last thing you want to do, and it's the wisest thing you can do: Say nothing. Do nothing. You want resolution now, and there isn't any.

The energy of anxiety and worry works like a big ocean wave—just allow yourself to ride with it as each wave comes and goes into and out from your awareness. Watch as the wave rises until it reaches its peak, staying strong and powerful for a while, and then eventually settling back down and drifting away. Continue to sit still with the energy in this situation and let the worry wave run its course.

Then gently return to the worry situation and take a final inventory. What are you left with here? What do you see? If you look closely, you'll see two things: the pain and hurt that fueled your worry to begin with and your values.

See if you can turn your attention to the pain and hurt underneath the worry. Give that pain and hurt a label. If you have a hard time identifying the hurt, ask yourself, "What would I have left to feel if I didn't get caught up in worry in this situation?" Take a moment to really take stock.

Perhaps you see hurt, fear, abandonment, loneliness, inadequacy, loss, guilt, vulnerability, or shame. There is no need to trap these feelings or cover them. They're part of you and belong to you without being you or defining who you are. Just allow them to be. Make space for them.

As if they were an open wound, take care of them by bringing kindness, care, and compassion to your experience and to this moment. Forgive yourself for burying and rejecting your pain for so long, for acting in ways to push it from view.

If at any time you feel like stopping and stepping back inside your worry armor, thank your mind for that option and simply return to your experience. If you notice judgment or resentment popping up again, place them into their own bubbles and let them go, floating upward.

Next, gently turn your attention to your values lying close by. Which ones do you see? Pick one or two that are important to you. Now ask yourself this question: "If worry and doubt are between me and moving in the direction of those values, am I willing to have them and still do what matters to me?" If you're willing, worry is no longer a barrier. It's just a thought.

Now think of a situation where worry had gotten in the way of you acting in accord with your values. Then go ahead and imagine yourself doing what you value and bringing your hurt and pain with you.

That probably feels strange and it also feels vital because you're moving toward what you care about in life. Here, you're exerting control where you truly have it. Take time to really connect with this. This is what it's all about!

Then, when you're ready, gradually widen your attention to take in the sounds around you in the room you're in. Take a moment to make the intention to bring this sense of compassion and forgiveness into the present moment and to the rest of your experience on this day.

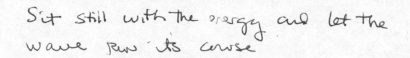
Sit still with the energy and let the wave run its course

Doing this exercise isn't easy. At first, you may have trouble taking an observer's perspective. Don't beat yourself up over this or other "failures" or difficulties. Being compassionate isn't about perfection. Continue to do the work, be patient, and relax with yourself. Commit to doing the exercise again tomorrow and again the next day. Do the best you can.

Repeat the same worry episode once a day until you can more readily adopt a Wise Mind perspective as you stay with the negative energy and hurt that shows up for that episode. Then move on to different worry episodes and cycle through the same process as before.

Continue practicing this exercise with worry episodes until you can stay with the bodily discomfort and hurt (using compassion and forgiveness) and with minimal entanglement in judgment. This may take several days or even weeks. The key is this: stay on the path!

FEEL Exercise for Disturbing Images

Being able to imagine—to visualize—is a great gift. We can paint in our mind's eye portraits of experiences that once were or that may be, and we can do this anytime and anywhere. We can also create "realities" that aren't real and treat them as if they were.

Our minds can turn any word into an image, and we can also put most images into words. Think the word "sunset" and you may find yourself being able to see one in your mind. Read the word "jerk" and you may be able to visualize a person who treated you or others poorly.

You have these capacities and need them. These same processes are at work when you experience joyful and serene images and thoughts and when you experience disturbing or fearful thoughts. Here's a powerful way to learn to hold your WAF images more lightly.

EXERCISE: KIND ALLOWING WITH PAINFUL IMAGES AND THOUGHTS

Start by generating a few sentences describing troublesome or disturbing WAF images. Here are a few examples:

- My children drowned in the bathtub, and it was my fault.

- I feel sick to my stomach, and my heart is pounding.

- I'm living on the streets because I'm incompetent, weak, and unable to think.

- I'm in a psychiatric ward because I'm crazy.

- My hands are shaking, I'm disoriented, and nobody understands me.

- I'm being attacked and I'm frozen in fear.

- If my husband's health gets worse, we might lose our home or he might die.

You may be having difficulty coming up with images. If you've suffered a past trauma, the images you may have are hard to open up to. Or if you're on constant worry autopilot, you may find it difficult to imagine anything because you're so caught up in a stream of worrisome thoughts. And if you've struggled with disturbing obsessions, you may find your images particularly nasty and unacceptable. You may even believe that thinking a thought or image may make it come true.

These are normal reactions for many people. In each instance, though, you'll need to ask yourself whether the reaction is serving you well or not. So if you've tended to blot out or shut down to thinking about upsetting images, you may ask yourself if "not thinking" is working for you.

What does your experience tell you? Will more of the same—shutting down, closing up—get in the way of your effort to change in more vital ways? Can you be willing to flip your willingness switch on? We know you can. You simply need to decide to do it and see how it goes over time. Are you willing to create that list now? If so, continue.

Once you have your list, go over it with both eyes fixed on willingness. For each image, ask whether you are 100 percent willing to have the WAF image just as it is. Remember, it's okay if you don't like it or if the image makes you uncomfortable. The willingness question is not about liking it. The question is: are you open to having that image and the discomfort that goes along with it, and without doing anything about it?

Next, get settled in a quiet space, your kind practice space. Close your eyes and become centered on the breath. Then, when you are ready, select an image that you are 100 percent willing to have and hold that image gently in your awareness.

Recognize the image as an image and label it as such: "I am having the image of. . . ." Bring kindness and compassion to the image as if you were holding something that you care about deeply. As you do, notice that these passengers on your Life Bus are just thoughts and images. You, not they, control the gas pedal, break, and steering wheel. You, not they, control what you do.

Allow yourself to bring an attitude of kind allowing to the image for at least five minutes beyond the point at which the image is vivid. Then you may move on to the next image or plan that for your next practice. It's best to stay with one image until you can do it with your willingness switch in the on position most of the time. Then you're ready to move on to a different image.

Go through all the images you rated as ones you'd be willing to have, and then practice with the ones that you were unwilling to have. Be patient and take your time. Follow FEEL steps 1 through 7 from chapter 16. Track your progress with the FEEL Thought and Imagery Form.

If you continue to have difficulty bringing kindness to your unpleasant thoughts and images, you may use prompts from newspaper stories or may look to photographs or movies to help you practice simply being with unpleasant imagery without trying to resolve it in any way.

FEEL Exercise for Painful Memories

Painful memories are reminders of what once was. They can be linked to all sorts of things going on inside you and can be triggered by situations happening in the world around you. Yet the memory is just that—a collection of images, thoughts, physical sensations, and emotions. These can show up in an instant. The hurt you reexperience is real, but the source of that hurt right now is only your mind doing its thing. A painful memory is not the same as the hurtful or life-threatening event you once endured. This can be hard to get.

If you step back, you'll see that the memory hurts and seems real, but there's nothing you can do now to undo it, change the outcome, or to bring about any resolution. And there's nothing you need to do either. The event is in your past. You are in the present. This is what we mean when we say "Painful memories are not the event." The only thing repeating is the emotional pain, right where you are now.

This is a critical moment. Your brain and nervous system have no delete button. This means that normally what goes into the mix, stays in the mix. What you can do is change the mix by adding something new to it. You do that by *doing* something new with your painful memories when they show up. That something is forgiveness.

Before beginning the exercise below, we'd like you to find a quiet comfortable place where you can set up a candle. Light this candle as a symbol of your commitment to forgive. This candle represents someone or an event that caused you pain or hurt. You will be focusing on the flame as you go through each step.

This exercise is likely to be difficult for you at first. Steps 3 and 4—bringing compassion and letting go as you extend forgiveness to the source of hurt or pain—are particularly tough. Be gentle with yourself if it feels like it's too much or too difficult. Your mind will give you all sorts of reasons why you shouldn't do it. Acknowledge these doubts, apprehensions, and uneasiness about extending forgiveness and see whether you can be willing to have them for the sake of living the life you want.

It takes practice to cultivate forgiveness. Give yourself time to get the hang of it. If you've suffered trauma and you experience a lot of painful memories and images, we suggest you do this exercise every other day for several weeks. You can do it in two ways: either just listen to and follow the instructions on the CD, or record the text below in your own voice at a slow pace and then listen to it. You could also try both options and see which works better for you.

There's one final thing to keep in mind before you start. Forgiveness doesn't mean condoning what happened to you. You may ask, "Why should I forgive those who harmed me?" The answer is simple and practical: forgiving yourself and others is the only path to healing.

If you don't let go and forgive others for the harm they did, they and their deeds will continue to haunt you, harm you, and have a hold on you. Every moment you hang on to your resentment, you hurt yourself one more time. So by not forgiving, you hurt yourself. Remember, this practice is for you, not for people or circumstances that once hurt you!

EXERCISE: THE CANDLE OF FORGIVENESS

Go ahead and light the candle and then get in a comfortable position in your chair. Sit upright with your feet flat on the floor, your arms and legs uncrossed, and your hands resting in your lap. Allow your eyes to focus on the candle flame and simply watch it.

As you watch the flicker of the candle flame, bring your attention to the gentle rising and falling of your breath in your chest and belly. Like ocean waves coming in and going out, your breaths are always there. Notice the rhythm of the breath in your body with each passing inhale . . . and exhale. Notice the changing patterns of sensations in your belly as you breathe in and as you breathe out. Take a few minutes to center yourself as you breathe in and out.

Step 1: Awareness of the Wrong and Hurt Beneath the Painful Memory

Now allow your awareness to shift to a painful memory or traumatic event. See if you can allow yourself to visualize the scene fully as if you were watching a movie in slow motion. What happened? Who else was there? Watch the candle as you acknowledge the painful situation unfolding in your mind's eye. Focus on your breathing as you watch the situation unfold. See if you can slow the painful situation down, slower and slower with each passing breath.

As you do, bring your attention to any sensations of discomfort that show up. As best you can, bring an attitude of generous allowing and gentle acceptance to your experience right now. See if you can make room for the pain and hurt you had then and that you may be reliving now. Soften to it . . . as you breathe in . . . and out . . . in and out.

As best as you can, open up to all of it: the hurt, pain, sadness, regret, loss, and resentment. Allow yourself to become aware of your hurt and painful emotions, and simply acknowledge the hurt you experienced and the hurt you may have caused. There's no need to resist or fight or blame. Simply acknowledge and become aware of your experience.

Step 2: Separate Hurtful Actions from Your Hurt and Its Source

Visualize the person or event that hurt you. As you begin to visualize that person, allow them to drift over and become the candle. Focus on the candle and visualize the person or situation that hurt you. Now remember and visualize what happened. As you focus on the candle, notice what your mind machine is doing with the images and sensations that show up.

You might see your mind making a judgment . . . blaming . . . having feelings of sadness . . . bitterness . . . resentment. As these and other thoughts and sensations come into your awareness, simply label them as you did in previous exercises—"There is judgment . . . blame . . . tension . . . resentment"—and allow them to be. Bring a gentle and kind awareness to your pain and hurt as you breathe in . . . and out . . . in . . . and out . . . slowly and deeply.

Next, create some space between the actions that made you feel hurt and angry and the person or situation that created them. If it helps, you can visualize the action that hurt you as the flame, and the person or situation who committed the hurt as the candlestick.

Notice the difference between the flame and the candle. The flame is not the candle. The actions of the person who hurt you are not the same as the person who committed them. As you breathe in and out, give yourself time to connect with this difference.

Bring each hurtful action into the flame one by one and notice it, label it, and then see the difference between the hurtful action and the person. Visualize what was done, not who did it.

Then, after you spend some time noticing each action, allow it to disappear up into the smoke, leaving the candle flame. Keep watching any tension, discomfort, anger, hurt, or whatever else your body may be doing. Make room for what you experience as you return your attention to your body and your breathing. Don't change or "fix" anything.

Step 3: Bring Compassionate Witness to Your Hurt

Next, bring your attention back to the human being in the candle—the perpetrator of wrongs against you. Notice how he or she is also a human being and vulnerable to harm just like you are. At a basic human level, the two of you are not that different.

See if you can allow yourself to take that person's perspective as a compassionate witness and see what life might be like through his or her eyes. Connect with that person's hardships, losses, missed opportunities, poor choices, faults and failings, hurts and sadness, and hopes and dreams.

Without condoning their actions, see if you can connect with that person's humanity and imperfections as you connect with your own humanity and imperfections, hardships, loss, pain, and suffering.

As a compassionate witness to this other human being, see if you can connect more deeply with that person as another human being. Notice the offender's thoughts and feelings, knowing that you've also experienced similar types of thoughts and feelings. What might it be like to have lived the life of the person who offended you? As best you can, bring an attitude of generous allowing and gentle acceptance to what you experience now.

Step 4: Extend Forgiveness, Let Go, and Move On

Now see if you can bring into awareness what your life would be like if you let go of all the negative energy you are holding on to—your grievances, grudges, bitterness, and anger. What would it be like to let go of the effort needed to shut out this painful experience from your past? Connect with the reasons behind why you want to be free from the painful memory, the anger, or the desire for revenge.

Allow yourself to visualize a new future, full of the things you've missed out or given up on by resisting the memory or holding on to your unwillingness to forgive. See if you can connect with your future without forgetting what happened in the past, and without carrying the weight of bitterness, anger, and resentment toward the person or event that hurt you.

Allow yourself to take the courageous step forward in your life by letting go of the memory, your pain, your anger, and your resentment. Take time to really connect with this relief as you imagine separating from the resentment and bitterness you have carried for so long. Allow all of it to drift away with each out breath, and with each in breath, welcome in peace and forgiveness as you continue to breathe in . . . and out, slowly and deeply.

When you're ready, bring into your awareness how you have needed other people's forgiveness in the past. Imagine extending that forgiveness to the person who hurt or offended you. What could you say to that person? As you think about this, notice any discomfort showing up and what your mind is doing here.

If the thought "The person doesn't deserve that" shows up, just notice that thought and gently let it go. Return your focus to your breathing as you remind yourself that kind and gentle acts of forgiveness are for you, not for others.

Imagine the weight of the burden being lifted from you as you choose to give forgiveness. Allow yourself to connect with the sense of healing and control that comes along with this. As you give the powerful gift of forgiveness, notice some budding feelings of softness where before there was only hardness, hurt, and pain.

Embrace this moment of peace as you return to the image of the person who offended you. Gently extend your hands as you say, "In forgiving you, I forgive myself. In letting go of my pain and anger toward you, I bring peace to myself. I invite peace and compassion into my life and into my hurt and pain. I choose to let go of this burden that I have been carrying for so long." Repeat these phrases slowly as you extend forgiveness.

Stay with and simply observe and label whatever thoughts and feelings come up as you extend this act of forgiveness. Sense the emotional relief that comes when the burden of a grudge is melting away. See if you can notice the peace and feeling of inner strength that comes about as you extend compassion and forgiveness in this moment.

Then, when you're ready, bring your awareness back into the room, to your body, and to the flicker of the candle flame. Finish this exercise by blowing out the candle as a symbolic gesture of your commitment to forgive and let go and of your readiness to move on with your life.

DEALING WITH URGES TO CUT AND RUN

We know how difficult it can be to face your discomfort squarely. You've had lots of experience doing just the opposite—pulling out, pushing away, or tuning out. The urge to act is powerful. It's a well-practiced habit for you. And it's natural that old cut-and-run urges show up as you consciously choose to move into your discomfort with an eye on doing what you want to do in your life. Anxiety News Radio wants you to tune in 24/7.

What you need to do is be patient and kind with yourself. Old habits may die hard, but they'll die much harder if you continue to rehearse them again and again. Remember that when you step in the direction of something you want, you'll risk discomfort and gain vitality in your life. Along with that discomfort will be the old urges that have kept you stuck.

Everything you've been learning up to this point in this book is teaching you skills to go against the old urges. Instead of pulling out of your discomfort, you're moving into it. Instead of hardening to your discomfort, you're softening to it. Instead of seeing the world through the blinders of your critical, judgmental mind, you're learning to see your mind for what it is.

The next exercise (Hayes et al., 1999) can be enormously helpful during those times when you find yourself trying to resist urges and other unwanted WAF thoughts.

EXERCISE: PUTTING THOUGHTS AND URGES ON CARDS

This exercise can be done anytime and anywhere WAF thoughts and urges show up. All you need are small pieces of paper or some index cards. When the WAFs show up, simply label them, placing each thought, worry, sensation, urge, or image on its own card.

A moment ago the thoughts and urges were inside your head. They probably seemed really hard and heavy in there. Now they're out, exposed, and you can look at them. Now see them for what they are. Notice that you have a choice to do what the card says and struggle, or you can allow what you wrote to be just as it is . . . a thought . . . a sensation . . . an image . . . an urge to act.

To get a sense of the struggle, place the card with the thought or urge on it between your hands and push against your hands really hard. Do this for at least thirty seconds and then stop. Gently place the card on your lap. Notice the difference in effort between pushing against the thought or urge compared to the experience of the card gently resting on your lap.

You can practice holding your thoughts and urges and carrying them with you too. To do that, place the cards in your pocket, purse, or briefcase as you go about your day. Notice that you can move with them. Notice that you can take them out and look at them. Notice that you can choose to engage them or engage something else in your life. The choice here is yours. If you look to your experience, you will know what to do. It's time to trust your experience, not the cards.

We suggest you keep putting your thoughts and urges on cards and take them with you wherever you go every day for as long as you wish. If you like, you can change the cards from time to time. Some people we've worked with tell us that they prepare a stack of index cards. Then, every morning, they pick four or five different cards and take them along for the day.

Remember, every time you happen to touch or read a card during the day without getting tangled up in what it says, or doing as it says, you're developing an important skill. The cards will be there anytime you wish to attend to them, just as your old history is always with you.

The next exercise will help you get more practice being with your WAF urges and not doing what they compel you to do. This exercise can be helpful during your FEEL practice and anytime that the urge to cut and run shows up.

EXERCISE: STAND SILENTLY WITH YOUR URGES

Old urges to act will show up in a flash. And, in the heat of the moment, it can be difficult to remember that you have other options. So let's keep it simple: *do nothing and practice patience*. Just be still with what you experience in that moment. Here's what you can do specifically.

Say and Do Nothing

You do have a choice here: You can do what your mind and body compel you to do. Or you can make a choice that seems ridiculous and as unnatural as pushing into the finger traps—you can choose to act with patience. You can stop, be still, and wait until the hardness of the stirring, raucous, and searing energy gradually softens and drifts away.

You aren't suppressing here. You're just being honest with the fact that you're uncomfortable or hurt or sad or lonely or fearful or whatever you're experiencing at the moment. And you stay with it, without feeding it or reacting to it. This will give you time to think about what you really want to be about in that moment and what you want to do.

Watch Your Mind Machine as an Observer

We guarantee that the mind machine will be in overdrive doing its old thing. Don't get tangled up in what it's doing or respond to it. Just watch what it's doing from the compassionate-observer perspective and meet that stirring energy with gentle acceptance. You don't need to get hooked. This will give you space to consider other, more vital options.

Ride the WAF Tiger

This is really tough. Sitting with the discomfort and doing nothing while you feel like exploding or running is like riding a wild horse or a tiger; and it's very frightening. In that moment, bring attention to the physical experience of anxiety. Is there pressure? Is there tightness or contraction? Where, specifically, do you feel it? Does it have a shape?

Here, perhaps for the first time, you can make a choice to sit and stay with the raucous energy and not do what you've always done. And you can do so in your daily life. Once you are still, you can bring compassion and curiosity to the energy and pain.

Look deeply into your experience without attempting to resolve it, fight it, or suppress it, and without acting on it. As you look, see if you can find the pain. Once you locate the pain, as in the previous exercises, look more deeply into it. And then let it be.

Approach this act of patience with softness and curiosity. You do have a choice to hold on here or to let go. This quality of patience is very much like the practice of extending forgiveness.

We mentioned resolution and relief earlier. Doing what your WAF urges compel you to do will bring no lasting relief. Doing something new by doing nothing at all can bring a sense of enormous relief, relaxation, and connection with the softness and tenderness of your heart.

The next exercise is another opportunity to develop space between your judgmental mind and your experience. Again, the easiest way to practice is to listen to the audio version on the CD.

EXERCISE: LEAVES ON A STREAM

Start by getting centered and focus on the breath as you've done before. Just notice the gentle rising and falling of your breath in your chest and belly. There's no need to control your breathing in any way—simply let the breath breathe itself. Allow your eyes to close gently.

Then, after a few moments, imagine that you're sitting next to a small stream on a warm autumn day. As you gaze at the stream, you notice a number of large leaves of all colors, shapes, and sizes drifting along, each at its own pace, one by one, in the slowly moving current. Allow yourself to simply be there for a moment, watching.

When you're ready, gradually bring your awareness to what's going on inside you. As you do, gently notice and label each experience that shows up—thoughts, feelings, sensations, desires, and impulses. Pay attention to what's happening in your mind and body and then label what's going on. Perhaps one of those thoughts is "I don't have time for this."

As each thought, feeling, memory, or impulse comes along into your mind, notice them and gently place them one by one on each large leaf passing by. Observe as each leaf comes closer to you. Then watch as it slowly moves away, drifting along as it carries the contents of your mind and body out of sight downstream. Return to gazing at the stream, waiting for the next leaf to float by. Continue placing each thought, feeling, memory, or impulse on its own large leaf. Watch each one as you let them just float away downstream.

When you're ready, widen your attention to take in the sounds around you. Open your eyes and make the intention to bring gentle allowing and self-acceptance into the rest of your day.

Do the Leaves on a Stream exercise every other day for a couple of weeks. As you get better at it, you can start practicing it during real-life experiences with your eyes open. You can also allow yourself to take the perspective of the stream, just as you did in the chessboard exercise. Being the stream, you hold each of the leaves and notice the thought, feeling, memory, or urge that each leaf carries as it sails by. You need not interfere with them—just let them float by and do what they do until they are eventually carried out of sight. And notice how you're learning to be an observer.

LIFE ENHANCEMENT EXERCISES

For the next two weeks, make the following activities a priority on your self-care to-do list:

- Practice the Acceptance of Anxiety exercise (from chapter 14) once a day, with or without the CD audio.

- Practice the exercises in the FEEL Exercises to Unhook Your Judgmental Mind section; record your commitment and progress with them using the FEEL Thought and Imagery Form.

- Practice noticing and being with urges to cut and run from your hurt.

- Practice mindfulness and observer skills and also kindness when anxiety shows up. Remember: do the best that you can.

THE TAKE-HOME MESSAGE

Developing comfort with your judgmental mind is one of the most powerful ways to end your WAF suffering. The acceptance exercises in this chapter and the entire book let you experience that your WAF flies are always on barbless hooks. You and you alone can choose to let go, even after you've been tricked into biting. The take-home message here is that if you stop struggling, you can get off the hook. This will give you freedom to swim in the direction of your values.

My Mind Is Not the Enemy

Points to Ponder: My mind is not the enemy. It is what I do with it and because of it that can hurt me.

Questions to Consider: Am I willing to face my painful thoughts, memories, judgments, and urges as they are? Can I take the bold step to let go and bring compassion, kindness, and forgiveness to my hurt and pain? Am I willing to make room for something new?

CHAPTER 18

Moving Toward a Valued Life

The journey of a thousand miles must begin with a single step.
—Chinese proverb

In chapter 12 we described values as the shining light in the sea of life. Values act like a beacon. They point you in a direction—toward what's important. This is crucial when you feel pulled and pushed around in a sea of worry, anxiety, panic, and doom and gloom. The next step is to take control of your actions and start moving in vital directions. You'll do that by focusing on specific goals. Goals are like destinations that you'll visit along the way toward living out your values.

The wonderful thing about values is that you can live them. The key to living out your values is to break them down into incremental steps. Living a rich life is all about taking steps, however small or large, each and every day, toward achieving your goals and living your values. You must commit yourself to taking those steps. You do that by setting goals and following through with action.

By taking charge of your behavior, you take charge of your life. Are you ready and willing to take these steps?

SETTING AND ACHIEVING GOALS

Go back to the Life Compass you completed in chapter 13. Now is the time to decide which of these values you want to have more of in your life right now. Choose a value that's important to you—a value with a high importance rating and a low action score. Perhaps you put this aspect of your life on hold because of anxiety-related barriers. This would be a good place to start. If you sense that you're not yet ready to confront barriers in this important area, then choose a different area and make that your ready-and-willing starting point.

For now, we'd like to walk you through one area to give you an idea of how the process works. Later you can go through the same steps for the other value domains on your Life Compass. Once you've chosen a value, write it down on the top line of the Value and Goals Worksheet that appears at the end of this chapter and on the CD.

Our colleagues developed a five-step behavioral program to help people achieve goals (Addis & Martell, 2004). For purposes of this workbook, we've simplified these steps, boiling them down to four key ones. Let's go over these steps one by one:

1. Identify concrete and achievable goals.

2. Identify steps and arrange them in logical order.

3. Make a commitment and take the step, no matter how you feel (and don't forget to pat yourself on the back after you complete a step!).

4. Practice living your values in difficult situations.

Identify Concrete and Achievable Goals

As you start thinking about goals, you'll find that some are short-term goals you can attain in the near future. Others are long-term goals you'll only be able to attain further down the road. Both types of goals are important, and achieving one may lead you to the next.

For instance, suppose you value your health and want to increase your fitness level. So you commit to walking each day. Your long-term goal might be to walk to a telephone pole one mile up the road from where you live. Between your house and that pole are a number of other poles, all spaced about the same distance apart. A short-term goal here might be getting to the first pole. The next day you commit to getting to both the first and the second pole, and so on. If you keep at it, you'll eventually reach the pole at your one-mile marker—your long-term goal. This is how short- and long-term goals work—they get you moving on a valued path.

It's important that goals meet certain criteria so that you avoid ending up on a dead-end street. Steven Hayes and Spencer Smith (2005) give some good advice in this regard. They advise that setting goals is all about workability. If you don't make your goals workable in the context of your life, it's unlikely you're going to get very far down the path of your values. Choose achievable, obtainable actions that can realistically fit with your life. Doing this makes it much more likely you'll actually be able to live your values every day.

In the space below (or on a separate sheet of paper), write down some goals related to the first value you chose on your Life Compass. Be sure that they are concrete and achievable—in short, something you could do and then tick off your to-do list:

_____   _____

_____   _____

_____   _____

We suggest that you start with up to three goals. One of those goals should be a short-term goal—something you can start working on this week. Ask the following questions for each goal to make sure it's achievable:

- Is the goal concrete, practical, and realistic?

- Is it obtainable (something I can do and have control over)?

- Does it work with my current life situation?

- Does this goal lead me in the direction of my value?

If you can answer yes to all questions for a goal, write it in the second row (near the top) of the Value and Goals Worksheet at the end of this chapter. You'll also find a copy of the worksheet on the CD. If necessary, revise and clarify the goal until you get a "yes" answer to each question. You'll want to have several copies of this worksheet handy so that you have plenty of blank copies for other values that you'll want to work on later.

Identify Steps and Arrange Them in Logical Order

Having settled on goals, you've put the first guideposts on your road map. Now focus on the incremental steps you need to take to get you there. Start with the short-term goal and break it down into smaller intermediate steps. Think of each step you need to take to attain your goal. Then write those steps down in the space below (or on a separate piece of paper):

_____   _____

_____   _____

_____   _____

Now think about a logical order for the steps. What needs to happen first before the other steps can follow? If no particular order is necessary, then start with the easiest step. Copy the steps into the Value and Goals Worksheet in the order in which they need to be completed. Put the first step at the top. You can go through the same procedure for other goals you've identified.

Let's look at two examples. Suppose your goal is to change jobs and eventually become a manager with a larger corporation rather than the small outfit you're currently working for. This goal, in turn, includes smaller specific actions, such as checking relevant newspapers and internet sites for postings of managerial jobs, networking, updating your resumé, setting up an informational interview at a company that interests you, and making a job application for a potential new employer. Notice that the interview depends on the other steps happening first, including plain old brainstorming ideas.

Here's another one. Let's say you want to work on spending more quality time with your spouse or partner. This goal may be approached via several steps, such as doing something once a week with your partner that you both enjoy, like going to a movie or the theater, dining out, going away for the weekend, taking a bike ride together, or spending quiet time at home talking. Brainstorming ideas is another step. It's important that you do these things regardless of how you feel at the moment. Notice too that there's no logical order to some of the steps in this example.

Make a Commitment and Take the Step

Now it's time to make a commitment. Are you willing to commit to the values explored in chapter 13 and to the behavioral and life changes they imply? If so, commit to a day and time to begin step 1 on your Value and Goals Worksheet. Tell someone else that you've done so. Then, no matter how you feel at that time, do it. This is all about action and doing something different with your life. Unless you take action, nothing will change. You'll continue to get what you've always gotten.

Write in the date when you achieved each step. Put a gold star on the chart if you want to. Make sure to congratulate yourself: give yourself credit for what you've accomplished, no matter how small the step was. Review your Value and Goals Worksheet frequently. It'll give you valuable feedback on how you're progressing and will encourage you once you start ticking off your goals.

To give you some ideas about how to break down a goal into subgoals, take a look at the two examples below. They both refer to the same value—parenting. However, due to the nature of the anxiety problem, the barriers and strategies are somewhat different.

■ Jill's Valued Goals

Jill, a thirty-seven-year-old mother of two daughters, has suffered from panic disorder and agoraphobia for over fifteen years. She's missed every school concert and special occasion that involved being in a crowded school auditorium or gym. Here's how she completed a section of her Value and Goals Worksheet. Note how some steps can and should be repeated to provide more opportunities for practice.

VALUE AND GOALS WORKSHEET

My Value: _Being a good mom with my kids_

Goal I want to achieve: _Attending my daughter Mary's school concerts_

Steps toward achieving my goal	Barriers	Strategies	Date(s) achieved
1. _Go to quiet place every other day and imagine myself being at next school concert._	_Stress of knowing that eventually I'll have to attend the concert_	_Practice FEEL exercise & Wise Mind skills. Make a list why attending concert is important for living out my values._	_9/15 9/17 9/19_
2. _Attend an outdoor concert with family._	_Fear of everyone around me knowing that I'm nervous and may have a panic attack at any moment_	_Practice watching my mind as an observer. Practice WAF surfing if panic arises._	_10/15_
3. _Sit twice in empty auditorium to become familiar with the surroundings two weeks before concert._	_Fear (thought) that I'll feel so anxious that I won't be able to make it through the concert when people are around_	_Practice watching thoughts and feelings as an observer—from acceptance exercises. Keep eyes on value of being a good mom and supporting my kids._	_11/1 11/14_
4. _Go to two rehearsals when few people are around._	_Fear of not being able to escape without interrupting the rehearsal_	_Practice FEEL exercise & Wise Mind skills. Watch thoughts, feelings, and images. Remind myself of value._	_11/20 11/28_
5. _Attend daughter's school concert._	_Fear (thought) of embarrassing Mary if I have a panic attack during the concert_	_Let thoughts be, and focus on Mary's performance and the value of being a supportive mom. Practice WAF surfing if I feel panic._	_12/10_

It took Jill almost three months from taking the first step to completing the last one. This is fine. Some people move faster, and other people need more time. It really doesn't matter how long it takes you to reach any of your goals. The only thing that matters is that you stay on course and move in the direction you want to move in—at your own pace and with both patience and persistence.

■ *Eric's Valued Goals*

Below is the example of Eric, a forty-two-year-old father of a son and a daughter. Eric was diagnosed with obsessive-compulsive disorder at the age of nineteen. Here's how he completed a section of his Value and Goals Worksheet. Again, note how Eric was doing just fine at his own pace, and that he repeated some steps to provide more opportunities for practice.

VALUE AND GOALS WORKSHEET

My Value: *Being a good dad with my kids*

Goal I want to achieve: *Doing at least one outside activity per week that kids and I like*

Steps toward achieving my goal	Barriers	Strategies	Date(s) achieved
1. Make a list with my kids of activities we'd like to do together.	Stress of leaving the house and going outside my comfort zone	Drop the rope. Make a list of all the reasons why it'll be good for me and my children to do more outdoor activities.	6/1 6/5
2. Practice sitting outside in the grass three times and just noticing the urge to wash my hands and clothing without giving in to the urge.	Anxiety of having germs all over my body and not being able to wash myself	Put disturbing thoughts and urges on cards. Imagine intrusive thoughts and worries as leaves floating down a river. Be kind to myself and remind myself that I can live out my values and be anxious at the same time. I can be willing.	6/15 6/18 6/21 6/25
3. Do two low-anxiety-provoking activities or outings (different one each week).	Worries about children not having a good time because of my anxiety	Look at worries as thoughts; use bubble wand—just WANR again. Remind myself of how activities help me live the life I want for me and my kids.	7/2 7/14

4. Do two activities or outings that kids like. May bring on medium anxiety (different one each week).	Fear of not being able to reduce my distress if there are no sinks nearby	Drop the rope in tug-of-war with urge to wash, continue to do what I'm doing, and take the urge with me. Sit with it and do nothing—ride the wave.	7/21 8/5
5. Do two activities or outings that kids like and may provoke considerable anxiety (different one each week).	Fear of getting sick from all the germs at public places	Use an observer perspective when it feels like anxiety is going to overwhelm me, and practice urge and anxiety surfing when it gets strong. Focus on the moment and the value in the action.	8/15 8/20

Practice Living Your Values in Difficult Situations

The two sample worksheets also give you a good idea of how to practice living your values in difficult situations. It's quite likely that the old WAFs are going to show up as you embark on your road to valued living. The FEEL exercises in the previous two chapters were meant to prepare you for how to move with barriers in difficult situations. Now it's time to apply these new skills and the skills you've been learning from the earlier chapters. Remember, valued action is the life prize and the reason you've been doing all this work so far.

LIFE ENHANCEMENT EXERCISES

Practice valued living by following the steps outlined in this chapter. Use the Value and Goals Worksheet to plan activities and to prepare for the difficulties and barriers that may come up along the way. Start with one value and a set of related goals. Later, you can work on other values and goals in a similar fashion. Also continue to practice any of the earlier mindfulness and acceptance exercises as often as possible, including kindness toward yourself, when anxiety shows up during the day.

THE TAKE-HOME MESSAGE

To change your life, you'll need to commit yourself to changing what you do, pure and simple. You can get back on the road to a valued life by focusing on your values, setting goals, and then taking action no matter how you feel. Acceptance, compassion, and kindness will be your friends when you deal with barriers that will undoubtedly come up.

Putting My Values into Action

Points to Ponder: I can live my values by setting concrete and achievable goals one day at a time. Making commitments and practicing living my values—even in difficult situations—is what life is all about.

Questions to Consider: How can I put my values into action every day? How can I break up my goals into small steps so I can keep on moving?

VALUE AND GOALS WORKSHEET

| My Value: _____ |
| Goal I want to achieve: _____ |

Steps toward achieving my goal	Barriers	Strategies	Date(s) achieved
1.			
2.			
3.			
4.			
5.			

CHAPTER 19

Staying the Course

Where you end up isn't the most important thing. It's the road you take to get there.
The road you take is what you'll look back on and call your life. —Tim Wiley

You've come a long way! The fact that you've read this far and followed the program shows that you're determined. That's good. On many occasions, WAF barriers will show up to try to stop you from getting where you want to go and doing what you want to do. The risk of getting sidetracked by these barriers is great. So we'll review again some of the key strategies for how to keep on moving with the barriers that will spring up along the way and for how to approach setbacks and slipups gently with kindness and compassion.

HOW TO KEEP ON MOVING

As you embark on your journey of putting your values into action, there will be new obstacles, doubts, and setbacks. The old WAF obstacles and barriers will show up too. At times, you won't put your commitments into actions. Sometimes you'll slip into old WAF habits. Once in a while you may even take longer to reach a goal than you had hoped. All of this and more is just fine. We all move at our own pace. The most important thing for you is that you keep yourself moving forward in vital ways. In this section, we want to remind you of some of the strategies and skills you've learned in previous chapters. You can draw upon them when discomfort *difficulty* threatens to get in the way of discomfort *vitality*.

Recommit to Action After Breaking a Commitment

Following through with a commitment is difficult when WAFs are right in your face. When you make a commitment to an activity, or to practice compassion, it's important that you have a clear understanding of what commitment means. We're pretty sure that the passengers on your Life Bus will be shouting things like "You'll never make it!" "You'll just make a fool of yourself!" "You're going to get hurt!"

Knowing that you're bound to experience discomfort and doubt, are you still willing to commit to your chosen activity 100 percent and go through with it? Remember, commitment isn't something you can merely try or do halfway. You either make the commitment or you don't.

We're not asking you to commit to success or any other particular result or outcome like "being in a steady relationship by July 1" or "feeling better and less anxious." Many outcomes are beyond your control. They lie somewhere in the future and cannot be known until you take some action. We're only asking whether you're willing to commit to doing something that will work for you *and* taking all those passengers with you on your Life Bus. Will you do that and mean it?

GETTING BACK ON TRACK IS WHAT COUNTS!

The commitment is that you fully intend to follow through, not that you'll never fall short. In fact, we predict that you, like everyone else, will fall short once in a while. Your commitment is that if and when you do break a commitment, you'll recommit and mean it once again, and that you'll do what you can to stay on the path of your values.

Your choices and actions ultimately determine what happens with barriers and setbacks on your road to valued living. At times, all of us will fail to live consistently with our values. What happens then is critical. You make a choice. Learn from the experience. Pick yourself up. Let go of carrying the "failure" judgment and being strangled by it. And then you make a renewed commitment to take actions that move you in life directions you care about.

When you let a WAF barrier stop you from time to time, don't slide into thinking that this means that WAFs will take over your life again. That won't happen unless *you* allow it to happen. It's your choice either to give up or recommit to small actions that make your life meaningful—and then put those actions into practice. So long as you do that and keep moving, you'll be truly living a life that expresses your values.

This entire book has been about helping you make choices—every day and every moment of your life—that will keep you moving in the direction of those values. If you've worked the exercises so far, then you're not the same person you were when you first cracked open this book.

Move with Barriers and Setbacks

Remember that you don't need to overcome WAF barriers first before moving forward on the road to living your values. You don't need to get rid of them either. The key is to acknowledge the barriers and move *with* them—take them with you for the ride. Let your values show you the way. Make room for all the unwanted stuff. Don't let it stop you from doing what's best for you. Keep on nurturing your willingness to have what you have, and stop running from yourself.

The solution is to keep on driving your Life Bus in the direction you want to go without allowing your WAFs to sidetrack you. When in doubt, do the opposite of what WAFs seem to be telling you. Don't listen to Anxiety News Radio; tune in to Just So Radio by watching what's going on from a Wise Mind observer perspective. Cherish the moment as it is!

And don't miss watching what's going on inside you with some kindness and compassion for what you're experiencing. Nurturing friendliness and willingness will make it easier to move with your WAFs. They need not be your enemy—they are more like a wounded child that needs some loving-kindness. Take care of that child. Embrace it. Take it with you on your journey.

Don't Let the Mind Machine Trap You

The mind machine won't stop its chatter just because you've made a commitment to act and to take your WAFs with you when they show up. Sometimes you'll fall short of being accepting and following through with your commitments. Your judgmental mind may scorn you: "Stop all this acceptance and commitment BS. You just can't do it. The only thing you should accept is that you're a failure at acceptance and commitment!"

When your mind is throwing this and other old, sticky stuff at you, it's important not to get tangled up in all that chatter. This is just another example of your mind doing what minds do all the time: creating thoughts and evaluating. It's just more "blah, blah, blah."

Do you really need to argue with "blah, blah, blah"? Or can you make room for whatever your mind comes up with and let it be? This will free you up to move on with your life, no matter how strong or powerful the feelings are, no matter how loud the thoughts get. These are the times when you need to watch and expose your mind machine in action, as you've learned to do in the earlier exercises. The practice is always the same: you simply acknowledge and observe your mind doing its thing without struggling against it or believing everything it produces. This is how you can gradually learn to drop all the old story lines your mind loves to feed you. This will position you to use your mind wisely when it serves you well.

Watch for Idleness and Fill It with Active Vitality

You know what people do when they run out of room in their house or apartment. Many get rid of what they can to make space. Many more eventually upgrade to a bigger home. Now they have more space, or so they say. That's true for a while. What normally happens is that people end up filling that new space with more stuff. Your mind will do this too when you're sitting idle, not doing anything vital.

When you're doing nothing, you create a big void in your mind. And your mind will do what it can to fill it. You've probably noticed this yourself. These times can be high-risk situations for getting hooked. Idleness is a great setup for WANR.

You have two ways to go here. One path is to welcome whatever shows up and do nothing with it. The other is to welcome what shows up and get moving. We think the latter option is better for you. Doing something vital will clear out the old junk and make room for something new. So when you are stuck with nothing to do, ask, "What do I want to be about right now?" Then, go and do what it is you care about doing. This is how you can take charge and do something to make your life grow.

Practice Flexibility

Every time you do something new, something different, something out of your comfort zone, you practice flexibility. You become less narrow, less rigid, more open, and more adaptable. And you set yourself up to get the most out of your life. You learn new things.

There are several ways to practice flexibility. Here are a few suggestions:

■ **Freshen up your mindfulness practice.** You can do this by switching between the different types of exercises we put on the CD. You can also practice the exercises in places other than your usual, special kind space in your house. In addition, you can find new exercises in many books and CDs that offer them (some are listed in the Readings to Expand Skills for Moving in Vital Directions section at the back of this book). Or you can create new exercises yourself.

■ **When you're stuck in a rut, step out of that rut and do something new.** One of our clients noticed he'd been stuck in such a rut. Every time he'd go out to dinner, he'd order the same thing—steak. It didn't matter where he went. He finally decided to consider the whole menu of options and choose something different. He now enjoys crab. Life is like a menu too. It gives you many offerings. Look for them, step out of your ruts, and follow your bliss.

- **Feed your mind and experiences with vital news.** If you're the type of person who's glued to the news, the Internet, or other sources of stimulation, it might be a good idea to cut loose. Give yourself a break—quiet time away from the negative noise of the world around you. Turn off the TV, the cell phone, and the radio, and do something you value. Stillness creates opportunities for peace and gives you space to think and move. You can fill that stillness with something other than negative news coming from your old history or the media. Fill it with valued action.

Are You Moving Forward or Backward in Your Life?

Whenever you encounter barriers and you're unsure whether your planned action is good for you, ask yourself one simple question: "Is my response to this event, thought, feeling, worry, or bodily sensation moving me closer to or further away from where I want to go with my life?" Below are some variations of this crucial question:

- If that thought (emotion, bodily state, memory) could give advice, would the advice point me forward in my life or keep me stuck?

- What advice would my value _____ [bring to mind a core value of yours] give me right now?

- What would I advise someone else or my child to do?

- If others could see what I am doing now, would they see me doing things that I value?

- In what valued direction have my feet taken me when I listened to this advice?

- What does my experience tell me about this solution? And what do I trust more—my mind and feelings, or my experience?

Asking questions like these when faced with adversity and doubt is far more helpful than listening to what your unwise WAF mind comes up with or what the surging impulses seem to be telling you. The answers will remind you that past solutions have not worked: you now have the opportunity to choose to do something different.

EMOTIONAL DISCOMFORT IS YOUR TEACHER

WAFs, along with other emotional pain and hurt, are not your enemies. They are your teachers. Think about that for a moment. Without experiencing disappointment, you'd never learn patience. Without the hurt and frustration you receive from others, you'd never learn kindness and compassion. Without exposure to new information, you'd never learn anything new. Without fear, you'd never learn courage and how to be kind to yourself. Even getting sick once in a while has an important purpose— strengthening your immune system and helping you to appreciate good health.

Moments of adversity and pain provide you with opportunities for growth and change. They teach you important skills. They give you perspective on life. You need them. They offer you great opportunities to expand your response-ability when faced with pain, hurt, or feelings of inadequacy, loneliness, or sadness.

When these feelings show up, they'll pull your eyes off of what you can control and make you focus on what you cannot control. Start by acknowledging feeling stuck, look at what you're doing, and then be response-able. Focus on what you can control to have your needs met and to keep you moving forward in directions that you care about. This is something you can do. Be specific here and write down a plan that keeps you moving forward even in the face of adversity.

We suggest you apply your Wise Mind, compassionate observer skills to each of those painful experiences. You can choose to open up to and embrace them when they show up and learn to bring compassion and forgiveness to them. The payoff is this: your emotional pain will no longer be fertile soil for your WAFs and won't sidetrack you from moving in directions you care about.

A MEANINGFUL LIFE IS BUILT ONE STEP AT A TIME

Sitting still with your WAFs and not getting all tangled up with them is one of the toughest parts of practicing courage on a day-to-day basis, and so is letting go of the internal dialogue and struggle. Over time, you'll get more skilled—so long as you keep practicing loving-kindness toward your own slipups, limitations, and all-too-human inability to be perfect.

Begin each day with this commitment: *today, to the best of my ability, I'm going to act with kindness and courage.* Then follow that with an intention to make your day a value-rich day. In the evening, go back and examine your day with loving-kindness. Don't beat yourself up if your day ends up being filled with some of the same old things you've always done. Look for the new and vital things you did that day too.

Compassion, softness, flexibility, and courage are vital. Recognize that you're only human and that you're going to make mistakes and experience setbacks. You're never going to be able to be courageous and accepting all the time; and still, you keep moving in directions you care about, one day at a time. What matters is that you are taking steps to bring acceptance and compassion to yourself and your worries, anxieties, and fears. The small steps eventually add up. Sooner or later you'll find that loving-kindness and patience will become a habit in your life. Give yourself time. Working through and with this book is not completed in a matter of weeks. It takes months to become really familiar with the exercises and to start to move in valued directions—continuing the journey takes a lifetime.

The important thing is to keep practicing the skills you've learned in this book. By now you will have found out which exercises and metaphors have been particularly helpful in keeping you unstuck and moving forward. Revisit them and focus on them. Alternatively, you could also start doing one or two exercises that you may not have done yet and see what happens if you practice them for a while. It may also be helpful to keep on examining your remaining WAF sticky spots—thoughts, images, memories, bodily sensations, and situations that tend to get you stuck—and then focus your mindfulness and acceptance practice on them. If you ever feel discouraged, we suggest you revisit your epitaphs and particularly focus on your Valued Life Epitaph—you could even rework or expand it.

It's risky to make changes. Things sometimes do go wrong or don't turn out as intended. Yet the biggest risk in life is taking no risk at all. There are few things in life that are certain. The future is, by definition, not knowable. Most choices involve risk for this very reason. Choosing to play it super safe is a surefire way to guarantee that nothing will change. You can count on that. And if nothing changes, you'll end up going where you've always headed before—a place where you're stuck, suffering, and waiting for your life to begin. Risking living your life, while you can, is risky business, but the payoff is huge—you'll get more of what you want. You'll risk living out your dreams.

THE CHOICE IS YOURS

When you first opened this book, you were probably looking for a new gold shovel that would finally dig you out of your anxiety hole so that you could get on with your life. We've done our best to show you that this isn't necessary. By now, we hope that you are experiencing this for yourself and doing what the image below shows. Remember that image from chapter 1? If you need to, go back and review that cartoon series and reflect on just how far you've come.

The most vital thing you can do to create a life is to put each moment of every day to good use. How you decide to use your precious time and energy from this day forward is up to you. You don't have to conquer anxiety when it shows up or endure it with brute force of will. Instead, you can apply the skills of acceptance,

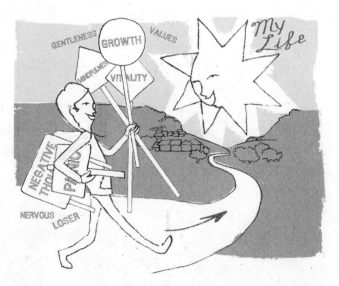

compassion, and wise observing to whatever is going on. These skills are your friends to help you stay on track.

It's your choice. Use your time wisely. There's no going back, no way to carry over until tomorrow the lost moments of today. In the end, it all adds up to what you'll call your life. Make the most of it. Make it about something bigger than your anxiety. We know you can do it. You have the skills. Continue to nurture them. Allow them to grow. Make your values a reality. This is what matters and what, in the end, leads people to say, "Now there was a life lived well."

Staying the Course for the Long Haul

Points to Ponder: I can live my values *and* take my WAFs along for the ride. My greatest barriers are those that my mind creates. I need not let them stand in the way of where I wish to go with my life.

Questions to Consider: How can I best keep on moving with my barriers toward a valued life? Is what I am doing now moving me forward or backward in my life? Is what I am doing now what I want to be about?

References, Further Readings, and Internet Resources

Below we list the materials we've used for writing this book. We've also included items that we suggest for further reading if you'd like to learn more about the ACT approach to anxiety and other related concerns. We particularly recommend the book by Steven Hayes and Spencer Smith for more examples and suggestions for how to use ACT in your life. We also know of several other forthcoming ACT books (that will be available within the next year or so) on the subjects of anxiety, worry, trauma, and depression. Many of these books and others like them are published by New Harbinger Publications. We also recommend that you check out books by Pema Chödrön—a great source of strength, courage, and practical advice on how to approach emotional pain with its most powerful antidotes: compassion and patience. Books by Thich Nhat Hanh, Jon Kabat-Zinn, and Jeffrey Brantley contain practical advice on achieving self-transformation using mindfulness and on how to nourish the positive seeds in you and in others, while starving the negative ones. Lastly, the Internet is a hub for resources on mindfulness. We've listed a few sites that provide text and audio exercises. Use them to enrich your skills and expand your practice.

REFERENCES

Addis, M. E., & Martell, C. R. (2004). *Overcoming depression one step at a time*. Oakland, CA: New Harbinger Publications.

Allen, D. (2002). *Getting things done: The art of stress-free productivity*. New York: Penguin.

American Psychiatric Association. (2000). *Diagnostic and statistical manual of mental disorders* (4th ed., text revision). Washington, DC: Author.

Antony, M. M., & McCabe, R. E. (2004). *Ten simple solutions to panic*. Oakland, CA: New Harbinger Publications.

Barlow, D. H. (2002). *Anxiety and its disorders: The nature and treatment of anxiety and panic* (2nd ed.). New York: Guilford Press.

Borkovec, T. D., Alcaine, O., & Behar, E. (2004). Avoidance theory of worry and generalized anxiety disorder. In R. G. Heimberg, C. L. Turk, & D. S. Mennin (Eds.), *Generalized anxiety disorder: Advances in research and practice* (pp. 77–108). New York: Guilford Press.

Brantley, J. (2003). *Calming your anxious mind: How mindfulness and compassion can free you from anxiety, fear, and panic*. Oakland, CA: New Harbinger Publications.

Chödrön, P. (2001). *The places that scare you*. Boston: Shambhala Publications.

Craske, M. G. (2003). *Origins of phobias and anxiety disorders: Why women more than men?* Elsevier: Oxford.

Dahl, J. C., & Lundgren, T. L. (2006). *Living beyond your pain: Using acceptance and commitment therapy to ease chronic pain*. Oakland, CA: New Harbinger Publications.

Dalai Lama XIV [Tenzin Gyatso]. (1999). *The path to tranquility*. New York: Penguin Putnam.

Dyer, W. (2005). *The power of intention*. Carlsbad, CA: Hay House.

Eifert, G. H., & Forsyth, J. P. (2005). *Acceptance and commitment therapy for anxiety disorders: A practitioner's guide to using mindfulness, acceptance, and value-based behavior change strategies*. Oakland, CA: New Harbinger Publications.

Eifert, G. H., & Heffner, M. (2003). The effects of acceptance versus control contexts on avoidance of panic symptoms. *Journal of Behavior Therapy and Experimental Psychiatry, 34,* 293–312.

Eifert, G. H., McKay, M., & Forsyth, J. P. (2005). *ACT on life, not on anger: The new acceptance and commitment therapy guide for problem anger*. Oakland, CA: New Harbinger Publications.

Hanh, T. N. (2001). *Anger: Wisdom for cooling the flames*. New York: Riverhead Books, Penguin Putnam.

Hayes, S. C. (2004). Acceptance and commitment therapy, relational frame theory, and the third wave of behavioral and cognitive therapies. *Behavior Therapy, 35,* 639–665.

Hayes, S. C., Follette, V. M., & Linehan, M. M. (Eds.). (2004). *Mindfulness and acceptance: Expanding the cognitive-behavioral tradition*. New York: Guilford Press.

Hayes, S. C., Luoma, J. B., Bond, F. W., Masuda, A., & Lillis, J. (2006). Acceptance and commitment therapy: Model, processes, and outcomes. *Behaviour Research and Therapy, 44,* 1–25.

Hayes, S. C. (with Smith, S.). (2005). *Get out of your mind and into your life: The new acceptance and commitment therapy*. Oakland, CA: New Harbinger Publications.

Hayes, S. C., Strosahl, K. D., & Wilson, K. G. (1999). *Acceptance and commitment therapy: An experiential approach to behavior change.* New York: Guilford Press.

Hayes, S. C., Wilson, K. G., Gifford, E. V., Follette, V. M., & Strosahl, K. (1996). Experiential avoidance and behavioral disorders: A functional dimensional approach to diagnosis and treatment. *Journal of Consulting and Clinical Psychology, 64,* 1152–1168.

Kabat-Zinn, J. (1994). *Wherever you go, there you are: Mindfulness meditation in everyday life.* New York: Hyperion.

Kessler, R. C., Berglund, P., Demler, O., Jin, R., Merikangas, K. R., & Walters, E. E. (2005). Lifetime prevalence and age-of-onset distributions of DSM-IV disorders in the National Comorbidity Survey Replication. *Archives of General Psychiatry, 62,* 593–602.

Leonardo, E. D., & Hen, R. (2006). Genetics of affective and anxiety disorders. *Annual Review of Psychology, 57,* 117–137.

McKay, M., & Sutker, C. (2007). *Leave your mind behind: The everyday practice of stillness amid rushing thoughts.* Oakland, CA: New Harbinger Publications.

Salters-Pedneault, K., Tull, M. T., & Roemer, L. (2004). The role of avoidance of emotional material in the anxiety disorders. *Applied and Preventive Psychology, 11,* 95–114.

von Oech, R. (1998). *A whack on the side of the head: How you can be more creative.* New York: Warner Business Books.

Wegner, D. M. (1994). Ironic processes of mental control. *Psychological Review, 101,* 34–52.

Wilson, P. (1996). *The little book of calm.* New York: Plume.

READINGS TO EXPAND SKILLS FOR MOVING IN VITAL DIRECTIONS

Brantley, J. (2007). *Calming your anxious mind: How mindfulness and compassion can free you from anxiety, fear, and panic.* Oakland, CA: New Harbinger Publications.

Chödrön, P. (2001). *The places that scare you: A guide to fearlessness in difficult times.* Boston: Shambhala Publications.

Eifert, G. H., & Forsyth, J. P. (2005). *Acceptance and commitment therapy for anxiety disorders: A practitioner's guide to using mindfulness, acceptance, and value-based behavior change strategies.* Oakland, CA: New Harbinger Publications.

Eifert, G. H., McKay, M., & Forsyth, J. P. (2005). *ACT on life, not on anger: The new acceptance and commitment therapy guide for problem anger.* Oakland, CA: New Harbinger Publications.

Hayes, S. C. (with Smith, S.). (2005). *Get out of your mind and into your life: The new acceptance and commitment therapy.* Oakland, CA: New Harbinger Publications.

Kabat-Zinn, J. (2005). *Guided mindfulness meditation (audiobook).* Louisville, CO: Sounds True.

LeJune, C. (2007). *The worry trap: How to free yourself from worry and anxiety using acceptance and commitment therapy.* Oakland, CA: New Harbinger Publications.

McKay, M., & Sutker, C. (2007). *Leave your mind behind: The everyday practice of stillness amid rushing thoughts.* Oakland, CA: New Harbinger Publications.

INTERNET RESOURCES

ACT-Relevant Books and Materials

www.acceptanceandmindfulness.com
This website contains information on other New Harbinger books, including some of our own, in which acceptance and mindfulness approaches are applied to many forms of human suffering.

ACT for Anxiety Disorders

www.ACT-for-Anxiety-Disorders.com
This is a website for this book and the professional guide that came before it. You'll find information on workshops, contact information for the authors, and additional information about the book and the ACT approach in general.

Acceptance and commitment therapy

www.contextualpsychology.org
This website is the hub for professionals and members of the public interested in acceptance and commitment therapy and other newer cognitive behavioral therapies. It contains many useful resources for those interested in learning more about ACT as well as those actively engaged in ACT research and application.

http://groups.yahoo.com/group/ACT_for_the_Public/join
You might especially benefit from joining a listserv (called "ACT_for_the_Public"), which is a kind of online support group of readers and professionals who are working to help one another with the concepts in popular ACT books like this one. It's not a substitute for therapy, but it's a help when

you get stuck with the ideas in ACT. The archive of messages is great if you're new to the work. The site also keeps a worldwide listing of ACT therapists. To search for one, just click on the "Find an ACT therapist" tab.

Beliefnet

www.beliefnet.com

This website hosts information on a number of spiritual traditions. If you follow the links, you'll find an excellent section of meditation and mindfulness practices, including several text and audio exercises that are freely available. This is an excellent way to expand your skills.

Center for Mindfulness in Medicine, Health Care, and Society, at the University of Massachusetts, Boston

www.umassmed.edu/cfm/index.aspx

This is the website for the Center for Mindfulness in Medicine, Health Care, and Society. This site is dedicated to furthering the practice and integration of mindfulness in the lives of individuals, institutions, and society through a wide range of clinical, research, education, and outreach initiatives. One of these initiatives is the Stress Reduction Program—the oldest and largest academic, medical center–based mindfulness program in the country.

Pema Chödrön

www.shambhala.org/teachers/pema/#

On this website, you will find information about Pema Chödrön's teachings, additional exercises, and forthcoming talks and books. Pema is a leading exponent of teachings on meditation and how they apply to everyday life. She is widely known for her humorous and down-to-earth interpretation of Tibetan Buddhism for Western audiences. Pema is the resident teacher at Gampo Abbey, Cape Breton, Nova Scotia—the first Tibetan monastery for Westerners—and has authored several books, including: *The Wisdom of No Escape, Start Where You Are, When Things Fall Apart: Heart Advice for Difficult Times, The Places That Scare You, No Time to Lose,* and *Practicing Peace in Times of War.* Her books are available from Shambhala Publications.

John P. Forsyth, Ph.D., is associate professor of psychology, director of clinical training, and director of the Anxiety Disorders Research Program in the Department of Psychology at the University at Albany, State University of New York. He has published numerous articles on acceptance and experiential avoidance and the role of emotion regulatory processes in human suffering. He has been doing basic and applied work related to acceptance and commitment therapy (ACT) for more than fifteen years. He is a clinical fellow of the Behavior Therapy and Research Society and a licensed clinical psychologist in New York. He serves on the editorial boards of several leading clinical psychology journals, and is associate editor of the Journal of Behavior Therapy and Experimental Psychiatry. He is coauthor of *Acceptance and Commitment Therapy for Anxiety Disorders* and *ACT on Life, Not on Anger*.

Georg H. Eifert, Ph.D., is professor and chair of the department of psychology at Chapman University in Orange, CA. He was ranked among the top thirty researchers in behavior analysis and therapy in the 1990s, and he has authored over 100 publications on psychological causes and treatments of anxiety and other emotional disorders. He is a clinical fellow of the Behavior Therapy and Research Society, a member of numerous national and international psychological associations, and he serves on several editorial boards of leading clinical psychology journals. He is also a licensed clinical psychologist. He is coauthor of *Acceptance and Commitment Therapy for Anxiety Disorders* and *ACT on Life, Not on Anger*.

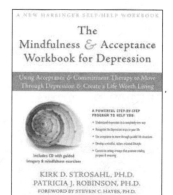